HONDA GP RACERS

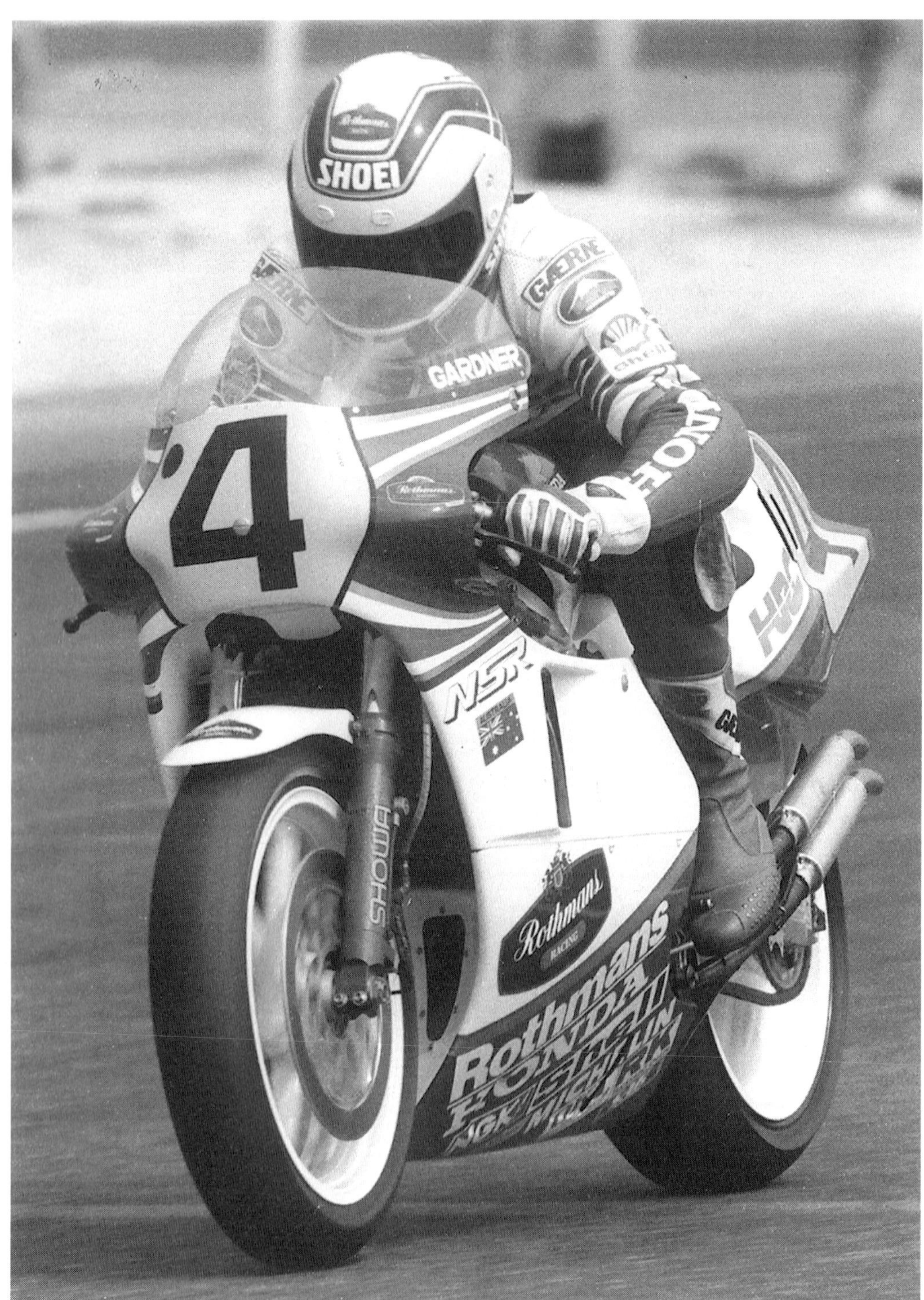
SHOEI
GAERNE
GARDNER
4
HONDA
NSR
SHOWA
Rothmans
RACING
Rothmans
HONDA

HONDA GP RACERS

Colin MacKellar

The Crowood Press

First published in 1998 by
The Crowood Press Ltd
Ramsbury, Marlborough
Wiltshire SN8 2HR

British Library Cataloguing-in-Publication Data
A catalogue record for this book is available from the British Library.

ISBN 1 86126 073 3

Picture Credits
The author and The Crowood Press would like to thank the following photographers, copyright owners and publishers for their assistance in the preparation of this book: Honda; Joost Overzee and Derk Jan Wolsink of *Motor* magazine; Dorna; Ton Kannekans; Henk Keulemans; Mick Nicholls; Mick Woollett; Yves Jamote.

Photograph previous page: Wayne Gardner on a 1986 NSR.

Typeface used: New Century Schoolbook.

Typeset and designed by D & N Publishing
Membury Business Park, Lambourn Woodlands, Berkshire.

Printed and bound by The Bath Press, Bath

Contents

Acknowledgements

The creation of this book, more than any other I have written, has only been possible because of the assistance, encouragement and generosity of a number of people who have worked with me. I wanted to place the emphasis on the factory GP racers, and realized I would have to penetrate the depths of HRC racing department to get to the source of the development information I needed. Two people are responsible for making it possible for me to talk to two generations of Honda GP engineers. A chance

Although only 'Supreme Advisor' to the company bearing his name, nothing kept Soichiro Honda away from the birth of the NR500.

encounter with Yoko Togashi, interpreting for Honda management at the 1996 Dutch GP, was a critical moment. Realizing immediately how crucial it would be for me to talk to the Honda engineers, she worked with Suguru Kanazawa, director at HRC, to find a way for me to visit HRC at Asaka, where I spent a week talking to those responsible for twenty years of Honda racers. My deep gratitude goes to both of these people, and to HRC engineers Seiki Ishii, Kazuo Honda, Gen Irie, Takashi Kudo, Shigeru Hattori, Satoru Horiike, Masuo Noguchi and Syuhei Nakamoto, for making it possible to get the story at first hand. HRC Managing Director Heijiro Yoshimura gracefully accepted my presence at HRC in the busy days before the start of the GP season, and Katsumasa Suzuki looked after me and got me to the right place at the right time.

While I was in Japan, Yoko also made it possible for me to talk to Yoichi Oguma, long-time Honda GP race team leader, with the delicate task of acting as conduit between the factory and factory riders. I was also able to claim an invaluable hour with Shoichiro Irimajiri, Honda Motorcycle R&D vice-president when the NR500 was created, and essentially its 'Godfather'. All the Japanese people I talked to were as open and forthright as they could be, limited solely by the difficulty of communicating in a foreign language.

Having heard the engineer's side of the story, it was fascinating to listen to the rider's view of the same set of events. I was fortunate in being able to talk to many of the men who have brought Honda fame and glory in the GPs over the last twenty years. Takazumi Katayama gave me a unique insight into the early days of the Honda team as they struggled with the NR500 and triumphed with the NS500. Yorkshireman Mick Grant was typically direct and frank, even-handed with both his praise and criticism. Ron Haslam, valued by Honda as one of the best test riders they have ever had, dug deep into his memory to recall the feel of the NR500, NS500 and early NSRs. Talking to Wayne Gardner, it became clear to me how ungenerous history had been to him, with his single 1987 world title. Sito Pons had a unique view of the first NSR250s and of the challenge of transition to the late-1980s NSR500. Hans Spaan was an RS125 rider and tuner from the first hour, later becoming the technical force behind Haruchika Aoki and his two world titles. What Spaan doesn't know about the RS125 isn't worth knowing. Finally, Mick Doohan took an hour to recount his experience of nine years of NSR500s – sixty minutes of the most articulate and concisely conveyed information I have ever received from a rider.

The third angle on the story comes from the guys caught in the middle – the team managers. Three people were, between them, able to cover the last twenty years of Honda racing. Gerald Davison set up the team that campaigned the NR500 from 1979 and spoke of the hopes and fears, few highs and many lows of the race team running the NR. Erv Kanemoto managed to allocate me a couple of hours from his frantic GP schedule and, together with George Vukmanovich, recounted the glory of the Spencer years with the NS500 triple and NSR V4. Moving on to work with other riders, Kanemoto has been involved with NS and NSRs that have claimed seven world championships. His record is only rivalled by that of Jerry Burgess, the force behind the Australians for the last twelve years, with five 500 championships as reward. Jerry spent many hours running through the year-on-year changes of the NSR500 for me, and the successes and failures that came from them.

There were others whose names may be less well known, but whose contribution was no less important. Marcus Schneider of HRC in Belgium helped me to establish contact with Japan. Mac Mackay allowed me to plunder his collection of publicity photographs dating from the Rothmans Honda days. Henk Keuleman's career as a motorcycle racing photographer neatly coincided with the period of the sport I wanted to cover, and the majority of this book's superlative photographs come from his collection. The photos in Chapter 1 came from the archive of the Dutch magazine *Motor*, whose staff members Joost Overzee and Derk Jan Wolsink helped me gain access. Guus ten Thije assembled an impressive collection of articles and Honda literature from his circle of friends and acquaintances. Melvyn Hiscock, my editor at The Crowood Press, inherited the project, and calmly planned and re-planned as I blew deadline after deadline, with never a hint of exasperation in his voice.

Lastly, there's the family. Cara and Marian have been through this a couple of times before, but Niall could never quite figure out why he had to quit playing Actua Soccer on the PC as I had something more important to do. It's all yours now.

1 The Story So Far

Honda GP Racing in the 1960s

Sunday 12 August 1979 may well have been the most disappointing day in the rich life of Soichiro Honda. Racing motorcycles had always been in the blood of this extraordinary man and his team's racing achievements during the 1960s had carved a place for his fledgling company at the centre of the motorcycling cosmos. In his hands, racing was an instrument of progress – technological, educational and promotional. It had been a weapon that had been wielded with incredible success as Honda moved out of their home market. Twenty years later, attempts to use the same strategy to put the fire back into the company name ended in the dust and dirt of the 1979 British Grand Prix at Silverstone.

ISLE OF MAN 1959

Honda's assault on the European motorcycle market was spearheaded by the Grand Prix season of 1960. A limited outing to the 1959 Isle of Man 125 race to test the waters had brought Honda the team prize, with sixth, seventh, eighth and eleventh places in the race. The bikes – called RC142s – had twin-cylinder double-overhead camshafts with four-valve heads. The camshafts were driven off the crankshaft via spur gears and a vertical bevel shaft on the left-hand side of the engine. Flat-slide Keihin carburettors, magneto ignition, a dry clutch and six-speed gearbox rounded them off. Although the bike was not extraordinary in comparison with contemporary 125 racers, the technology was impressive. With hindsight, many of those who took the time to check out the Japanese team's headquarters on the Isle of Man in June 1959 claim to have seen an inkling of the greatness to come. In reality, it was more likely that they were impressed by the thoroughness and professionalism of the Japanese team at a time when 'Made in Japan' was considered to mean poor quality and unreliability. Soichiro Honda was aware that the team would be under intense scrutiny as the first Japanese team to participate in European road-racing and was determined that they would not be faulted on their professional approach. Their maxim was 'When Honda go racing, they do it properly'; later, it became 'Honda races, Honda wins'.

THE RC160

If Euro-pundits were impressed by the technology they had seen in 1959, they would have been startled by the path Honda's development was taking back in Japan. Convinced of the philosophy of multi-cylinder four-valve technology, the company produced the first of the famous small-capacity four-cylinder race bikes and used it to win the open class of the last of the Asama races in August 1959. The RC160 was a doubled-up RC142, with the same bevel shaft drive (now moved to the right-hand side of the engine), dry clutch, and five-speed gearbox. Battery and coil ignition was used and the whole engine was housed in a pressed-steel spine frame that was very similar to that of the 125. Sadao Shimazaki rode the bike to victory in a race made controversial by the boycott of Yamaha and other manufacturers in protest at the change of rules that no longer required a street bike pedigree for the racers.

It took several months before news of the four-cylinder bike reached the European motorcycle press. The accompanying photos of the racer kitted out in the eccentric (to Western eyes) clothes of the Asama competition machine, may have disguised the wolf in sheep's clothing. The implication of the pending arrival of the four-cylinder 250 for a full season of GP racing was hardly mentioned in the press. When the bike did arrive prior to the Isle of Man TT, it proved to be totally different to the RC160 that had been raced once and put aside. The aim of the Honda team was to learn the science and engineering of race machinery. The European adventure of 1959 had given them enough knowledge for a significant evolutionary step towards a bike that would bring them GP glory.

MORE POWERFUL ENGINES – FOUR-STROKE ENGINE DESIGN

The development of racing machinery in the 1960s was dominated by the drive to produce more powerful engines. Through empirical methods, an understanding was developing of the forces at work within two-stroke and four-stroke engines. For the two-strokes, this centred on the process of scavenging the engine of exhaust gases, through the pressure waves forming in the tuned exhaust pipes. Higher engine speeds were less important for the two-strokes as there was so much potential for power increase through improved scavenging. With the four-stroke, scavenging was less of an issue, since the pumping action of the piston should deliver a relatively clean combustion chamber before the fresh charge is sucked past the inlet valves. However, it needs to turn the engine twice for each power stroke of the piston, whereas each rotation of the engine in a two-stroke is a power stroke. Honda had to concentrate on getting high engine speeds without the engine self-destructing.

Generally, higher engine speeds for a given engine capacity can be obtained by a shorter stroke, with a limit being set by the maximum average piston speed possible before failure of the conrod big end or small end bearings. The larger bore also enabled larger-diameter valves to be used, with the intention of flowing more charge into the combustion chamber. But it was discovered in the 1950s that there was a limit to the over-squareness of the engine. If the bore was more than 30 per cent higher than the stroke, the efficiency of the combustion process suffered and there was a loss of power. The only way to shorten the stroke even further was to increase the number of cylinders. Now the crankshaft could safely spin at higher speeds, but the problem shifted to the top end of the engine and the valve train. Two-valve heads could no longer be used as the inertia of the heavy valves made it impossible for them accurately to follow the profile of the cams using conventional valve springs. The move to the lower inertia of four valves solved the problem of high valve-train speed. With the four-valve technology firmly part of Honda's design philosophy, the key to greater power for a given capacity was further cylinder miniaturization.

THE RC161

The 1960 RC161 looked quite similar to the 1957 Gilera 500-4 that had taken the world

The first four-cylinder 250 Honda to be seen in Europe was the RC161, but the MV twin still had the edge.

title that year. The vertical bevel shaft for the overhead camshafts had been replaced by a train of gears driven from the centre of the crankshaft. The engine had been tipped forward 35 degrees, to provide better cooling than the ducting that had been used on the first engines, and to provide some downdraught for the new flat-slide Keihin carburettors. A racing magneto provided the sparks and an extra gear had been squeezed into the box, for a total of six gears. The mould had been cast for the engine that would power a generation of Honda racers that were to dominate racing during the 1960s. It took Honda another year to produce the duplex frame that was needed to match the dominant power plant, and from 1961 the bike reigned supreme in its class, until the Yamaha two-strokes started snapping at its heels in 1964.

FURTHER DEVELOPMENT

In the 350 class, Honda swiftly dispatched MV, with a bored-out version of the 1962 four-cylinder 250, the RC171. Under pressure from the two-strokes in the smaller, 50cc and 125 classes, the pace of development was quicker. The 1962 single cylinder

(Above) *Tom Phillis took the RC144 to a 1961 world championship in a bitter and controversial battle with Ernst Gegner on a two-stroke MZ.*

Honda domination of the 250 class was absolute in 1961. Here Takahashi (100) beat Redman (107) to the flag and victory on the RC162 at the West German GP.

50cc racer, the RC110, produced 9 bhp at 14,000 rpm, but was overshadowed by the new two-stroke Suzukis. By the end of the season, Honda had a 50cc twin ready that produced an extra 2 bhp at 17,500 rpm. It was raced to victory by Tommy Robb at the end of season Japanese International race at Suzuka, but not raced in the GPs in 1963. During the race, won by half a wheel from Hugh Anderson on the Suzuki, Robb revved the bike out to 22,000 rpm with no damage to the engine. Faster engine speeds seemed to be the solution to the two-stroke challenge and, by 1963, the 125 twin was outpaced by the Suzuki twins. For 1964, the four-cylinder RC146 was given to Luigi Taveri to re-take the 125cc world title for Honda, spinning at 18,000 rpm and producing just under 30 bhp.

THE RC166

Honda had bitten off more than they could chew, by starting up a Formula 1 car project that drained money and engineers from the race-bike development. The R&D effort had been enough to get a new 250 off the drawing board quickly, but not enough to de-bug it.

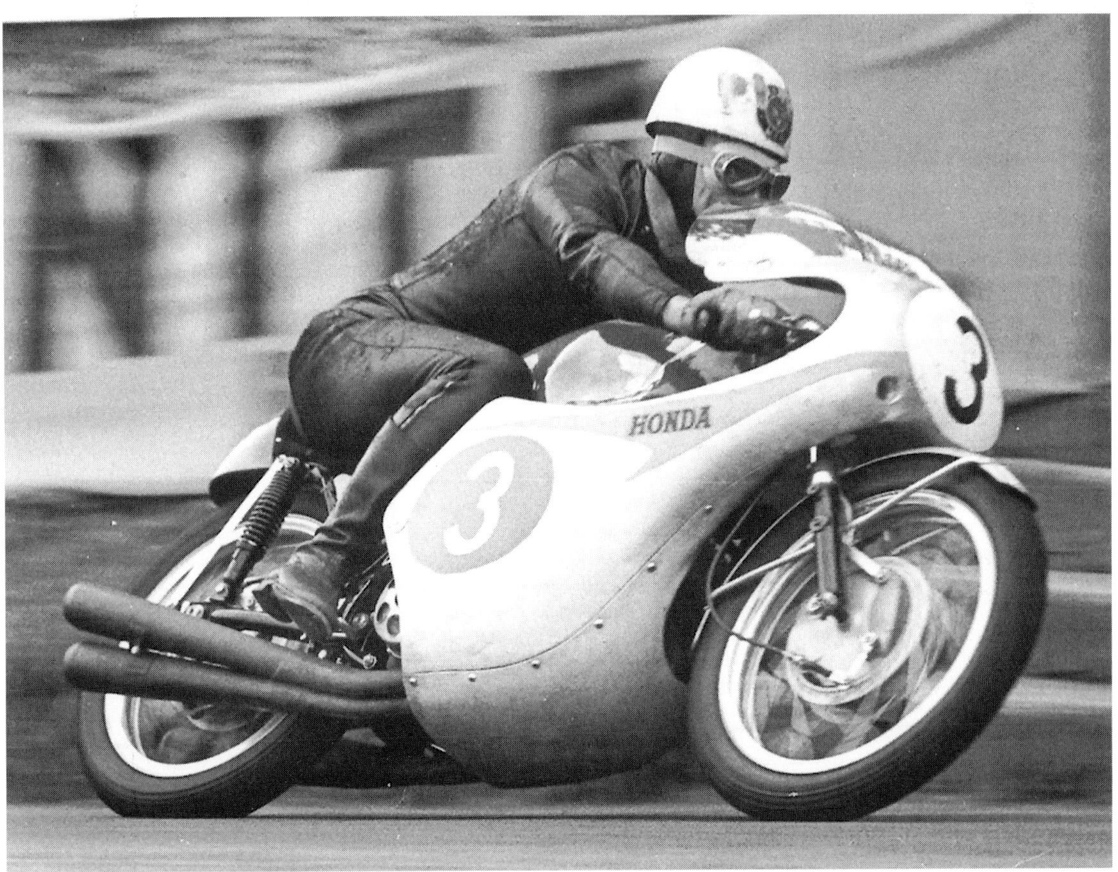

At the 1961 Lightweight TT, Bob McIntyre came within a whisker of setting the first 100mph (160kph) lap on a 250 machine, but his RC162 overheated and he retired.

The result was that one of the most famous racing engines ever created had a disappointing start to its career. The RC166, a six-cylinder 250, was beaten by the rotary-valve 250 two-stroke from Yamaha, the RD56, at its first race at Monza in 1964. On home territory a few weeks later, for the Japanese GP at Honda's own Suzuka circuit, it triumphed, but the title had passed to Honda's greatest competitor, Yamaha.

THE 1965 AND 1966 SEASONS

The consequences of the strain on Honda's R&D resources continued into 1965, when Redman was unable consistently to beat the Yamaha twin, and Phil Read retained the title against the odds. The Suzuki twins outclassed the RC146 to regain the 125 title. Honda's only bright spots were the 350, in which Redman held off the MV dream team of Agostini and Hailwood, and the 50 class in which Ralph Bryans held off the two-strokes on the finest miniature four-stroke engine ever built. The RC115 was the ultimate refinement of Honda's tiny twin. The stroke was shortened, enabling it to spin up to 24,000 rpm, although the 14 bhp it was claimed to produce came in at 22,500 rpm. Honda managed to shave off 6½lb (3kg) to bring the dry weight down to just 110lb (50kg), 22lb (10kg) lighter than the RK65, Suzuki's twin cylinder two-stroke competitor. It was an extraordinary piece of engineering and marked the zenith of Honda's participation in the 50cc class.

With their eyes on Mike Hailwood and a challenge for the 500 class, Honda decided to drop the 50cc racers from their stable. But their engineering brilliance was to live on in the 1966 125 machine that was built for Luigi Taveri to beat the Yamahas and Suzukis. The RC149 used five of the cylinders from the RC115 to produce 35 bhp at 20,500 rpm, with eight speeds in the gearbox to keep it in the razor-sharp power band. At the end of 1966, however, Taveri retired from the sport, and Honda withdrew from the 125 class to let the two-strokes fight it out amongst themselves.

In only its second race, the 1964 Japanese GP, the six-cylinder RC165 was ridden to victory by Jim Redman; in the same race, Luigi Taveri on the same bike passes Hailwood on an MZ.

Not an RC166, which Hailwood rode to glory, but a late model RC165, on which Redman was only occasionally able to beat Phil Read on the Yamaha twin.

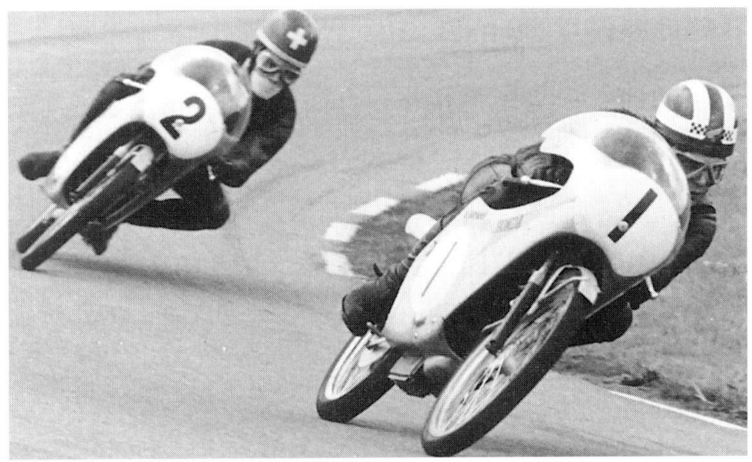

(Right) *The miraculous jewel-like RC116 50cc twins were untouchable at the 1966 Dutch TT.*

Although a masterpiece of miniaturization, the 1966 RC149 in the hands of Luigi Taveri was only just able to beat the combination of Ivy and Yamaha.

HAILWOOD JOINS THE TEAM

As was to happen later in Honda's racing history, it took the arrival of new blood in the team for the company to realize that there is more to a successful racing bike than a good engine. Mike Hailwood's reaction to his first test session on the RC166 – apparently, he asked the mechanics to remove the rear shocks so that he could examine them, then walked over to a nearby pond and threw them in – may have been the first time Honda became aware that it was the package that counted rather than incidental superlative components. The token acceptance of Girling shocks as a replacement to Honda's own shocks was the only response to the criticism made by Hailwood, but it set the company on the path that was to lead to the RC166 and big brother RC173 becoming the best balanced Japanese racing package of the 1960s.

While competitor Yamaha struggled with its new four-cylinder 250, as unbalanced a package as can be found in the inventory of 1960s racing bikes, Hailwood took the RC166 to ten wins from twelve GPs during 1966. The story was the same in the 350 class, with wins in all the six races that he finished. Unfortunately, Honda hadn't realized that it was a balanced motorcycle design that had made this possible, as they went into the development of the 500cc motorcycle that was to bring them the prestigious 500cc crown.

Perhaps Honda had become a little complacent. After all, they had conquered every class they entered, and victory had been especially easy when pitted against MV Augusta. The RC170 and 171 had done the trick, winning the 350 crown in 1962 and, since 1963, Jim Redman and the RC172 had developed a stranglehold on the class that not even the Giacomo Agostini and Mike Hailwood team could break.

Honda were not complacent, however, about their choice of riders for the team. Recognizing the fact that Redman's dynasty at Honda was surely drawing to a close, and capitalizing on his frustrations within the Italian team, Honda enticed Mike Hailwood to leave MV Agusta. With the arrival of Agostini, it had become clear that Count Domenico Agusta would like nothing better than to have an Italian world champion on his 500cc machine. None of the nine crowns MV had achieved in the 500 class up to the end of 1965 had been obtained by an Italian. Agostini clearly had the ability to become the first, with only team-mate Mike Hailwood in his way. With the swing of interest in the MV team, and the promise of championship-winning 250 and 250 machines, as well as the challenge of the 500, Honda seemed to Hailwood to be a very attractive proposition.

The classic combination of the 1960s – Hailwood and the RC166.

THE NEW 500

Honda decided to model the new 500 on the RC172 that had consistently beaten MV in the 350 class. The competition they were facing was dated, MV having been unchallenged in the 500 class since Gilera officially withdrew from racing at the end of 1957. The four-cylinder MV that won the 500 crown in 1965 was overweight and underpowered, when running against a competitive multi-cylinder bike. It seemed to be an easy match for Honda, but MV had finally realized that their bikes needed a radical redesign and the 1965 season had seen the first 350 four-cylinder running four-valve cylinder heads. It had been almost enough to give Agostini the 350 championship that year, the title struggle going down to the last GP in Japan. The ignition had failed whilst Agostini was leading comfortably and the title remained with Honda and Redman. MV decided to use the three-cylinder 350 as the base for their battle with Honda to retain the 500 crown. The initial bike had a capacity of just 420cc, but this grew through 1966 to reach 489cc by the season's end.

The RC181 had a traditional Honda four-cylinder engine, with the drive for the double overhead camshaft via a train of gears located between the middle two cylinders. Both the cylinder heads and barrels were cast as single units. They were fed by a bank of four Keihin magnesium carburettors, with flat-slides but integrated floatchambers. The initial RC181 was supplied with magneto ignition, although there were some rudimentary transistorized ignitions tried throughout the life of the bike. Although the bike was to produce power in a generally broad profile, Honda slipped six gears into the gearbox. The traditional wet sump used by Honda was present and correct, containing 3.5 litres of oil. There were twin outboard oil coolers located just wide of the engine and fitting into ducts cut into the alloy fairing. The engine ran up to 12,000 rpm and initially produced about 80 bhp. This was surely enough to defeat MV.

As it turned out, it wasn't enough. The same philosophy that had been applied to the 500 engine was applied to the 500 frame. The 350 frame was assumed to be adequate, with some token extra gussetting for strengthening. In January of 1966, Hailwood was already commenting that it didn't 'seem like a good idea to be sticking the engine into the old 350 frame'. The one concession Honda made to the higher power of the 500 was to use a full duplex frame, with detachable tubes passing down from the engine mounts on the cam box to those at the back of the gearbox. Honda's own Showa suspension was used front and rear, with double twin-leading shoe-drum front brakes and a single twin-leading shoe-drum brake in the rear wheel. The bike weighed in at a rather heavy 340lb (155kg) at the start of the 1966 season. Hailwood decided that it was also a bit of a 'camel' when he got to race it against Agostini:

> Nobody at the factory knew just how bad the 500 was, because nobody there had ridden it anywhere near as fast, or under the same conditions as I had to ride it. They had a test rider – a good man and a fair racer in Japan – and he took it out just the once. He came back after a quick spin and said it was perfect. Then he left the factory to go and work somewhere else. He wasn't so bloody daft! They never saw him again. When I first tried out the 500, in Japan at Christmas 1965, Honda agreed to cobble up a new frame. I went back three months later to try it out, and it wasn't much better. But we figured it had so much horsepower that nothing would get anywhere near it, and, having the legs on the other bikes, it should get

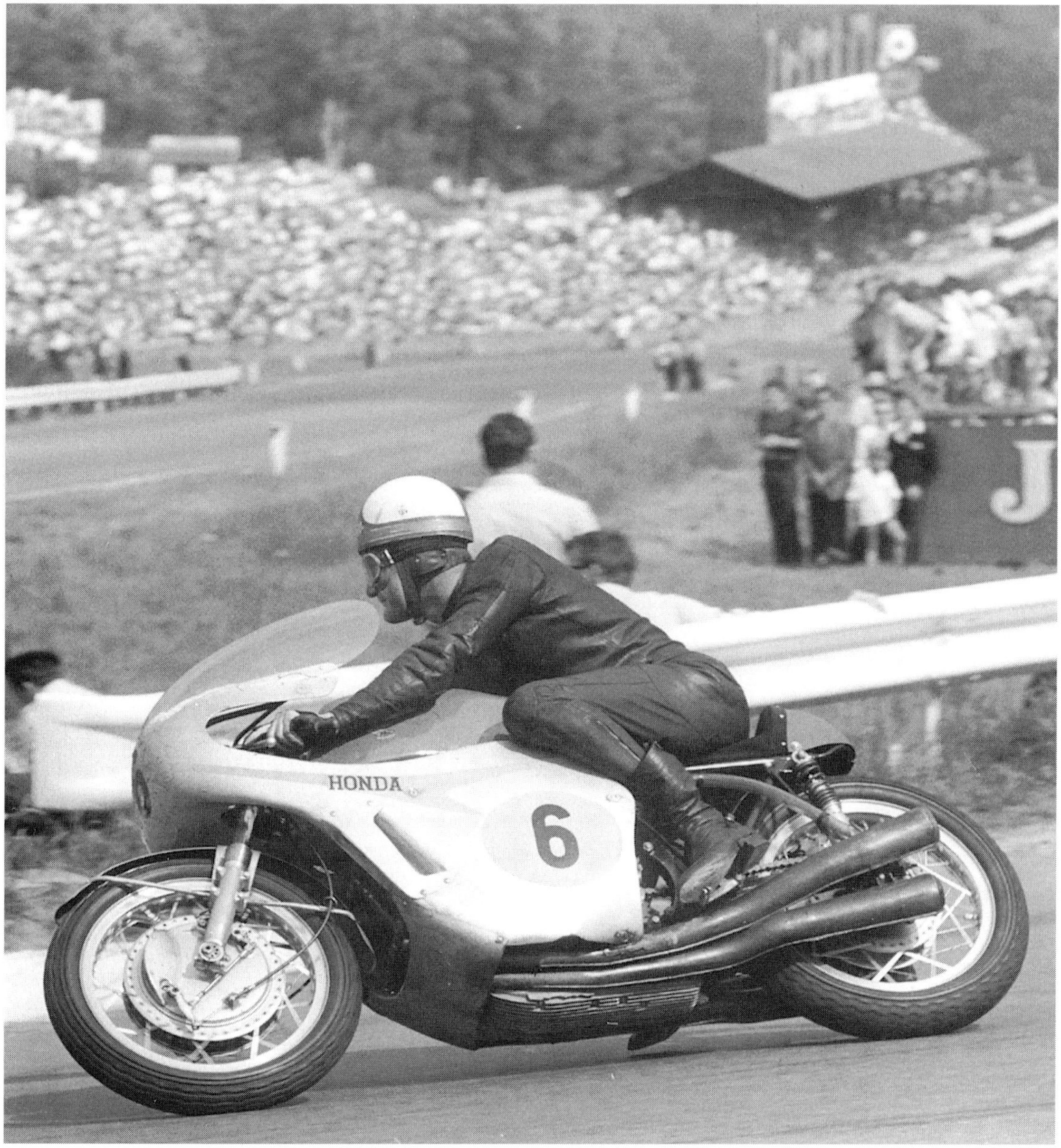

Hailwood on the RC181, Honda 500 at Spa in 1967; somewhere ahead is Agostini on the MV.

through the season quite successfully. Anyway, my feeling later was that I wasn't going to ride it, Jim [Redman] was. He'd made up his mind that he wanted the 500 title, even though I'd been signed by Honda to race the big bike. Jim got his way. None of us at Honda thought that anybody would come up with anything to beat the 500, however

> badly it handled. But when the new MV was introduced, it was only about two miles an hour slower than the Honda – and a far better handler. The old MV had been something like 25 horsepower down on the Honda. I would say that riding ability counted throughout 1966 and 1967 more than for a long time. I had to ride as I'd never done before to give the big Honda any chance at all against the MV.

The history books show that Hailwood and Honda came very close to beating Agostini and MV in both years they fought for the 500 crown. The RC181 was not an especially reliable bike, the gearbox causing Hailwood problems during at least three of the races in 1966. Despite the plain language Hailwood had been using about the bike's flawed handling, most of the winter development effort went into squeezing 93 bhp out of the engine at 12,650 rpm. No new frame was produced, although some extra gussets were welded around the headstock. This lead to the midnight run that Hailwood made with an RC181 engine, back to the UK, where he asked Colin Lyster to design a new frame around the engine. With the mock-up, they approached Reynolds the UK tube manufacturers, who quoted 2 months for the delivery of the new frame. According to Hailwood,

> That was far too long to have to wait, so Colin and I went to Italy to see a man [Belletti, who

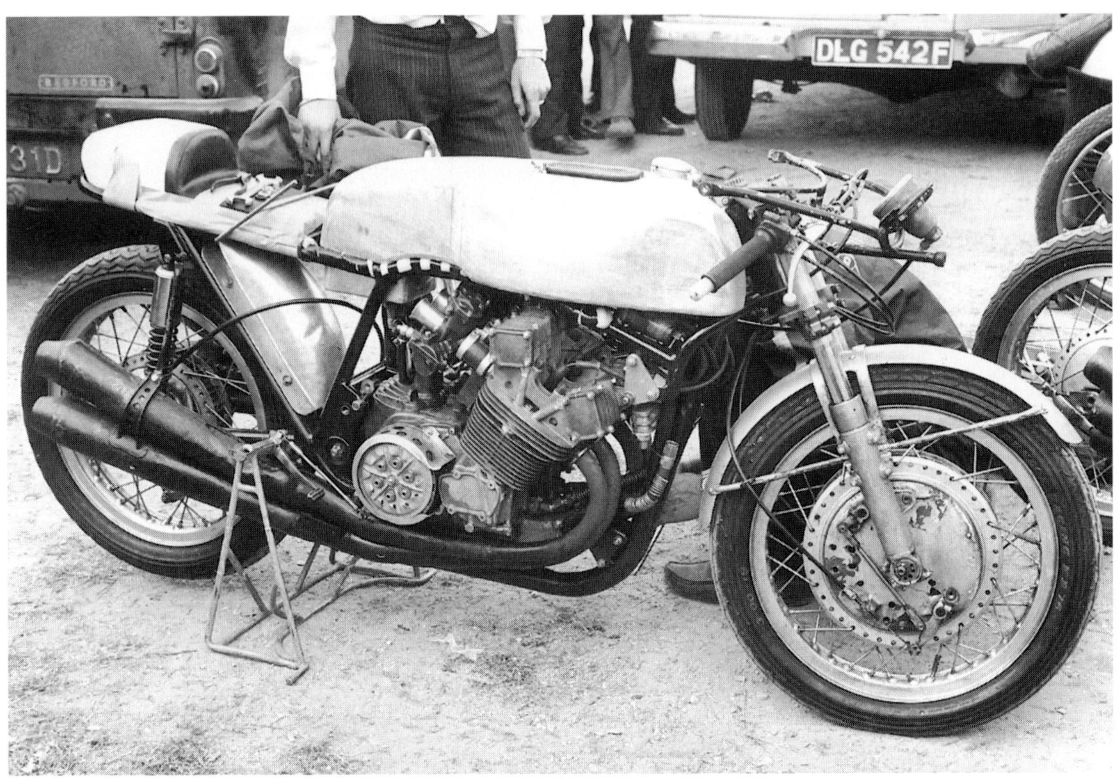

The ultimate version of the Honda 500 was this Reynolds-framed RC181, commissioned and ridden a few times by Hailwood in 1968.

built frames for Guiseppi Pattoni] who had a welding business outside of Milan. Everyone told us he was a brilliant welder and a fair hand with frames. I took the best tubing I could find and the Honda engine. He really got to work and produced a frame in sixteen days. We almost lived on his doorstep to make sure he hurried things along. I rode the Honda with the new frame at Rimini before the Grand Prix season started. I managed to win and the frame stood up to the test better than the standard one would have done. It was obviously only a question of time before the new frame was absolutely right, but time

At the International race at Rimini in 1968, Hailwood took out the big four for the last time and was leading Agostini until he slid off on the tenth lap, re-mounting to finish second.

was something I didn't have enough of. I couldn't risk using it in the world championships. The fact that I was using a new frame leaked out to the motorcycle press and Honda were furious. They sent me a strong letter emphasizing that they like to keep everything they do secret. But I still couldn't get them to commit themselves about making a better frame. They knew as well as I did that I couldn't afford to use it in the championships, so it stayed in my van. I'm still convinced it could have been successful if Honda had given me some assistance; I couldn't do it alone.

THE 1967 SEASON

The 1967 season was, for Honda, very similar to the previous year, with some wins, some defeats, and some mechanical failures – a crankshaft in West Germany, the gearbox in East Germany and, most disappointingly, the gearbox at the Italian GP when leading with just two laps to go. That win would have given Hailwood the world title but, as it turned out, Hailwood and Honda were not destined to take a 500 world championship together.

HONDA'S RETIREMENT

Honda announced their retirement from GP racing in February 1968, although they did lend their contracted riders, Ralph Bryans and Mike Hailwood, bikes that could be used in non-championship events. Hailwood commissioned a new frame for the RC181 from Reynolds, and rode it at a couple of races before dropping it in favour of the RC174, the 300cc six-cylinder. This had become Hailwood's favourite Honda, with a little under 70 bhp and weighing 260lb (118kg) it was fast enough and agile enough to beat all comers, except the MV 500 triple.

So the curtain dropped on a performance that had played to packed appreciative audiences around the world for eight years. The investment made by the company had been enormous, the returns more so. By 1968, Honda had produced more than ten million motorcycles and was easily the largest motorcycle manufacturer in the world. Some of the race technology was to rub off on the street bikes with the arrival of the Honda CB750, the first production in-line transverse four-cylinder motorcycle. This was, however, an incidental benefit of Honda's involvement in racing; the main aim had been to achieve recognition of Japanese excellence in engineering, and to change the Western countries' negative opinion of Japanese products. Soichiro Honda had been an engineer first and a businessman second. In the early days he had smarted at the widespread view that the Japanese were a nation of plagiarists, incapable of original research and development. At the Swedish GP of 1961, with Mike Hailwood winning the 250 race and with it Honda's first world championship, Mr Honda made a short speech to the assembled world press. He acknowledged the influence that Western technology had had on his early designs, but proudly drew their attention to the technological achievement that had culminated in his machines proving themselves to be the best in the world. Honda's engineering excellence had been proven.

Honda themselves had set the four-cylinder framework for the next generation of road bikes that were to come to dominate the market. Racing had served its purpose, and now there was a business to be run.

2 A Bike is Born

The Conception of the NR500 Four-stroke (1978–79)

WORLD LEADER IN MOTORCYCLE MANUFACTURE

Four-stroke Technology

During their years of self-imposed exile from world racing, Honda consolidated their position as the undisputed world leader in motorcycle manufacturing. They had a substantial advantage over their fellow Japanese manufacturers, having adopted four-stroke technology from the start. As concern for environmental standards developed in the USA, strict emission rules began to be drafted, and it became clear that the two-stroke engine would not be able to pass the new legislation. The transition from two-stroke to four-stroke engines was to occupy the other three big companies at least into the mid-1970s, giving Honda the chance to identify, create and supply different market segments. One milestone in motorcycling history was the release of the Goldwing in 1974, with an innovative new design that created overnight, and largely captured, the touring market segment.

The UJM

Honda's other flagship model, the CB750, released at the close of the 1960s, was to evolve into the model for what was later to be defined as the 'Universal Japanese Motorcycle' (UJM) – a bike that was adequate in most ways, reliable enough, fast enough, comfortable enough, economical enough. The UJM was designed to be 'enough' for most people, ignoring the fact that motorcycle owners were very different. Each of the 'Big Four' was to produce its share of UJMs, but during the 1970s Honda's range of street bikes was dominated by them.

CHALLENGES TO HONDA'S DOMINANCE

Supersports

By 1976 it was clear to the directors of Honda that this strategy was flawed. The success of the Goldwing had drawn their attention to the existence of different market segments, and they had forfeited one of these to Kawasaki. For most of the 1970s, there was only one supersports bike that was worth owning – the Z1. Kawasaki dominated this market from the model's introduction in 1972 to the last years of the decade. With a heritage that was also based on four-stroke powerplants, Kawasaki had been able to adapt to the change of technology faster than Suzuki and Yamaha, with their two-stroke legacy. Kawasaki had also built a reputation as the supplier of ultra-sports models with their legendary H1 and H2, two-stroke triples. The Z1 was the four-stroke equivalent, with a superb bullet-proof engine in a questionable chassis.

Those looking for a high-performance four-stroke knew where to go. Honda decided to identify a strategy to enable them to challenge for this segment of the market.

The Japanese Market

In addition, Honda's previously undisputed leadership of the Japanese market was under attack, with arch rivals Yamaha promoting their sports image well through their success in the world of GP racing. During one month in 1975, Honda's share of the domestic sales of motorcycles dropped below 40 per cent for the first time in fifteen years. The 'Honda-Yamaha war' broke out in Japan at this time, with the two companies fighting for position at the top of the Japanese commercial motorcycle market. Against this background, a new R&D manager – Irimajiri – was appointed for the Honda motorcycle division, with a directive calling for an innovative sports street bike.

INNOVATION OF THE 1970s

Mid-range Revolution

Again, Japanese engineering excellence was to be demonstrated to the world. There were some early results from Honda's R&D department. Irimajiri remembers:

> Within R&D we started a new project that was called Mid-Range Revolution. At the start, we developed very experimental 400 and 500cc sports bikes, which ended up as the CB400 and CX500. In parallel there was a small project in endurance racing which was isolated from R&D. This was RSC, led by AikaSan. It was strange that we had a racing activity outside of R&D. There was no racing from within R&D.

The CBX

Another project was to result in the CBX1000, the six-cylinder masterpiece derived from the RC166 GP bike, designed by Irimajiri when he had been the GP engine designer during the 1960s. Although conceived as the ultimate sports bike, it was too offbeat ever to fill that role, and never sold in large numbers. Nevertheless, it was important in making such a bold statement indicating that Honda were going to break out of the UJM mould and compete with all comers in all areas of the market. The CBX was in the vanguard of a strategy for targeting the sports bike market, which bore fruit in the 1980s.

A RETURN TO RACING?

The Freedom of the 1960s

More was required to put Honda back in the spotlight. A return to racing seemed a tempting way of demonstrating engineering excellence. During the previous racing era, engineering excellence and racing success had become synonymous. If a team was not winning, its engineering was not good enough, and development was essential. This philosophy had worked for Honda in the 1960s, and its spirit still permeated the corridors of Honda's R&D centre in Asaka, although the engineers who had applied it were long gone. However, racing-bike designers had enjoyed a special freedom in the 1960s. There were no regulations restricting combustion principles (although supercharging was banned), engine configuration, number of gears, or exhaust noise. (There *were* restrictions on the fuel that could be used.) The freedom enabled the engine designers to produce radically different engines relatively quickly, leading to a diversity of design and configuration.

Changes in Regulations

The Fédération Internationale Motocycliste (FIM) felt that this freedom was actually restrictive, because it led to the rapid development of new engines, requiring a level of investment that was too high for small manufacturers. In 1969 and 1970, therefore, it introduced regulations restricting the number of cylinders that could be used in each class. It was a misguided step that didn't significantly lower the cost of building a racing motorcycle. It did, however, hammer the final nail in the coffin of the four-stroke GP racing motorcycle; the multi-cylinder strategy could no longer be applied to increase the four-stroke's engine speed, to allow it to remain competitive with the two-strokes. MV Agusta managed to stave off defeat in the 350 and 500 class for a few years, helped a little by the tragic death of Jarno Saarinen in 1973. Yamaha would have claimed the 500 crown that year, but for Saarinen's accident. It was to be another two years before Agostini, of all people, used a Yamaha to wrest the crown from the Italian company that had held it for sixteen years.

During 1976, with the MV still being run, but looking barely competitive, the FIM put the company out of its misery by introducing noise restrictions that could not be met by the MV without sacrificing vital engine power. At the last GP of 1976, Agostini, reunited with the team with which he had been so closely associated for most of his racing career, wheeled out the final version of the most famous racing motorcycle of all time, the MV500. Fittingly, this last race took place at the old fourteen-mile Nürburgring in Germany, a circuit at which MV had never been beaten. At the start of the last lap, Agostini had a lead of more than a minute. On the notorious track, slick from the rain that had started to fall a couple of laps before, the roar of what many thought would be the last four-stroke GP 500 racing bike faded into the gloom of the Eifel woods.

Four-stroke or Two-stroke?

Honda was a four-stroke company, heart and soul, although the head had told them to build a two-stroke racing bike when necessary. Their first forays into Motocross had been with the two-stroke Elsinores, and they had won championships with them. Honda's ideal was to use a four-stroke, facilitating a link between racing excellence and street bike excellence. MV were still winning as Honda's plans for a return to GP racing began to crystallize, so the gap between four-strokes and two-strokes didn't seem that wide. According to Honda, it was just a question of engineering excellence, and since it had worked in the past, why shouldn't it work again?

This was certainly the philosophy of Soichiro Honda who, although officially retired from the operational aspects of running the business, was still a powerful figurehead in his role as Supreme Advisor. Kiyoshi Kawashima, successor to Soichiro Honda as president of the company, was also a four-stroke man, having been personally involved in the legendary battles of the 1960s. As far as they were concerned, there was no choice; it would be a four-stroke 500cc racing bike.

The Announcement of the Return

The announcement of the return to racing came out of the blue. Gerald Davison, heading up the Honda UK racing effort, was in Japan in December 1977, when it was made. He remembers it like this:

> We were having a very big press convention in Japan. President Kawashima was to make a speech. It wasn't unusual in situations

> like that, when I was in Japan, for me to write speeches for him. I went to head office one day to draft this speech for him and I had by then been arguing for a serious return to GP racing for three or four years. So I sat in his office and he was telling me what he wanted to say that evening and I was starting to draft the speech. Then he said to me, 'and the next part is we have taken the decision to return to GP racing with a four-stroke'. I was just astounded. I just couldn't believe what I was hearing. He looked at me and said, 'and you're going to do it'. I said, ' No, I'm not. I have a wife and two young children. That's not my sort of life these days.' I'd raced as a youngster, I'd been with Honda for many years but, to cut a long story short, a few weeks later I finally agreed, knowing that I didn't have much choice.

It was an emotional decision by Honda. They were going back into GP racing and they were going to do it with a four-stroke. The problem was whether it could be done.

DEVELOPING THE NEW FOUR-STROKE

The Project Leader

Irimajirib was given the challenge of designing the new four-stroke racer. He recalls,

> I don't know what happened in the upper management of Honda before the announcement. I remember one day Mr Kawashima coming to R&D and saying to me, 'We'll start now.' I was assigned as the project leader, without any resources. He said to me, 'your job is to collect some people and make a team'. He knew that I was in charge of the entire motorcycle development business, so he knew that I had the obligation to the motorcycle business itself. I needed to balance human resources between the racing and commercial programme. It was a good strategy. Also Mr Kawashima knew about racing. In the 1960s, when Mr Honda was deeply involved in GP racing and Formula 1, he put almost all the resources to the racing programme. One day Mr Fujisawa, executive VP Honda, realized that there was no output from R&D to the commercial business. Kawashima knew that racing can be a drag on other projects. He realized that there was a danger that all the resources would be spent on the racing project.

The Challenge of the Design

It was time to start with a clean sheet of paper. The challenge of designing a four-stroke that met the FIM restrictions, and produced power that would be competitive with respect to the Suzuki and Yamaha opposition, was a tough one. A number of design parameters were indisputable. The engine was going to have to run at a very high speed to make the horsepower figures it needed to obtain. At the end of its days, the MV500 had been tuned to run at 15,000 rpm, with just over 100 bhp produced at the crankshaft, and reliability had been marginal. The bike was a fully developed in-line four, with all of the characteristics that Honda had used in 1966 and 1967. It was just not enough and there was nothing radical that could be done to that design to make it competitive. An alternative needed to be conceived.

The Calculations

Without the FIM regulations, the most logical engine to build would have been a V-8 or V-12. The V-12 would definitely be adequate to get the engine speed up to the 20,000 rpm mark to produce the 115 bhp it would initially need to beat the two-strokes. It would also conceivably be possible with a V-8, but this could be marginal, since the longer stroke that would be needed would raise the piston speed to well over 4,500 ft/min, considered at the time to be an absolute maximum for a reliable engine. A small group was formed to do the maths, calculate the stress curves on the engine components, and make a recommendation of how to proceed.

Irimajiri remembers,

> At that time, the new Asaka R&D was just started and there were only 500 or 600 people, much smaller than Yamaha, which was just motorcycles. Most of our resources were dedicated to the automobile projects. I could not afford to re-assign people. The only thing I could do was put some young inexperienced people in the GP programme and collect other people from other areas in the company. Initially we had about ten people and it grew to about twenty-five. Only KamiyaSan was experienced.

The Engineers

In addition to Irimajiri himself, there were a number of key engineers working on the project. Takeo Fukui was the engineering project leader for the new machine, with Kamiya the chief designer for the chassis, and young graduate Suguru Kanazawa working with his more experienced colleagues on the engine design.

It took eighteen months of blood, sweat and tears before the NR500 could be wheeled into the studio for its official portrait.

Delays and Difficulties

The project got off to an inauspicious start when it was decided that the existing buildings housing the R&D centre at Asaka were too small to support the new racing team work. It was decided to extend the building at the site but, when foundations were laid, it was discovered that they were building on a site of ancient interest. A number of old artefacts were uncovered, the local prefecture administration was called in, and a building restraint order was imposed to give archaeologists six months to investigate the site. There was no way to absorb this delay in the schedule and the plans to start racing at the start of the 1979 season suddenly seemed over-optimistic.

Progress on the design gave no cause for increased optimism. For many weeks the team racked their brains about the problem, looking at trying to squeeze more valves into a cylinder, fuel injection, and desmodromic valve operation. The wildest ideas were considered, but none offered any solution within the restriction of the four-cylinder regulations. The breakthrough came from an unexpected quarter – the evening rush-hour traffic.

The Idea

Irimajiri recounts how the idea came to him:

> In those days I was thinking through the problems day and night – how to increase the engine speed, valve area, horsepower. I drew lots of different configurations and I was so tired. On my way home one evening, I stopped at an intersection and saw the horizontal oval traffic lights with three round lights, and it clicked that this was the answer. I went back home very fast and all through the night I drew some very rough sketches. The next day I brought them to R&D and told Mr Kanazawa that this was the new engine design he should use. He was not happy. He said it was a crazy idea.

The FIM regulations stipulated the number of cylinders, without saying anything about their shape or form. By adopting an elongated oval form, it would be possible to produce an engine in which one piston would have a surface area comparable to that of two conventional pistons. Four oval cylinders would be as close to an eight-cylinder engine as it was possible to get. The spark of innovation had flashed and opened Honda's path to a successful return to GP racing.

The Engine

The pistons that were used on the NR500 were 93.4mm wide and 41mm long. The extreme width of the piston resulted in the need for a double conrod to ensure lateral stability, to stop the piston rocking in its bore and compromising the piston ring seal. Magnesium pistons and forged aluminium were tried, before aluminium alloy was finally used. Exotic materials abounded – the crankcases were cast in magnesium and the cylinders were aluminium, with a hard chrome plating on the walls for oil retention. The small end wrist pin was 12mm in diameter and the big end 26mm.

A total of eight valves, with twig-like shafts of 3.8mm diameter, and two tiny 8mm spark plugs were located in each cylinder head. The 18mm inlet valves were slightly larger and placed closer to the vertical than the 16mm exhaust valves, with an included angle of 65 degrees. Each pair of inlet valves was fed by the inlet manifold connected to a twin-choke 30mm downdraught carburettor. The geartrain drive for the camshafts was taken off the end of the crankshaft on the right-hand

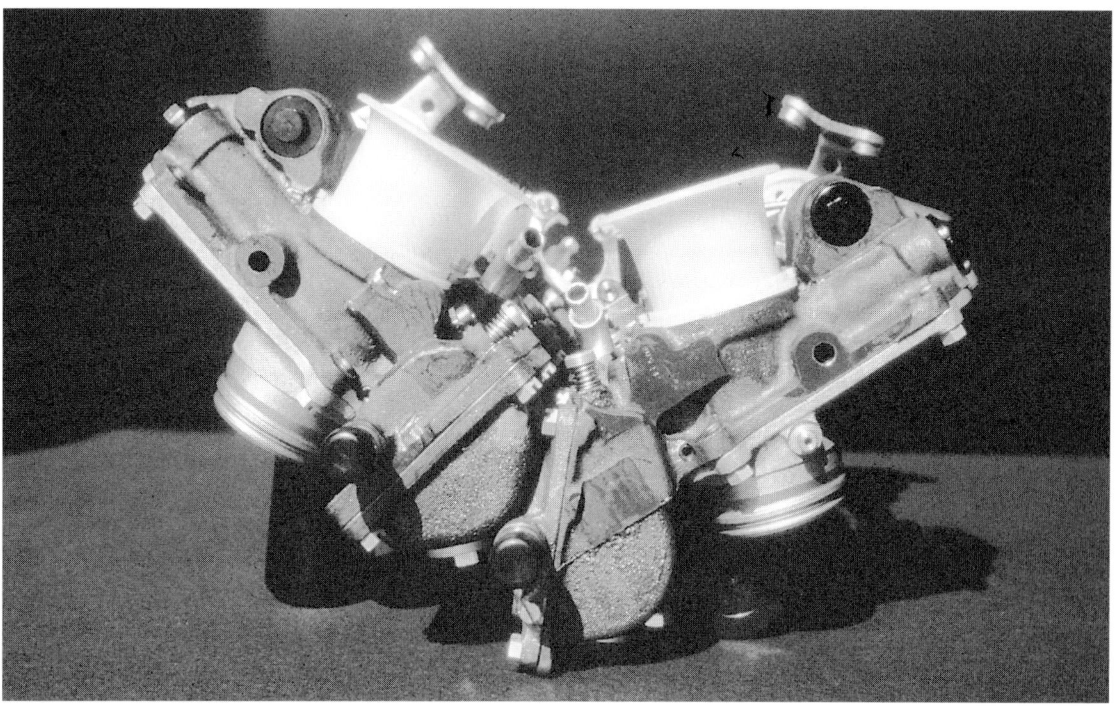

A set of these magnesium-bodied 26mm carburettors went missing at the 1979 French GP, never to be seen again.

side of the engine. A central gear on the crank drove a jackshaft taking power through to a dry clutch on the right-hand side of the engine, with the drive for the water pump also coming off this shaft. With the V configuration that Honda had chosen, water-cooling was an obvious consequence. The angle between the cylinder banks was slightly wider than the fully balanced 90 degrees that is optimum for a V-engine. At 100 degrees, extra room was available between the cylinder banks for the carburettors and there was no noticeable increase in vibration from the engine. The engine had conventional wet sump lubrication, the main bearings being fed via oil passages in the crankshaft. Full electronic CDI ignition was used to generate the 300 sparks per second generated by this engine.

Testing

A testbed was set up in the workshop to prove this exotic new technology, starting with the oval piston and cylinder and eight-valve head. This was a single cylinder configuration using the crankcases of an XL125 as host, and was given the code name K00. The new piston design was christened UFO, standing for 'Ultimately Formed Oval'. Despite this unfortunate name, it worked, the single cylinder testbed managing to produce 20.5 bhp at 12,000 rpm in February 1979. It functioned sufficiently well for the team to get the go-ahead to build the entire engine. Irimajiri remembers,

> When I initially created the oval piston concept, there were very few people who

thought it would work. We built a single cylinder experimental engine and ran it. Really it ran quite well, but there were several problems. The torque was lower than we expected and it was very difficult to increase the engine speed due to the vibration caused by the single piston. Most people thought that piston ring sealing caused most of the early problems and also the idling and low engine speed problems. It was not. It ran quite well at low revs. The problem was that the torque was not as high as calculated. We thought that this was due to the shape of the combustion chamber. We had two plugs, so we realized that we needed to improve the combustion chamber shape. We experimented with different shapes. We also tried three plugs and different plug lengths. There was a big difference between one and two plugs, but with an extra third plug there was almost no difference.

The Chassis

On the other side of the workshop, the chassis design team was coming together. Seeing what was happening in the engine department, the chassis designers were anxious to show how innovative they could also be. In particular, one engineer had a dream that he desperately wanted to see become reality. According to Irimajiri, it was Kamiya's dream to make a monocoque chassis. There was a lot of discussion within Honda whether such a radical chassis should be used. Irimajiri's thought was that, if the engine was so experimental, they could hardly stop the chassis designers from experimenting. The project leader encouraged Kamiya to realize this concept.

The 1970s had seen some considerable experimentation with alternative frame design. The single shock rear suspension had been introduced on a broad scale for Yamaha's racing models and the first rising-rate designs were appearing. There had also been several attempts to improve on the tubular Featherbed design that had become largely universal on racing bikes during the 1960s.

Some of the most radical new chassis designs had come from the John Player Norton team struggling to hold back the two-stroke tide in the early 1970s. Technical director and rider for the team was Peter Williams, who had, among other things, been one of the first riders to use light alloy electron wheels instead of spoked wheels on his Arter Matchless. For the 1973 version of the bike, powered by a vertical twin engine with roots in a design dating from 1948, Williams directed the building of a monocoque chassis, the engine suspended from a double-skinned sheet of mild steel. This enabled the frontal area of the bike to be reduced and resulted, with a carefully designed fairing in a very low drag coefficient. These changes, as well as some other changes to engine position and front suspension damping, resulted in a bike Peter Williams was happy to ride. He was later quoted as saying,

> That weight distribution, together with the low centre of gravity and rigid monocoque frame, made the 1973 JPN the most superb motorcycle it has been my privilege to ride. People won't believe me when I say that I could lay it over, get the rear and the front wheels sliding, then put the power on and put in a two-wheel controlled drift round any corner faster than Druids at Brands. It was a really wonderful little machine – smaller than almost any 500, yet quite powerful enough and with perfect steering.

The next year, the monocoque chassis was gone, replaced by a triangulated space frame that Bimota and Ducati were later to adopt. The reasons for the change were never fully revealed, although engine access for the mechanics was a severe problem with the monocoque design. Peter Williams felt that the John Player Nortons had been hugely successful, claiming, 'We demonstrated that a 78 bhp four-stroke twin could be competitive with 120 bhp two-stroke by gaining a clear advantage in other areas.'

Honda felt it was the right approach as well. A compact frontal area and optimized aerodynamic form were put on the list of requirements for the bike. But first they needed to design the monocoque chassis they had decided to use. They designed a true monocoque that would have been recognized and understood in the aeroplane industry in which the technique originated. The complete front end of the motorcycle, from the top of the headstock to the rear engine mountings, was a stressed double-walled skin of aluminium. The headstock was positioned at the apex of the two sheets of aluminium, with another sheet of aluminium forming an enormous gusset behind the headstock. The engine itself was a stressed member of the frame and was held in position between the monocoque halves by a dozen bolts on each side into the engine casings. With these retaining bolts removed, the complete engine and rear half of the bike could be wheeled out of the monocoque and front end, something that needed to be done even to get to the carburettors to change the jetting. This was not going to be an easy bike for the mechanics to fine-tune during GP practice.

The chassis therefore acted as the lower fairing and was also used to mount the radiators that were located on the side of the bike. Keeping to a compact frontal area meant no room for a radiator of the size that was needed to cool the 20,000 rpm engine. The theory was that the radiators would benefit from the 'venturi' effect that would occur when the bike was at speed – airflow along the side of the monocoque would produce a lower pressure over the radiator fins, and the slight raised pressure within the monocoque would result in the air being sucked through the radiators. It would also mean that the carburettors, housed in the relatively dead space between the cylinder bank V, would not be breathing warm air that had already passed through a radiator mounted in the nose of the fairing or chassis. On paper, this new machine was beginning to shape up into something really special.

The Wheels and Tyres

The search for a lower frontal area lead the Honda team to look at the universal standard front wheel size – this had been 18in diameter for several decades. They came up with 16in wheels front and rear, and inadvertently sparked a re-evaluation of tyre and wheel sizes throughout the racing sport. The lowered frontal area also resulted in a lower centre of gravity, making the bike easier to turn into a corner and change direction. There are also several other benefits to be gained with smaller wheels, such as the lowering of the gyroscopic effect of the rotating wheels, which can work against the change in direction the rider is trying to force. Once they were convinced of the advantages the 16in wheels should bring to the racing package, the Honda team contacted Dunlop and Michelin and asked them to develop racing tyres for the new bike. Honda's influence in racing meant that the 16in tyres went straight on to the development programme of both companies.

Although all of the racing manufacturers had chosen cast magnesium wheels, Honda endorsed their own design of wheel, the Comstar. These had first appeared in 1977 on some of the new Honda street bikes and were considered strong enough to do the job on the new racer. Short aluminium struts were riveted between the hub and lugs on the rim of the wheel to form a five-point star or pentagram. Disc brakes provided the braking all round, with only the mounting of the calliper in front of the forks deviating from conventional contemporary thinking.

The Front End

Another innovation was to be found on the front end of the bike. The conventional telescopic front fork was scrutinized, found wanting and a new design was made. This involved the fork slider being attached to the front wheel axle rather than the upper yoke and triple clamp of the steering head. The thicker fork stanchions were now attached to the triple clamp and bars, resulting in an upside-down fork. In addition, the spring was mounted externally in front of the tubes, simplifying adjustment, but, more importantly, oil and the air within the fork could

What a challenge the NR500 engine was for a young engineer just out of university! Suguru Kanazawa is now a Director at HRC, but the NR500 remains close to his heart.

be kept separate to reduce frothing. A further oddity was to be found at the front end, with a trailing front axle mounted behind the forks. The theory behind this was that the forces working on a leading axle when the bike passed over a bump would not be fully absorbed by the reactive forces from the frame, and the result would be twisting force into the forks. What seemed to have been overlooked was the fact that this was putting a lot of weight ahead of the steering axis, the forks themselves with springs in front of them as well as the brake calliper that had also been mounted in front of the forks. This could be expected to make the steering heavy, although with the smaller 16in wheels and their tendency to quicken the steering, the two might have cancelled each other out. Later, the almost complete change of front-end design was to make the task of de-bugging the bike an especially difficult one for the riders.

The Rear Suspension

The rear suspension, by contrast, was almost conventional in layout. As the bike took shape on paper, the world of racing still seemed to be undecided with respect to the use of single shock rear suspension. Yamaha had lead the way with the introduction of its monoshock suspension in 1975 and for a time they had been the sole proponents of single shock rear suspension. Then Kawasaki also rejected the twin shocks for their new 250 and 350 tandem twins when they were introduced in 1977. Kawasaki had taken the principle a step further by designing a linkage system that progressively increased the spring compression rate as the suspension was compressed. The intention was to provide a soft spring rate on small compressions, which would stiffen up as the spring was compressed further. The leverage provided by the geometry of the linkage would provide this. Yamaha's monoshock was simply a single shock, potentially enabling softer suspension due to the greater swing-arm travel possible and greater stiffness due to the triangulation that the monoshock mounting wishbone provided. Suzuki were still persevering with dual shocks, laid down at an acute angle with the swing-arm, with progressively wound springs or Kayaba shocks using nitrogen as the spring.

Honda decided that the single shock was the way to go, and designed a system that looked very similar to Yamaha's design. In fact, there was a subtle change that resulted in rising-rate suspension. The U-form wishbone positioned above the conventional swing-arm was pivoted at both the lower connection to the swing-arm and the upper apex. The lower end of the shock was bolted to the upper apex of the wishbone, as was a tie rod that was attached to a lug on the engine casing above the gearbox. The tie rod ensured that the movement of the rear wheel resulted in the pivoted shock/wishbone connection travelling in an arc, providing rising rate of suspension. The upper end of the suspension unit was bolted to the sheet headstock gusset.

The conventional rear swing-arm was just a little unconventional in that it pivoted on bearing carriers integrated in the monocoque frame that were coaxial to the rear drive sprocket. During the 1970s there had been some designs that achieved this, the new Italian Bimota company making it something of a trademark with their racing and road chassis. This was considered desirable because the coaxial location with the drive sprocket eliminated any variations of drive chain tension as the rear suspension was compressed. Although it undoubtedly achieved this, it did so at the cost of a wider and heavier swing-arm.

How to disassemble a monocoque NR500 in six easy steps, as demonstrated by Carlo Marelli and Sugihara. (They got a lot of practice changing engines at Le Mans.) First, hook up the engine to a transverse paddock stand straddling the bike; undo the nine bolts holding the monocoque to the engine.

Pull the front half of the bike with the monocoque forward and away from the engine and rear section; the NR has started to grow in length.

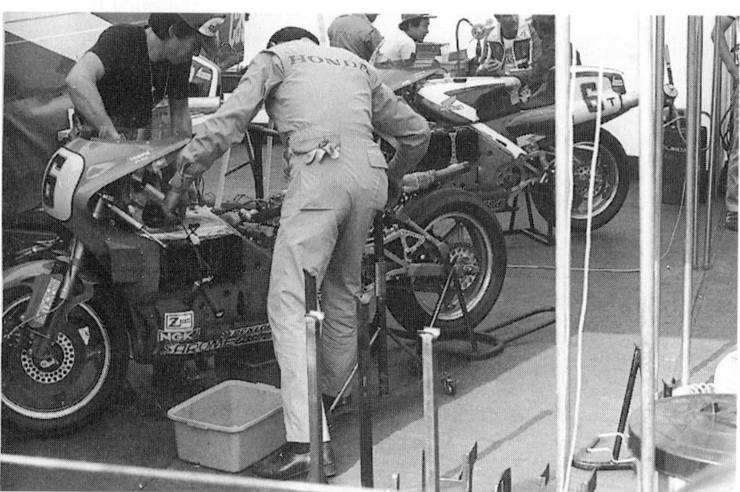

Now the NR has grown by a foot and the front end is almost clear of the engine.

The monocoque can now be separated from the engine and assorted cables can be fed through it.

The monocoque now gets lifted away on to a separate stand.

(Right) *A new engine is wheeled up and the process can be reversed.*

THE NEW BIKE TAKES SHAPE

Dummy Engines and Early Problems

The new four-stroke bike package gathered shape in late 1978 and early 1979. The first dummy engine with XL250 crankcases and an oval piston and cylinder was fired up in July 1978. Six months later, in February 1979, the first full engine was running, but there were problems with the sealing of the piston rings. Blow-by along the sides of the piston, although not severe, was resulting in the destruction of the oil film in the chromed cylinder walls. The initial K0 engine used the same piston ring design as conventional circular pistons – a scraper ring sitting over a rippled expander ring that should force the out scraper ring against the cylinder walls. With a circular bore, the radial tension of the rings, plus the gas pressure within the cylinder, keeps the rings seated against the cylinder walls. At high rpm – this engine could be expected to work at 20,000 rpm – ring flutter can break the gas seal and, if there is inadequate radial tension in the springs, blow-by will occur. This was to continue to be a problem for the new bike for the first eighteen months of its existence.

The first conventional oval ring in the K0 engine was replaced by a ring that was cast with considerably greater tension, with the open end of the ring centimetres apart when uncompressed. This helped a little, but Honda finally fixed the problem later only by careful machining of the piston grooves to maintain gas pressure at high rpm.

Testing Begins

By April 1979, the first full bike was built and it was time for test riders to start the development programme. Honda decided to call the bike the NR500, the acronym appropriately standing for 'New Racer'. The riders who were called to travel to the test circuit in Japan were Englishman Mick Grant and Japanese rider Takazumi Katayama.

A NEW GP TEAM

Honda International Racing Company

While the NR had been taking shape in the Asaka R&D offices, the infrastructure needed to run a GP team in Europe had been put together. Within Europe, France and Britain were the two countries where there were active Honda organizations involved in national racing. From their French and British bases, Honda had mounted a successful challenge to Kawasaki in the niche sport of endurance racing. Honda first entered the world championship races in 1976, and the French team took the first of four consecutive titles.

A year later, Honda supported the inaugural one-race Formula 1 'world championship' that the FIM had awarded to the Isle of Man, after the GP status was transferred to Silverstone on the British mainland. They also sponsored a single marque 125 championship for the MT125 production racer Honda had produced.

This was to continue in 1978, and a nine-round National Formula 1 series was organized, narrowly won by Kawasaki from Honda. Both France and Britain had the makings of a racing infrastructure that could be extended to include the GPs. Honda President Kawashima chose Gerald Davison to start preparing for Honda's return to GP racing.

The first step was to create a new company, the Honda International Racing Company (HIRCO), to run the GP on behalf of the

Honda company in Japan . It was decided to set up an operation completely separate from the main Honda UK company, which was based in Chiswick in London.

Gerald Davison remembers, 'We needed a new site for the GP team as the Chiswick workshop was too small. We needed somewhere where we could be testing engines late into the night, away from our commercial activities to maintain some secrecy. We wanted to keep away from prying eyes.'

Mick Grant

The next job was to find a rider who was skilled enough to help in the development of the NR500 and talented enough to win GPs. Mick Grant was an obvious candidate on the British racing scene. His career had started at the beginning of the 1970s, with a British 350cc championship in 1972 and membership of the John Player Norton team in 1973 and 1974. In 1975 he had joined Kawasaki and spent four years running their water-cooled 750 triples against Barry Sheene in the British Superbike series. He won the series in 1975, but the growing strength of Sheene's RG500 and lack of development of the antique KR750 left Grant runner-up in subsequent years.

During 1977, Grant had also shown his ability to compete at GP level, when he won Kawasaki's first 250 GP in Holland with the new KR250 tandem twin. He followed that up with another win in Sweden and a very close second place in Finland, demonstrating his ability to perform at circuits he had never ridden. Grant had been contracted to ride the GPs for 1978 alongside his commitments in the British Superbike series, but suddenly there were a number of Kawasaki riders, with Kork Ballington, Greg Hansford, Jean-Pierre Balde and Anton Mang all getting support. Initial results were disappointing and then a crash in Austria broke some bones in his foot and ruined the rest of the season. By the Powerbike International meeting in October at Brands Hatch, he was fully recovered from his injuries and had a wonderful meeting, taking the 250 and 350 races, beating Sheene in the Superbike race and finishing second in the Powerbike race. One of the spectators was Gerald Davison.

Mick Grant recalls, 'The press published a photo of Gerald Davison and me talking behind my van at the October 78 Powerbike International meeting at Brands Hatch, where I won the 250, 350 and 750 races. It was an *MCN* [*Motor Cycle News*] scoop: "HIRCO set to sign Mick Grant?"'

Davison had already been briefed about the decisions that had been taken on the NR500, and he was anxious to impress Grant with the effort that Honda were going to put into the project. Grant's memory of his conversations with Davison are quite clear:

> It was a bit frightening really as I'm someone with both feet on the ground. I'm always very suspicious when I hear claims of things that don't really make sense. If things don't sound logical, I'm a bit wary. At that Brands meeting, Gerald was telling me that it was a revolutionary new four-stroke, with oval pistons that revved to 21,000 rpm. They would be using a lot of ceramics. There were all sorts of ideas, even considering not using radiators. They were looking at using some sort of nitrogen and letting that seep away and dissipate the heat during the race. When they started talking like that, I just got a little bit worried about it. Gerald had not yet seen the bikes and was going on what he had been told. Gerald is more a salesman than an engineer and I found some of the things he was saying a little bit hard to believe. It was clearly going to be a very experimental bike, but some of the ideas seemed to be too crazy to be possible.

Just before Christmas 1978, Grant signed a two-year contract with HIRCO to develop the NR500 and ride the Formula 1 Honda bike in the Isle of Man and UK races. Davison says he had a lot of faith in Mick, who he believed to be a sound engineer:

> When you are working on a new machine, you need someone who can come in and tell you what is happening out on the track. He needed no convincing. This was Honda. Everyone thought we were going to take the dust-covers off something on a starting grid somewhere and win a GP.

Takazumi Katayama

Earlier that year there had been an unexpected phone call received by Irimajiri. Takazumi Katayama, Japan's most successful GP racer, wanted to join the Honda GP effort. In 1973 Katayama had become Japanese 350 champion and the next year he started his GP career at the mid-season Dutch TT. He was not the only non-European debuting in the 250 race, and he made as vivid an impression as Kenny Roberts, who finished third, while Katayama crashed contesting the lead. A week later in Belgium, he finished third and two weeks later he won the 250 race in Sweden. The GP regulars were astonished by his cut-throat attitude that did not include any room for compromise during the race. Complaints streamed in about his aggressive riding style and he was admonished by the FIM, but still finished fourth in the championship table despite just half a season of competition.

In 1977, he rode the Yamaha Europe home-brew 350 triple to a world championship win, becoming the first-ever Japanese motorcycling world champion. For 1978 he was one of the three riders supported by Yamaha in the 500 class, ending the year in fifth place. For most of his racing career he had had a very close relationship with Yamaha, working as a test rider for the factory. His inclusion in the team would be an enormous psychological advantage to the engineers; he was a gifted racer speaking their own language, with years of experience developing competition machines.

Irimajiri received a call from Katayama, expressing an interest in joining the team, having heard rumours about the NR racing programme. He told Irimajiri that he was interested in the four-stroke racing machines and wanted to be involved in the development stage. Irimajiri was surprised, as Katayama was so successful, but he remembers Katayama saying that that he was not afraid to throw away his career.

Katayama recalls the situation slightly differently:

> There was an international race at Donnington Park in 1978 and there were a few Japanese people watching. Barry Sheene and Kenny Roberts were strong and I finished close behind Barry. One of the Honda people came to my caravan and started talking about Japan. We agreed to meet again when I returned to Japan. Honda had been working quite secretively, so I did not know what exactly was going on. I thought that if Honda would return to racing they would win. Everyone thought that. It had always been my dream to ride for Honda if they returned to racing. I admired Mr Honda very much. I read his book when I was ten years old. I realized that a four-stroke would be tough to win with, but I had confidence and their engineering skills. I signed a contract for three years. I expected the second year to be very competitive, something that many people at Honda said. The first year was going to be a very tough development schedule, the second competitive, and the third world champion.

FINISHING THE BIKE

Continuing Problems

The NR riders were chosen, but there was still no bike for them to ride. It had taken the team more than a year to solve the enormous problems that their design mandate had presented. According to Gerald Davison, the problem was that they all thought that Honda, as a company, were infallible. The feeling was that all they had to do was screw the machine together, and they would have something to win with. It became clear early on, however, that many of their engineering problems were entirely new. They were at the cutting edge of technology and what really should have been a research project conducted in secret for two or three years was going to be a very public return to GP racing.

The whole NR story is characterized by differing views of what was happening within Honda. The race team thought that Honda were building a racing bike to become world champion. This was not completely accurate. The racing was actually just a part of a development programme that had other, more important goals. According to Irimajiri, the NR team had to achieve two things: create new technology that could be used in the future, and train a group of engineers who would then be very useful for future R&D work. He started the project with very inexperienced people and the four-stroke concept. It would have been easier to reach competitive level with a two-stroke, but a four-stroke engine would have much more of a future in commercial terms.

The first full V4 engine was fired up in April 1979, after much experimentation with the single cylinder engine. The first engine produced just 80 bhp at 14,000 rpm, due to the piston ring problems. With the re-designed rings the engine pushed out 95.8 bhp at 17,000 rpm. By raising the compression ratio from 10.5:1 to 10.7:1, the engine crept very close to the psychologically important 100 bhp.

Mick Grant had his own mechanics, Nigel Everett and Paul Dowes, over in Japan as part of the NR team as soon as possible after he signed his contract. They participated in the activity around the development of the bike, and Grant spoke to them on the phone from time to time. He remembers them describing what was going on and saying that there were still mechanical problems, but that the bikes were very revolutionary.

Those mechanical problems primarily related to the piston ring sealing, and to valve spring failure. The problem with the valve springs persisted for some time, occurring again on the full V4 engine when it was fired up in April.

First Tests

Finally, at the end of April 1979, a complete bike was assembled and the team set off for the JARI proving track at Yatabe. On 28 April 1979, Honda's test rider Hiroyuki Iida completed a few cautious laps on the NR500, until the test was cut short by boiling water pouring from a burst water hose. The pannier radiators were not cooling adequately, and redesigned units with a greater surface area were mounted shortly afterwards. A month later it was the turn of the GP riders and the team travelled to the Tochigi proving ground. Mick Grant had sustained a fractured pelvis in the North West 200 road race in Northern Ireland, so it was Katayama's honour to take the bike out for a spin. He was not impressed, and describes the first NR as 'ridiculous'. He recalls,

> It was impossible to fight with this bike. I was afraid to be as direct to the engineers.

> I understood that they loved the NR. They just did not realize how far off the pace the bike was. They thought we would finish the first race in the top fifteen. It was impossible. The 16in wheels and tyres were too new. The suspension was terrible, hopping all over the place. The rear swing-arm was flexing badly and the front suspension stanchions were also bending. The brakes were very weak

The bike he rode was producing just under 100 bhp at 17,000 rpm and weighed in at 275lb (125kg); at least, that is what was claimed by Honda. If it was true, the weight was an incredible achievement – the competing two-stroke 500s were 10–12lb (5–10kg) heavier, but they were also producing at least 20 bhp more. Even so, 100 bhp was a lot better than the 80 bhp at 14,000 rpm produced in the April test; the first engine also had a razor-sharp power curve, while the power curve of the second engine was more user-friendly, despite a bad flat spot between 14,000 and 15,000 rpm. All the same, Mick Grant recalls that it was not an easy bike to ride:

> The engine wouldn't tick over at anything under 7,000 rpm. Power started at 13,000 rpm and it was all done at 17,500, although it would rev on to 20/21. The engine never had flywheel on it. If you were running at 20,000 rpm and did a plug chop, it was like blowing out a candle. Whoof, and it was gone. When you rode, it didn't feel that it was running that fast, there was no vibration at all. Due to the lack of flywheel, shutting off the engine coming into corners would cause the back wheel to hop. You could either slip the clutch or rev it as you came into the corner. I talked to the Japanese and explained the problem and we eventually got it pretty good, after a couple of abortive designs.

More Problems

The difficulty of starting the engine demonstrated to Shinichi Sugihara, Katayama's mechanic, the lack of practical reality with which the GP adventure had been approached. Sugihara, based at the HIRCO's UK headquarters, was not involved in the preparation of the machine in Japan, but he remembers the problems:

> Opening of the throttle valve was very critical. It was 0.3mm or something; the engineer always checked with a small wire. If opened more, the engine did not start. Ignition was also not so good with wet plugs. I complained about it being difficult to start and an engineer told me that it was designed to be started when the bike had a speed of 5–10mph [10–15kph]. At Le Mans, the start is a little bit uphill, so it was very difficult to start it there. The second engine was much better.

The handling took a little getting used to as well, according to Mick Grant:

> The bike felt quite chubby, but I think that was because we had never ridden 16in wheels. The Dunlop tyres had been built for a machine that they had never even seen. At the best it was going to be a wild guess as to what they should be. Michelin had done the same. You didn't feel sure of your footing at all.
>
> The original monocoque chassis was in aluminium and it used to crack at the steering head. We used to go out for three or four laps then come in and they'd get the welding torch out and weld the cracks up. Every time you braked hard into a corner, you thought of the cracks growing and wondered if you'd finish your stint before the front end dropped off. I think they were trying to make a chassis like a car's. They

would have had in production two pressings, one for each side of the machine, one weld up the middle, with a headstock stuck in it. Imagine how cheap that would be to manufacture. They intended proving this on the race circuit, encouraging the general public to accept the design. Unfortunately, they went wrong in their use of aluminium – too soft and therefore prone to fatigue and failure. It had to be like that in order to get a headstock welded in. Had they made that chassis a little bit heavier, perhaps using steel, they may have had a chassis that worked.

According to Sugihara, the monocoque was not such a success. The riders complained that every time the chassis and engine was split and reassembled, the handling was different. Access was difficult and making changes to the geometry was impossible.

Satoru Horiike was a young graduate who had joined the chassis development team. He remembers well the handling problem of the monocoque NR. His first job was to make a scale drawing of the monocoque:

In those days we designed on boards and with pencil. I made a big scale drawing of the frame and an experienced race engineer came along and said 'Very interesting. What sort of fairing are you drawing?' I said, 'This is the frame.' He was amazed. The monocoque was very light and very stiff, using 3.2mm thick aluminium. It would crack at the engine mountings. We made a prototype, checked the stress via a gauge and some places we found, but not all. The main problems with the original monocoque were the cracks and the fact that the frame and engine were not properly locked together. There were too many tolerances in the engine mounting and this changed the feel of the bike every time the engine was removed.

THE RETURN TO RACING

A GP Programme for 1979?

Now that the bike was running, questions began to be asked within the company about whether they would announce a GP programme for 1979. It was obvious to most people on the race team that the bike was not yet competitive and there was still a big question mark over its reliability. The early bikes would not run for longer than twenty minutes before they failed. In addition to the sealing problems and valve spring failure, the cush drive, in which the middle gear in the cam gear train was mounted, would wear and the cam timing would slowly slip. The best that could be hoped for with a new fresh engine was a few warm-up laps, followed by a couple of fast laps.

Irimajiri remembers that there was no pressure from top management to go to the GP races. His own philosophy was that the machines would be improved through actual racing (even though the likely poor performances would be embarrassing), and that Honda should therefore go to races as an important part of the development programme. He recalls, 'There was a big discussion within the company and most people were of the opinion that Honda should not compete without a very competitive race machine. I understood this, but it was not my philosophy.'

According to Gerald Davison: 'We had to compete at Silverstone. If I had said to Irimajiri, "I'm sorry, this is not good enough to race", he would not have accepted that. The NR was operational – even though it was not competitive – so we had to race.'

The Isle of Man Press Conference

On 7 June 1979, twenty years after Honda's first appearance on the Isle of Man, a press conference was held at a hotel on the island, and the first official photographs of the NR500 were handed out to the press.

The Isle of Man was no longer an official GP circuit, and had not counted for points for the world championship since 1976. In 1979, therefore, although the public gathered in large crowds to see Mike Hailwood, who had been coaxed back on to a bike for the TT, only the British press was well represented. On the morning of 7 June, a small piece of paper was pinned up in the press room, stating that there would be photos of, and information about, the new Honda GP racer available at the hotel later that evening. A Honda UK dealers' convention was hijacked and, after a long speech underlining Honda's leading position in the motorcycle market, Eric Sulley, chairman of Honda UK, passed out two photographs and a specification sheet that stated that the bike was a V4 four-stroke in a monocoque chassis. That was all the information that was available. A couple of hours later in Japan, a second press conference was called with the same package of information.

With so little information, there was feverish speculation in the press as to how Honda could be competitive using a V4 engine. There were strong rumours that the engine was using a double-piston construction and that there were six valves per cylinder.

Two NR500s leave Japan

Following the announcement on the Isle of Man, Mick Grant and Takazumi Katayama were in Japan testing the bikes for an extended period of four weeks. It was decided to go for the last two GPs of the year, with the British GP at Silverstone on 12 August as the bike's baptism of fire. The French GP at Le Mans would follow three weeks later. Two NR500s were flown out of Japan on 27 July 1979, along with 20,000 spare parts!

Sugihara recalls that the real problem was that the Japanese customs required every individual part to be listed in the carnet. The X0 engine used uncaged needle rollers, so every bearing contained tens of 'spare parts' that had to be listed. Later, they managed to get the customs to agree that each needle size counted as a single spare on the carnet.

Testing in the UK

The Honda team decided that they needed all the testing in the UK they could get, so they hired Snetterton, an obscure circuit in Norfolk, far from the world press assembling at Silverstone. The main objective was to get some tyres sorted out for the GP, but there was the predictable engine carnage as well. Another day's testing was spent at Donnington Park, where Mick Grant felt he rode one of his best laps of Donnington ever. He remembers doing a lap of 1min. 17.8s:

> If I had to single out one lap of any circuit in my life that was an incredible achievement, that would be it. At that time on an NR, it was absolutely phenomenal. I came back in but the chief mechanic wasn't right impressed. I said, 'You couldn't do a better lap than that on the computer', and you couldn't have.

The problem was that Fukui was holding a little slip of paper. Written on it was the lap record set by Wil Hartog on the factory RG500 Suzuki. A couple of months earlier Hartog had stopped the clock at 1min. 15.4s. Two and a half seconds in a 75-second lap is an eternity.

Silverstone

At last the time had come to pit the new bike against the best 500cc machines in the

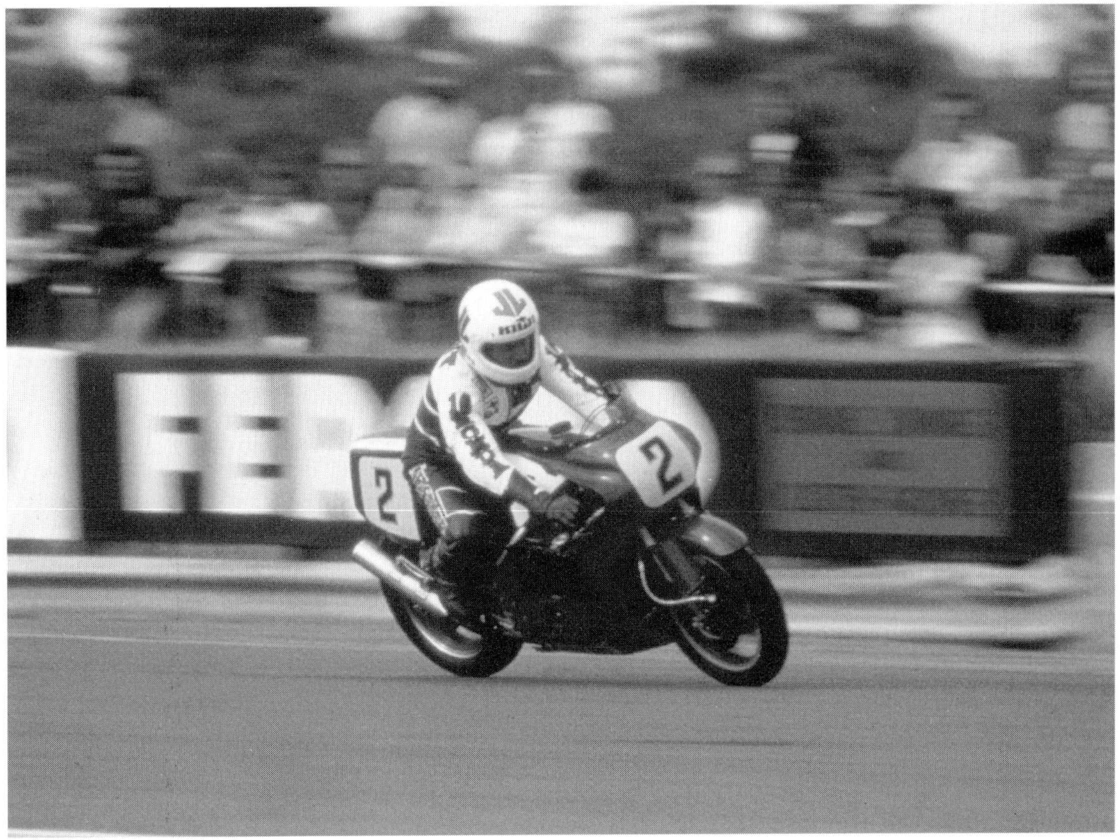

Mick Grant out for practice at the 1979 British GP at Silverstone.

world. The Honda team travelled to Silverstone and practice started. Their worst fears were confirmed. The bikes were hopelessly uncompetitive.

Mick Grant remembers that, on the way to the GP, the Honda team seemed to be quite hopeful that they would get some sort of result. Just before the GP, there was an open practice session with all classes out at once:

> I was going flat out down the Hanger straight on the NR and Charlie Williams on a standard TZ250 was pulling away from me at 3 or 4 mph [5 or 6kph]. That brought home the enormity of the task we had. I was riding really hard, on a bike that hadn't the power to slide the tyres, and still managing to slide both wheels through the corners. We were riding well.

Gerald Davison says that Silverstone was a very serious effort for Honda, who spared nothing in order to enter and finish the race. If they managed to finish, they would have made an enormous amount of progress, but they knew what they were up against.

Katayama qualified in 38th; Grant was 41st, the first reserve, and was able to start when another rider withdrew. The mechanics spent all weekend overhauling the engines. There was a new engine used for each session. According to Katayama, they only managed to qualify at Silverstone because the 500 class was not so strong, with some riders still using 351cc TZ Yamahas. He thinks everybody realized the bike was far from competitive, but no one dared say it aloud. Sugihara recalls,

> We seemed to do nothing but lap valves all weekend. After each session, the engine was swapped and heads were taken off for inspection. Each of the thirty-two valves needed to be re-lapped. It was a joke with Nigel [Everett, Grant's mechanic], how many valves a mechanic could lap in a weekend.

The team hid inside a large tent all weekend, with the probing cameras of the press kept outside at all times. Irimajiri had come over from Japan for the big event and was cross-examined by the press and an inquisitive Keith Duckworth of Cosworth fame, who was a pit-lane VIP. Irimajiri wasn't revealing anything about the engine, but seemed willing to discuss the obvious chassis design features. No one got to see anything substantial of the engine. It was easier to keep the engine a secret at Silverstone than at Le Mans: Sugihara remembers photographers crawling under the trucks at Silverstone to get shots of the bikes but, at Le Mans, it was too hot to keep the tent closed. 'It was like a sauna.'

The race day dawned at Silverstone, and Katayama and Grant lined up at the back of the grid. The team knew that the bikes could not finish in a decent position, even if they held together long enough, so the fuel tanks were only half-full. It was a tense moment for the team. As the flag dropped, the bikes were heaved towards the 15kph starting speed. Then disaster struck. Mick Grant's recollection is as follows:

> You had to push as hard as you could, hit the seat and, if you caught it the first time, you were away. Every time after that got more difficult. I was fit, but I missed it when the flag dropped. Takazumi just caught it and I had about three goes; for the first two, Takazumi was waiting for me. But finally he set off – it was taking me so long to get started. When it caught, I landed on it towards the back and it came up in the air. I climbed on and went through first, second, third gear with the front in the air; unknown to me, the oil was being pumped out the back through the massive breather pipe. I knocked it down to get round the first corner and the plastered rear tyre let go and down I went. The chief engineer complained, 'No more wheelies'. There were a lot of long faces within the team.

Katayama remembers waiting for Grant, and, as Grant came past pushing the bike, tried to help him by pushing the bike with his feet: 'I don't know if it was legal or not, but I wanted Honda to start. He couldn't start, so I went.'

Grant's smouldering NR got a liberal dusting from the fire marshal's extinguishers at Stowe as the badly winded rider was helped to the side of the track. After two laps, Katayama also pulled into the pits, with an ignition problem that caused a misfire and front brakes that were soggy. Honda's return to GP racing had ended in ignominy.

Le Mans

There were three weeks before the final GP of 1979 at Le Mans in France. The entire team of Japanese engineers and mechanics packed up and returned to base with the intention of working 24-hour days for two weeks to produce an engine with another 10 bhp and 22lb (10kg) less weight. After two weeks of blood, sweat and tears, the most obvious changes to the new engine that came out of the R&D shop were the flat-slide magnesium carburettors, whose throat diameter had grown from 22mm to 26mm. According to Honda's dyno, the engine was producing 108 bhp and they had managed to shave 10lb (5kg) off the weight, bringing it down to 270lb (122kg). Now they were on their way back to Europe to get some GP points.

Sugihara had stayed in Europe and he travelled to Le Mans to join the team flying directly to France. He remembers that there was no time to ship the bikes to France as cargo, so two complete bikes and two extra engines, plus spares, were brought over as hand luggage. He says,

> I can't imagine what it cost. It was all too large to get through baggage claim, so we had to pick everything up at the other side of the airport.
>
> Honda also brought an extra group of mechanics, who were excited at visiting France – the overhaul team. At the end of the practice we removed the engine, and the special engine overhaul team got to work. We had hired some extra garages and there the overhaul team stayed, repairing

Takazumi Katayama looks understandably concerned in the pits at the French GP of 1979.

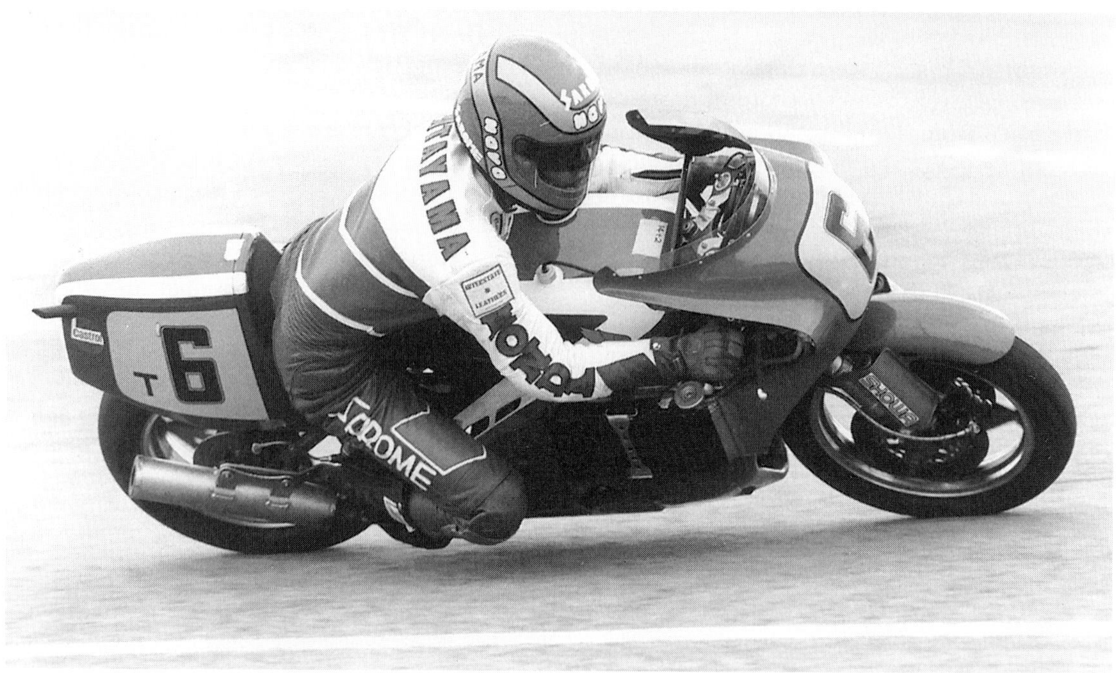

Viewed from this angle, the NR500 could almost be mistaken for a competitive racing bike. For the riders, the nightmare continued in Le Mans.

engines all night. In the morning, they returned to the hotel. They never saw anything of France, working all night and sleeping all day.

The engines may have been more powerful and the bike lighter, but the results were the same as at Silverstone – dismal. To make things worse, it was sweltering hot and the already marginal cooling of the NR was stretched towards failure. The engine was running far too hot, with the water temperature just under boiling point. Neither rider qualified, coming in first and second reserve. On race day they were allowed to join the warm-up lap; one French official said they could start, as two qualified riders had decided not to. This turned out to be inaccurate and a heated discussion ensued at the starting grid, as officials tried to get the Hondas off the grid, while the riders stood their ground. Eventually, the two NRs left the grid and were pushed back to the vans waiting to take them home. To make matters worse, a bank of the priceless 26mm magnesium carburettors had been stolen and was never recovered.

The period of the 1979 Silverstone and Le Mans GPs was the lowest moment for the team throughout the NR saga. Fukui was close to despair, after the intense work of the previous two weeks. He had crammed two months' development work into two weeks, but the result had been total failure. He now needed to re-evaluate the radical direction that had been chosen by the design team, and define a fine line between tradition that could prove inadequate and revolution that had proven unpredictable. It was going to be a long, hard winter.

3 Mission Impossible

The Development of the NR500 Four-stroke (1980–81)

MORE WORK AT R&D

The Engine

The second anniversary of Honda's announcement of their return to GP racing found the team working hard at the Asaka R&D headquarters. The team was still convinced that the bike needed a more powerful engine at its heart, and were trying some significant engine changes. The gear train drive was moved from the right-hand side of the engine to the middle of the engine between the two cylinders of the V. The original 65-degree included angle between inlet and exhaust valves was shrunk to just 55 degrees, enabling the compression ratio to be raised a little. The pilot and idle jets of the carburettors were re-designed to help the engine tick over at a normal engine speed. The clutch was re-designed to stop the phenomenal engine braking causing the rear wheel to hop. And most important of all, the whole engine was re-examined and re-engineered to give it sufficient reliability to stay in one piece for a complete race.

This patient work resulted in an engine that was producing 115 bhp by November 1979 and 118 bhp at 19,000 rpm by January 1980, with the engine running through to 20,000 rpm. The power curve was a useful one, with a steady build-up from 50 bhp at 12,000 rpm, and just a hint of a flat spot between 16,000 rpm and 17,000 rpm.

The search for power had pre-occupied the team from the start, but they had been slow to establish a benchmark at which to aim. It had been decided that a competitive figure would be 130 bhp, but the competition was moving faster than them. At the start, they had bought a standard production RG500 and put it on the dynamometer; not being two-stroke experts, they had not set it up for an optimum power run.

Mick Grant recalls,

> We had done some testing at Suzuka and we were always about four seconds off the lap record set by a 500 two-stroke. I was riding my own RG500, which was as quick as anybody else's, and it was clear that they were very short of horsepower. The RG500 that they had at the R&D shop was already a couple of years old – a Mark 2 – and I had a Mark 5. I asked Mr Fukui if we could put my Suzuki on the dyno. The best they had had out of the Mark 2 Suzuki was 96/97 bhp and the best NR500 at that stage was 103/104 bhp. They were pleased that they already had more horsepower that the Suzuki, but were not taking into account that the Suzuki was a few years out of date. I wanted to prove to them that if it was set up right, even the old Suzuki would be quicker than the NR500. I wanted to get some sense into them. Nigel [Everett] spent the previous day pulling the engine apart, putting new pistons and rings in, freshening the engine up. Went to the dyno

and got 98 bhp on the first run. Jetted it down, got 101/102 bhp. Jetted it down again and got 104/105 bhp. I said, 'We just need to do some more little changes and we're away', but Mr Fukui said there was 'no more time, no more time'. The next run on the dyno would have been about 107, which was more horsepower than they had ever seen. They didn't want to see that and I found that quite disturbing.

The Chassis

In some ways, the concentration on the engine development meant it was easier for the decision to be taken to scrap the revolutionary monocoque chassis, and return to a more conventional design. It was something for which Gerald Davison pushed very hard, recalling how, when Honda started in Europe, they only began to win GPs when they changed to English frames. In the end, Irimajiri reluctantly concurred, and Ron Williams was contacted to develop a Maxton frame.

Gerald Davison remembers that all the Japanese efforts were concentrated on getting the engine right, and suddenly it seemed that the rest didn't really matter to Honda. As he says,

> If I could source it from somewhere else, it was OK. So we ran Italian suspension, brakes, and so on. We put the monocoque

The season almost over, but the first GP of the year for Honda. The new frame from Ron Williams worked reasonably well, but the engine broke at the 1980 Finnish GP.

> chassis aside because, with a completely new concept for an engine and a chassis, you are never really sure which of the two is the problem. The third component is the rider. You need a proven rider; he doesn't need to be the fastest as long as you know what he is capable of on a quick machine. By running the Williams chassis, we knew we didn't have a chassis problem, unless the bhp exceeded anything that we ever encountered before. There was no danger of this as we were always about 10 bhp behind the two-strokes. We were always chasing a moving target.
>
> The race team had no chance of any input on the engines and we had some very clever engineers. We could give a lot of input on the chassis side. We commissioned Ron Williams to build frames for us, so he worked for us and we built frames in Slough.

Irimajiri's recollection of the changes is as follows:

> At the end of the season, we realized that the monocoque chassis could not become competitive in the racing world, because of some rigidity problems and also the inaccessibility of the engine. Modifying the chassis was very time-consuming, as the whole monocoque needed to be rebuilt to the new dimensions. We decided to reject the monocoque chassis, temporarily at least. Once we had decided to stop using the monocoque, we needed a tubular frame very quickly for the bikes. The Maxton chassis was already there so we decided to use it for the first half of the season, and we built our own for the second half.

Ron Williams had been involved in factory efforts in the past. Takazumi Katayama had commissioned a frame for the three-cylinder Yamaha that he rode in the season when he won the world championship. In the early days of the RG500, Paul Smart had used a Williams frame to turn the bike into a more competitive package. Now Honda were doing the same. Katayama, however, was not very enthusiastic about Maxton frames, despite using them several times. He thought that the Maxton frame was better, and stronger, but didn't like it very much himself, feeling that he didn't fit with it. According to him,

> Honda also didn't want to use it, but they had to. They decided to concentrate on the engine, and to use the Maxton frame. Charles Mortimer liked the Maxton and I had tried to adapt my racing style for the Maxton when I was racing Yamahas with him, but I never liked them.

The chassis was to change completely, not only through the use of a tubular frame instead of the monocoque, but also in the rejection of 16in wheels in favour of the 18in standard of the time. This was the first sign that the engineering team was willing to compromise its own goals of excellence through the application of innovative technology in the interests of producing a motorcycle that could win races.

The layout of the Williams frame bore a close resemblance to that of the last generation of Honda racers from the 1960s. It was a half cradle frame, with the engine functioning as a stressed member. The rear suspension was essentially of the same design as had been used for the monocoque frame, the upper end of the shock absorber bolted to a cross member between the two tubes tying the top of the headstock to the upper rail of the cradle.

Initially, the same upside-down front fork was used, with the external spring in front of the tubes, but, for the bike's first competitive outing in the middle of the year, this had been replaced by conventional Marzocchi forks.

The minimalist frame Williams had built for the NR500 is best seen from this angle.

The front brake callipers moved to their rightful place behind the front fork.

At first, the radiators continued to be mounted on each side of the bike. During the course of the 1980 season, they were replaced by a single vertical radiator at the front of the bike, and a supplementary radiator in the tail unit, using a venturi effect to suck air through the radiator elements.

Improved Reliability

The new, improved package began to come together slowly and, most importantly, the engines became much more reliable. It was becoming possible to run the bike for something approaching race distance during tests, without a catastrophic engine failure. It was still quite a long way from being competitive at GP level, with the lap record at Suzuka remaining at least an elusive three seconds away. It was not clear how this gap was going to be bridged. Mick Grant remembers,

> It was frustrating. Sometimes it seemed like the team almost didn't want the truth. After every practice session of a few days, we would have a debriefing. I remember one of these and it was always me first. All the technicians were there with notepads and Mr Fukui went to the blackboard. At that particular session I was the quickest and did 2 min 17.2s; Takazumi was about a second slower, and the local hot-shot was about a second and a half slower than him. Fukui put my time right at the top of the board and drew a big arrow to the bottom of the board where there was a time of 2 min 12.7s, the lap record on a Yamaha. He turned to me and said, 'MickSan, please tell me how do we achieve this?' I went through it all. The engine needs about 15 bhp more – that will give us 1.5 seconds – then the chassis needs this, the tyres need that, a quarter-second here, and a half-second

there. The last half-second took a lot of getting at. Eventually we got down to this lap record. What I was saying to them was that we actually had a very well-balanced motorcycle. Unfortunately, this meant that every bit of it needed a lot of improvement. They didn't like that. Takazumi was not at the debriefing, so it was the local test rider's turn. They asked him the same question and he stood up and said '30 horsepower' and just sat down. They were actually more receptive to that than they were to re-designing the motorbike. They believed that the powers that be, which were actually themselves, could find another 30 horsepower. To re-design the bike was a bit of a problem.

RACES IN 1980

Whatever techniques were adopted to bridge the gap between Honda and Suzuki, Gerald Davison felt that Honda should be allowed to apply them outside the spotlight of the publicity surrounding the GPs. In agreement with the engineering team, it was announced that Honda would not be competing in the initial GP races. Instead, a number of European International races were identified at which the NR could compete and, if necessary, fail with less accompanying publicity.

It was not only the bike that was evolving. During the winter break, Katayama had sensed himself undergoing a transition. He describes it thus:

> In 1979 I was not yet a Honda guy. I was still a Yamaha guy. Gradually, I began to tune into the Honda way of doing things. It's difficult to define the Honda way. It's the process that is more important than the result. Of course, you want to win, but it's the process that people are more concentrated on. I started to understand this and it caused some conflict within my own consciousness, as I was always a fighter. I came back to Japan and went to a Zen temple for ten days, just sitting from morning to night. This helped me enormously during and after my racing career. I had to realize that I could no longer attack with Honda as I had no bullet.

Ron Haslam

Katayama had broken a collarbone, and Grant an ankle, during testing, so a third rider was approached to help out with some testing and riding. Ron Haslam flew to Japan to do some tests and then was entered for the first race of the season at Donnington Park in June 1980. Haslam was the sort of person who could ride anything, but he was not too impressed with the first NR he rode. He remembers that when he first rode it, the maximum rpm was 24,000. He says,

> It was like a switch, though, as soon as you let the engine speed drop, it stopped. No spread of power at all. It did have a reasonable top end though. If you were riding quite hard and you missed a gear, the engine would stop before you could get it back again. A bit later during development, they got the revs back down to 18,000 rpm. That made it a bit easier to ride and spread the power a little bit, although the maximum power was down. You'd get a better lap time, but the maximum power was less. The initial engine was very unreliable, but the one with 18,000 rpm became a lot more reliable. It always had a reliability problem. Even during the last GPs, they never used a practice engine for the race as they knew it wouldn't last. It was a little bit better than an over-the-counter RG500. It was still a lot less than the works RG500.

Donnington Park

At the Donnington race, Mick Grant retired after two laps and Ron Haslam managed to hold on to ninth place until the engine expired with just a couple of laps to go. It seemed like progress, but the reason for failure raised tensions within the team.

Gerald Davison remembers,

> When we got back to Slough, my chief mechanic Ken Hull came to me at 1.00 am and said that the engine oil level was incredibly low. We only then discovered that the engineers had removed a lot of the oil to try and reduce the power loss through oil churn, but didn't tell anyone. They wanted to find out what performance it could give without a full sump of oil. Of course, the first time they went through a few corners, the engine ran dry. Both engines went. We had a lot of that. It was very very difficult.

Katayama and His Suzuki RG500

Katayama had been campaigning a private Suzuki RG500 in some of the early GPs, successfully arguing that he needed to keep his mind tuned to GP race speeds. He managed fourth place in Spain ahead of a couple of Yamaha and Suzuki works riders. Katayama recalls,

> I went to Europe with my RG500 so that I could race. I asked IrimajiriSan for his permission to keep up my racing skills using an RG500. I spent nearly 10 million yen on the bikes and the mechanics. Mr Irimajiri said that he could not give me permission, but that he could also not stop me. We agreed that the question had never been raised and we had a good arrangement. At the time, everyone was asking how Katayama could be racing Suzukis whilst contracted for Honda. I couldn't say anything at the time, but that's how it happened.

Misano

In the middle of July, Katayama went to an Italian International meeting at Misano and on 20 July 1980, the NR500 completed its first race, ending an encouraging third place behind Graziano Rossi on a factory Suzuki and Walter Migliorati on a private RG500. Only five seconds separated first and third place. The engine had run hot and the lower fairing had been removed for the race, but this was blamed at least partially on the 30-degree centigrade ambient temperatures in which the race was held. It was a moment for great optimism. At last, after all the frustrations, ridicule and hard work, it seemed as if the corner had been turned and a competitive Honda machine was emerging.

Imatra

It was immediately decided that the team should compete in the Finnish GP, due to be held just a week later at Imatra. A transporter with two bikes left Slough in England to travel the 2,000 miles (3,000km) to the venue, and the team members flew up from Italy. The optimism of Italy turned to bitter disappointment as Katayama only just managed to qualify in last place on the grid. To make matters worse, he suffered two seizures on the last day of practice, something that plagued many of the teams using the local high-octane fuel available at the circuit. This led to bitter disagreement between race team manager Davison and chief engineer Fukui. Fukui wanted to patch up the bike and send Katayama out for the race. Davison considered it pointless. Tensions that had been simmering between the race team and the engineers finally came to a head.

For Davison, the issue had become who was actually in control of the racing team. It was finally solved by Davison phoning Irimajira from Finland to tell him that there was a problem: he was not prepared to complete the race, but the engineers wanted to screw the machines back together overnight and enter the race. As he recalls,

> We didn't race. We packed up the team and returned home. It was becoming a farce. The engineers were interested in engineering and proving that the thing could work, and moving it forward. We were interested in racing. We did not have a race machine and all we would have proved was if it would do X number of laps or not. I suppose for the engineers that may have been a small advance. When we arrived in Finland, our tanks were not even big enough to carry enough fuel. I had people working away from the circuit, cutting up tanks and fabricating larger ones.

This was a painful experience for the Japanese engineers and they are still reluctant to talk about it. It was the apogee of the dispute between the race team and the engineers, aggravated by a clash of cultures and philosophy. At the end of the season, Gerald Davison transferred to another division within Honda; no other action was acceptable after the events at the Finnish GP.

The Last Two GPs

There were two more GPs to be ridden in 1980. The first at Silverstone saw Katayama complete the race in last place, having been lapped by winner Randy Mamola. It was still a major achievement on one of the fastest GP circuits of the time, with average lap speeds of 115mph (185kph). On 24 August the last GP of the year was run at the infamous old Nürburgring circuit, the daunting 14-mile (22km) armco-lined track through the German pine woods of the Eifel. This was to be the last GP at this classic venue that had hosted decades of racing. Katayama came home in twelfth place, outside of the points, but within three seconds of Kork Ballington, who was

Second and last GP for 1980 was the British GP at Silverstone; detailed differences can be seen from the bike ridden in Finland two weeks before (see page 48).

Katayama spent more time riding his Suzuki RG500 than the NR500, but at Silverstone he had to earn his salary. He finished dead last, but he did finish.

riding Kawasaki's two-stroke square four that had debuted in 1980.

Katayama remembers, 'During practice, the engine blew up at the end of the 2km straight as I went into the chicane. During the race, I watched the rev counter very closely and was feathering the throttle on the straight to save the engine. We almost beat Kawasaki.'

The NR had held together for almost an hour of GP speeds, whereas a year before it would have disintegrated within twenty minutes. Enormous improvements had been made during the twelve months, and similar continued progress through to the next season could bring the NR close to the competition. The team could but hope.

NEW TACTICS

Anything that could help the team was tried by Honda, leading to some tactics that seemed strange to Western minds. Gerald Davison tells the story:

> I wrote a very long letter to IriSan, setting out everything about what we were trying to do and the difficulty of doing it. We needed a sea-change to stop what we were doing, step back from it and have a look at it and realize that we did not have competitive racing machines. After this letter, Irijamiri and I met in Tokyo and I said, 'You need to get the key engineers like Fukui, send them to a Buddhist temple up in the

mountains to think about what we are trying to do. They have got to step back from it and realize we are trying to operate a racing team and we are struggling with these engineering problems.' He took me very seriously, and the next day he said, 'OK, we're going to do it.' I said, 'Do what?' He said, 'We're all going to a Buddhist temple.' I couldn't believe it.

You have to understand that the average modern Japanese is quite ambivalent about religion, but they hedge their bets. They will say they are not religious, but admit to going to a Shinto shrine or a Buddhist temple, just in case. We set off in a fleet of vehicles from Suzuka, about forty of us packed into a couple of minibuses and cars. The European team members couldn't believe what was happening. When we got everybody ready to leave, they decided to take a few bits of the bike and some racing leathers. So we took a couple of wheels. It was about an hour's drive to this beautiful temple in the mountains, at a wonderful location. A senior monk came out and talked to IriSan. A deal was done. You pay not so much on results, but on the size of who you are, so Honda had to negotiate an acceptable price.

We all went into this place. First, we had to give all our birthdays so that they could eliminate any unlucky people. It led up to a ceremony, which the Japanese took very seriously. It was difficult to control the Europeans, who had never seen anything like this. A couple of ladies came in and danced. A priest came in and chanted and shook things in the air. This went on for about an hour and that was it. Once we left, the Japanese relaxed again and were laughing; at the end of the day, I'm not sure they took it all that seriously. All in all, it wasn't really what I had meant in my remark to Irimajiri, but it was a wonderful experience.

I went to a Shinto shrine once in Tokyo. There was a new Toyota that they had somehow managed to get inside. All its doors and hood were open and the Shinto priest was chanting and waving his wand over it. Apparently, the problem was that this guy had got a bad car that was unreliable and had taken it along to the Shinto shrine to see if they could do something about it.

LAST RACE OF THE YEAR

The last outing of the year came at an International race at Misano, in Italy, where the NR appeared with a new frame. The Maxton frame had worked well, but it was a Ron Williams frame and not a Honda frame. Engineer Tanaka designed a Honda tubular frame to replace the British unit, at the same time changing to a Pro-Link rear suspension, Honda's version of rising-rate suspension that had started to appear on their street bikes. Horiike remembers,

> We were very disappointed in having to use the Maxton frame. The engine guys were busy trying new stuff and we were making engine mounting plates and sending them to the UK. It was very de-motivating. A chassis designer from R&D helped us to make a new pipe frame. The frame was called NRT, the 'T' standing for TanakaSan, the chassis designer who helped us. It was closely modelled on the CBX1000 frame.

Unfortunately the clutch failed at the start of the race, and Katayama retired.

CONTINUING THE DEVELOPMENT

There was still absolute determination within Honda to continue the development, and a list of improvements was set as a target for the winter of work ahead.

Weight

The weight of the bike had to be reduced. The NR2 had weighed 335lb (152kg) at the start of the 1980 season, about 45lb (20kg) heavier than the two-stroke competition. The engine weighed in at a hefty 142lb (64.5kg) The goal was to reduce the overall weight to 285lb (130kg), considered achievable as the new frame and rear suspension had already shaved 22lb (10kg) off the bike. The engine was planned to lose 15lb (7kg), mainly through the use of new magnesium crankcases and cylinder heads. Carbon fibre also began to appear on the bike. The strength and light weight of this material made it very attractive to the frame designers, who were planning its widespread use. Initially, they used it solely for the NR's wheels, but later it was to be used for the forks and swinging-arm, with the final version of the NR500 sporting a complete frame manufactured in carbon fibre.

Power

The original goal of 130 bhp had yet to be achieved, although 122.5 bhp had been recorded from an engine on the test bed during May 1980. In the past, tightening up the included angle between the inlet and exhaust valves had resulted in a measurable increase in power. The 40 degrees of the NR2 was reduced to 37 degrees for the NR3, and at the same time the diameter of the inlet valves was stretched by 0.5mm to 18.5mm.

A lot of energy was to be spent on the carburation, ending up with 30mm diameter flat-slide carbs, but with totally re-designed internals. The carburettors on the first two engines had a very narrow needle that was now widened. The wider needle improved the driveability of the engine. The Honda camp felt that there was an unacceptable delay in throttle response that probably cost them about one second per lap. Also, there had been cases of sticking throttles that were now fixed by running the slide in bearings. Improved carburation and lower crankshaft flywheel mass was felt to be the way to address the problem. Slow, painstaking fine tuning was the hard road ahead for Honda.

A New Rider

There was one other avenue open to the company. There are the three components in the package for success – engine, chassis and rider. Honda had links to the best road racer in the world, who, at the tender age of 19, was riding Honda Superbikes in the USA. Freddie Spencer was the hottest property in motorcycle racing and Honda had great plans for him. Spencer himself was certain that GP racing was a step he intended to take, and he was tempted by an offer Yamaha were making to team him up with Kenny Roberts for the 1981 season. Honda were anxious to hang on to him until the time was ripe for GP racing, but 1981 seemed to be too soon. They finally agreed a three-year contract that would keep him in the USA for 1981, riding Superbikes and a CX500-based dirt-track racer, but with the promise of GPs in 1982. It was also hinted that there would be something special available in 1982. Although it was not stated that this would be a two-stroke, this is what Spencer interpreted it to mean. Seemingly, doubts about the feasibility of the NR500 were beginning to creep in.

THE 1981 SEASON

A Poor Start to the Year

It was announced that Katayama alone would be competing in the GPs in 1981, and racing started early in the year at Suzuka

Spot the million-dollar GP racer. In a sea of production Suzukis and Yamahas, Katayama (51) waits for the start of the 1981 International race at Hengelo in Holland.

with a round of the All Japan Championship. It was not an auspicious start to the year, with Katayama crashing whilst in fourth place and Kiyama, just behind, ploughing into the debris and also falling. A month later Kiyama managed a fourth place in another All Japan Championship race, whilst Katayama tried his luck, in vain, at an early season Dutch International race at Hengelo. A week later, at the first European GP at the Salzburgring, Katayama was lapped but still managed to claim 13th place at the ultra-fast circuit. A split water hose in France sprayed water on the rear tyre and Katayama crashed, after qualifying 28th during practice, also preventing him from competing in Yugoslavia.

Win at Suzuka

After a disheartening series of results, the project finally got some good news with the 200km race of Suzuka, held in wet weather conditions on 14 June. Oguma was in charge of the two-rider team competing in the race, and he devised a race strategy that brought the NR500 its first and only race win. He calculated that it would be possible for the NRs to complete the race without coming in for fuel. The NR had a fuel consumption figure of about 7km/litre against the typical 5km/litre thirst of the competition. In order to conceal the strategy, the squad set up their quick-filler in the pit lane just like the other teams. Riders Kiyama and Abe stayed put when the warm-up lap started, so as to conserve fuel. The strategy worked, with the two-strokes pitting for fuel, leaving Kiyama to take the win, followed by a works Yamaha OW51, a factory Suzuki and Abe. The R&D department at Asaka went wild after the race with a big party. Oguma remembers,

> It was high drama and I really felt as if I was on the stage. I wanted to close the curtain on the NR project as soon as possible and I thought Suzuka would be the moment. After winning at Suzuka, I could honourably leave the project, with a successful result. Unfortunately, the management saw it differently. They said, 'You've done such a good job, you can stay on and bring us some more good results.' I was very disappointed that I could not go back to production bike design.

Better Performances

Things really did seem to be getting better, as Freddie Spencer had tested the NR500 at the end of May and set a lap time of 2 min. 14s, two seconds faster round Suzuka than

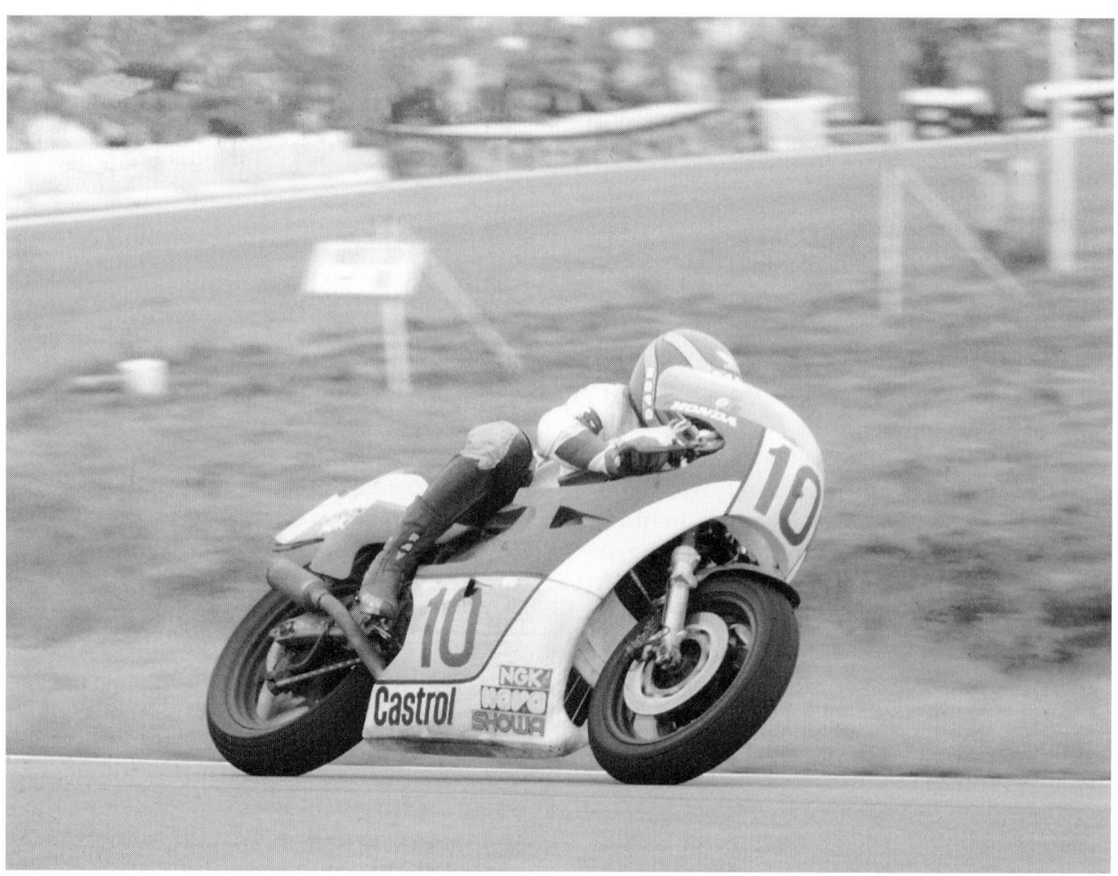

Katayama was holding tenth place at the 1981 Dutch GP going into the last lap, but ignition failure saw him rattle to a stop out on the circuit.

any NR lap of the circuit up to then. Perhaps it was a rider problem after all? At the Dutch GP it looked like Katayama would snatch the first championship point for the NR as he started the last lap in tenth place. Halfway round the lap, the ignition failed and he was forced to park the bike dejectedly at trackside.

Spencer had been impressed enough with the NR to elect to race it at the Champion Spark 200 in Laguna Seca. Later, he recalled,

> At first, I was about six seconds outside the lap record because I was trying to ride it like a normal motorcycle where you accelerate on the edge at around 13,000 revs. The four-stroke would rev to nearly 22,000 rpm and so eventually I narrowed the power band and brought the gears so close together that I was changing between 19,000 and 21,000 revs. I was shifting gears all the time, but you had to keep it in the power band if you were going to race it hard. Its great shortcomings were its weight and lack of torque.

Spencer won his heat race, beating Roberts in the process, but in both legs of the main race the NR broke, the valve springs failing due to over-revving of the engine. The maximum safe engine speed for the NR was still 21,500. It was decided to run the combination of Spencer and the NR at the British GP, but there were only enough engines for a single rider. Katayama was asked if he would be prepared to provide Spencer with his bikes. He recalls,

> I was initially a little angry that I had to give Freddie the room. We discussed the situation and Honda needed the result. I agreed to give Freddie the bike, also making clear that I was not happy. But they did not take the bike from me, they asked me if I would voluntarily defer the ride to Freddie. Freddie did very well in the race and everyone was very surprised. The bike broke when he was in fifth place. The bike could not survive with his riding style that would rev the engine very hard. There were not enough engines for two bikes. When they asked me for my bike, they already knew that Freddie would be breaking a lot of engines and there were not enough for two bikes.

The kid who could win on anything. Freddie Spencer seems unsure what to make of the NR500 as he prepares to take it out for practice at Silverstone in 1981.

Interest in the NR500 was resurrected by Spencer's ride at the 1981 British GP. He revved the engine to oblivion, but managed to get up to fifth place before it expired.

The push start was a problem:

> If you didn't hit it just right, it would skid the rear wheel, and I had such a sore chest after that weekend, banging the gas tank trying to get that thing started. In the middle of one of my practice sessions, Carlo, an old Italian mechanic who went on to work for Marco Lucchinelli, came across after watching my efforts and said, 'I will show you'. So this old guy took three or four steps and the bike started first time. I watched him and from that point on I didn't have a lot of trouble starting it.

As far as the GPs were concerned, this was the high point of the NR's performance on the track. The team contested no more races during 1981. Back in Japan, continued development had resulted in the goal of 130 bhp finally being achieved in September 1981 with an engine that weighed 122lb (56kg), just 2lb (1kg) heavier than the design goal of 120lb (55kg). However, it was all too late. A shattering but long-expected decision had been taken by Iri back in Japan: Honda would build a two-stroke GP racer to compete in the GPs alongside the NR during 1982.

The NR500 as GP trainer. Ron Haslam was given the opportunity to ride the last model of the NR500 in 1982 and test the GP waters.

(Left) *The very last NR500 produced 135 bhp at 19,500 rpm. Here is this technological wonder in all its gold-anodized, sand-cast magnesium glory.*

4 Independence Day

The Conception of the NS500 Two-stroke Triple (1982–83)

TIME FOR A CHANGE

When development of the NR500 started, Honda's unstated schedule called for a championship-winning machine within three years. Management, engineers and riders were unified in their collective confidence in Honda's ability to achieve this. By the end of 1980, with three versions of the bike behind them, it was clear that it was becoming increasingly difficult to make progress in extracting more power from the engine. The Honda team had to ask themselves how much more development potential there was left to exploit, and whether it would be enough to produce a race-winner.

For Irimajiri, it seemed that the four-stroke development exercise had achieved its goal of training new engineers, and investigating and applying cutting-edge technology that would benefit the company's commercial activities for many years to come. According to him,

> By that time, we had tried everything possible and realized that we must be approaching the true limit of the engine. We started to think that we would need to change the basic strategy from four-stroke to two-stroke. There was an MX racing team and the potential of those engines for high power outputs was tremendous. It was clear that if we used two-stroke for racing, we would have a big chance to win races. We started talking quietly about using two-strokes.

A TWO-STROKE FOR 1982

Miyakoshi

The quiet discussions about two-strokes involved the director of the Motocross development programme, Miyakoshi. Having been part of the Motocross programme since the mid-1970s, and masterminding the Elsinore and CR Honda crossers, Miyakoshi was the two-stroke expert within the company. In a world dominated by four-strokes and four-stroke devotees, Miyakoshi, a two-stroke man, had been something of an outcast. Now, his almost unique experience with, and insights into, the two-stroke engine were desperately needed. Irimajiri asked him to design a new racing bike for 1982, using a two-stroke engine.

Information-gathering

Once it was decided that a new bike was to be built, an observer was sent to Europe to gather information for input to the design process. Interestingly, the bikes that were targeted for observation were not only the Suzuki and Yamaha 500s, but the Kawasaki 350s. Oguma was sent to Europe to analyse the complete operation on Honda's side, and to get as much information as possible on the RG500 and OW, and on the Kawasaki KR350 as well. He recalls that, on his return to Japan, he was told to report his findings to Miyakoshi:

He came straight to the point and asked me what I thought about using a two-stroke, and I told him it was the right choice to make. At last I could talk seriously about the bike many of us had wanted to talk about for some time. Mr Miyakoshi had a design for the bike in his head, but it had never been put on paper. He had many ideas in his head when I met with him to discuss my report. We sat down, and he had his drawing book and we worked out a few ideas, one of which was the NS500. He asked me what the performance was of the OW Yamaha. I had never measured the performance directly, but I estimated it to be about 140 bhp. This seemed to have a lot of impact on him, and you could see his brain working through the calculations. I think he had two possibilities in his mind, either a V-twin or a triple, but not a four-cylinder. The four-cylinder had already been claimed by Suzuki and Yamaha. Honda needed to be different. This was our development philosophy at the time. If Mr Miyakoshi had developed a four-cylinder, he would have been kicked out. When we analysed these options, it became clear that the triple was the best choice.

Engineering Teams

As the design began to take shape, Irimajiri had some delicate staff management to attend to. He felt that the NR engineers had experienced many challenges and found some innovative solutions, and wanted to continue to motivate them, and not discourage them by suddenly announcing a two-stroke. Fortunately, most engineers realized that Honda could not win using the four-stroke, so the idea was already there. Miyakoshi was asked to develop a very simple two-stroke engine and, in fact, there were then two separate teams working on the two-stroke and the four-stroke; each team knew of the other's existence.

Valves

The four-cylinder engine had been universally adopted by Honda's opposition and, when Honda announced that they were to use a three-cylinder engine, there was a good deal of head-shaking. In fact, the most revolutionary difference in the Honda plan was the use of reed-valves to control the flow of charge in the inlet tract. Reed-valves had been in widespread use for over a dozen years and were considered to be essential for getting some torque out of two-stroke motocross engines. They had, however, only ever been used for two-stroke road racers by Yamaha on their TZ750; the common theory was that the reeds were too restrictive for engines that were tuned to the maximum, which the TZ750 certainly wasn't. Instead, the disc valve had been adopted, initially by Suzuki on the RG500, and then later by Yamaha and Kawasaki.

The disc rotating on the end of the crankshaft, with a cut-out that corresponded to the intake period of the crank cycle, presented no obstruction between carburettor and crankcase. It did, however, dictate a very wide engine for the four-cylinder 500s; Suzuki had been struggling to improve this, with limited success.

Deciding on a Triple

Clearly, if the new bike was to be a triple, it would need to be as compact as possible. The new plans caused Miyakoshi much concern. Katayama remembers being introduced by Iri to Miyakoshi after the last race of 1981, and being told that he would be taking care of next season. Katayama realized that this meant the four-stroke would have to stop. He recalls,

When we discussed the NS, before MiyakoshiSan drew up the engine, he only had

> the idea of the three-cylinder. When IriSan introduced me to him, he asked me my opinion on the three-cylinder. I said that if he could reach the ratio of 1 bhp pulling 0.9kg of bike, he would have a winner.

Configuration

Just as with the NR, it was important to concentrate on low weight and small frontal area. Once it was decided that the bike should be a triple, the idea of an in-line three-cylinder was ruled out as the frontal area would have been too wide. Instead, Miyakoshi decided to mount all pistons on the same crankshaft, with the two outer cylinders pointing vertically like a parallel twin, and the middle cylinder pointing forward and downwards. In this configuration, the engine was only marginally wider than a twin and could be wrapped in an aerodynamically efficient package. All three conrods were anchored to the same single crankshaft, in a design that was to become a Honda trademark. The single crankshaft would serve to save some weight but, more importantly, reduce the friction that would otherwise have been generated by the extra four bearings needed for a twin-crank engine. The vertical and horizontal cylinder were spread wide at 110 degrees, with the three carburettors nestling in between and connected to the four-blade reed-valve blocks feeding into the crankcase at the base of the cylinder. Bore and stroke were 62.6 × 54mm and the engine revved through to 11,500 rpm.

Power was passed to the clutch via a jackshaft just behind the crankshaft, which resulted in the engine running backwards (clockwise). This was a good thing, as the cylinders themselves had been turned 180 degrees, with the exhaust ports pointing to the rear of the bike, so that the piston skirt was not pushing up against the gaping inlet port. The exhaust port was bridged, to prevent the piston rings from bulging into the port and snagging on the roof of the port. The jackshaft was also put to use as a balancer shaft with a weight rotating to balance the resonances set up by the three-cylinder power unit.

The right-hand end of the jackshaft drove the clutch, behind which were the two transmission shafts, which could be removed from

The first NS500 publicity shot. It didn't look like championship-winning material.

the crankcase as a cassette, once the clutch basket had been removed. A total loss battery ignition was driven off the left-hand end of the crankshaft, as was the water pump. As the carburettors were located at the front of the engine, the radiator had to be split, with the main unit above the carburettors and a small V-shaped vestigial radiator below them. Magnesium alloy was used throughout the engine for crankcases and engine covers as well as the 34mm Keihin carburettors.

Frame and Wheels

Surprisingly, the initial round-section frame for the NS500 was made from steel, possibly because it was likely that changes would need to be made, and they could most easily be performed on a steel alloy. Honda called the frame layout the 'diamond frame', presumably referring to the shape of the twin loops of tubing that passed from the top of the headstock back down around the rear engine mounting position, along the bottom of the engine and up to the top of the headstock. A large cross-section bracing strut was welded between the two sides of the loop, about halfway down the run from the headstock to the rear engine-mounting plates. The bottom of the headstock was tied in by two tubes that swept around the top of the engine to the bracing strut, and welded to the front and rear down tubes of the main twin loop cradle.

The initial NS500 had a round-section, steel chassis. It didn't need the bright red paintwork to get heads turning.

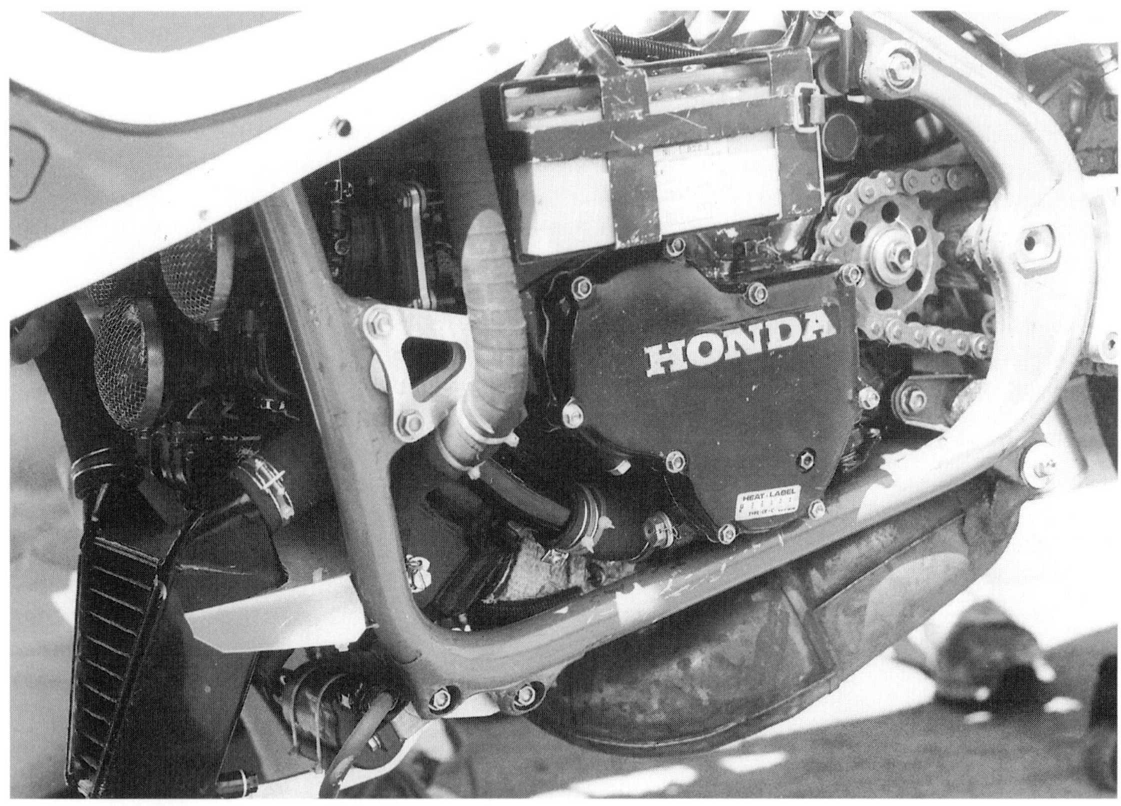

The three forward-facing carburettors of the NS500 can be seen nestling above the lower radiator. The massive battery was dropped on the 1983 model.

Rear suspension used a near-vertical shock absorber with rocker arms attached to the rear swinging arm. Aluminium Comstar wheels were used front and rear, with 16in fronts marking a return to Honda's racing specification.

Building the New Engine

The first NS500 engine was built very quickly. It was desperately needed to convince Freddie Spencer that he could and should run it in the GPs for 1982. Honda had decided that their GP effort would be centered around the young superstar who had been sweeping all before him on the US roadracing tracks during 1980 and 1981. He, in turn, had made it clear that he would only compete in the GPs if accompanied by his friend, mentor and chief mechanic Erv Kanemoto. However, Spencer was more enthusiastic about running a Honda GP effort than Kanemoto. According to Kanemoto:

> When we decided that Freddie was coming over, we talked to Yamaha and Suzuki. At one point it looked like it would be Yamaha. Freddie was leaning towards Honda. I could see him dragging his feet. He said that he felt obligated to go to Japan to tell Honda that he would not be riding for them and he asked if I wanted to go with him. I said that

if he was just going to tell Honda that, I wasn't going. I later remember getting a call from Japan. It was Freddie and Mr Irimajiri in a meeting and Freddie said, 'I can't believe it. You should see this place. They're working on this bike and there are so many people here.' Of course, he had seen the whole R&D operation, maybe 2,000 people, but the race bikes is just a small part of the operation. He was very enthusiastic and I could see that he really wanted to ride for Honda. I had worked with Barry Sheene the year before and knew a lot of Yamaha people. I had nothing against Honda, but it is hard for me to move. I felt that he would be able to do well on the Yamaha and the new three-cylinder Honda was less of a certainty. I was a little sceptical – a new bike and a two-stroke. Then he came back to California and we talked. He asked me what I thought and I said, 'Whatever you want to do is fine with me.' I knew that if everything went well he would do well. If he got on something that he did not feel comfortable with, he would not perform.

Running the New Bike

A mock-up engine was boxed and carried over to the US for inspection in September 1981. Then Kanemoto went to Japan in December, and remembers the Honda team starting the bike for the first time in a meeting room. Kanemoto and Spencer had gone there to test the new bike, but Honda were so far behind on it, in the end they could only ride the NR at Suzuka. The first time Spencer rode the NS was at Laguna Seca, a couple of months later.

They found the bike to be very small and light, but well down on power – the very first NS engine had shown a disappointing 112 bhp on the dynamometer. The complete bike weighed in at 282lb (128kg), which was well under the target weight to power ratio of 0.9:1. The bike was very peaky, with a power band of just 1,500 rpm, from 9,500 to 11,000 rpm. There was no over-rev capability, the power dropping very fast over 11,000 rpm. There were some serious concerns about the ability of the NS500 to compete with the much more powerful Yamaha and Suzuki competition, despite the weight advantage.

CONCLUDING THE NR PROGRAMME

Although the NS500 had been chosen to lead Honda's GP effort, there were still one or two things left to try on the NR before the development programme could be concluded. The psychological goal of 130 bhp had been achieved, but the goal of a power to weight ratio of 1.0 was still just out of reach, with the bike weighing 308lb (140kg). A new camshaft gear train was designed, with the crank driving a single central spur gear that itself drove spur gears in each of the cylinder banks. This spur gear was offset so that it drove only the camshaft controlling the inlet valves, which itself drove the camshaft for the exhaust valves. This lowered the weight a little and reduced friction losses.

The last generation of carburettors for the NR was designed, using a box-shaped slide rather than the flat plate that had previously been used. Throughout 1982, 28mm, 29mm and 30mm bore carburettors were used. The steel frame was replaced by an aluminium frame built to the same geometry, with carbon-fibre swing-arm and wheel rims and spokes. The whole package came down to about 300lb (135kg), with power around 132 bhp. There was no hurry to campaign the NR in the GPs, and it was only at Assen in mid-season that Ron Haslam was entered to ride the bike.

Rushing to Finish the NS500

The situation surrounding the NS500 was very different. Honda had suffered three years of scorn and ridicule in the motorcycle racing world, and they were now determined to win races and world championships. They were rushing to get the bike ready on time, and development continued right up to and into the season.

Kanemoto arrived at Asaka when two bikes were almost ready, and the team was starting to pack them up. He remembers they then decided to pack just a single bike, as they were going to cut the back off the other, having decided to re-locate the shock:

> That is when they pivoted it from the centre of the thing, like a steering damper. We spent a couple of days re-assembling the bike. It was just an idea that they had, not a response to our comments. Mr Miyakoshi wanted the weight as low as possible, so

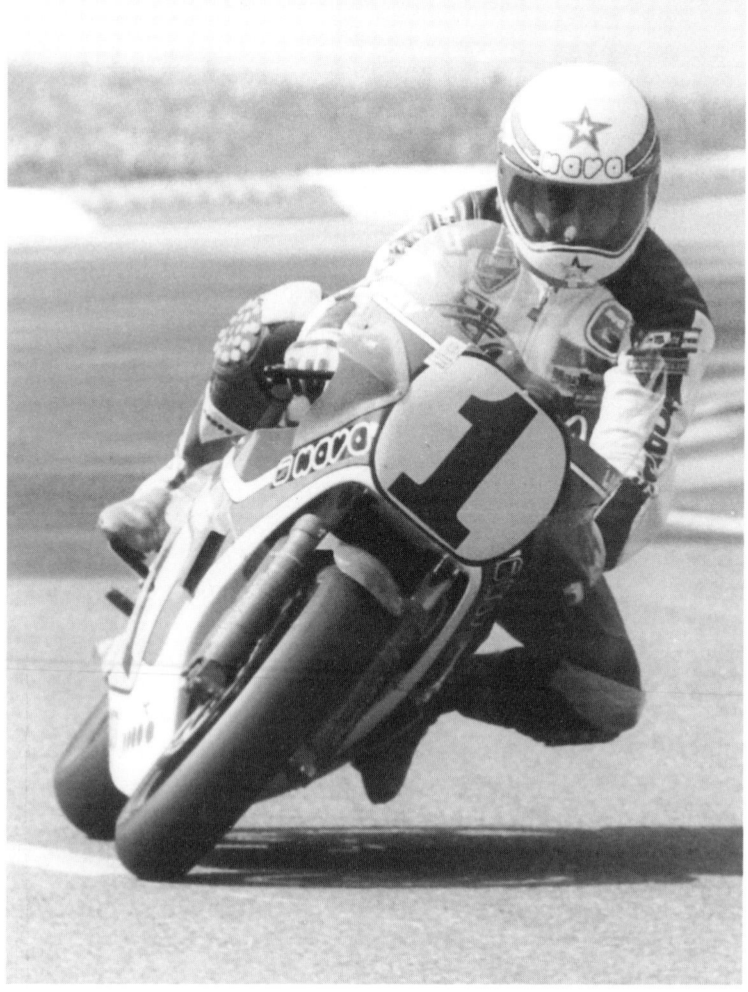

It's nice to debut a new bike with the Number 1 plate. Marco Lucchinelli was enticed away from Suzuki to ride the NS for Honda.

> rather than the shock being high in the thing, they could lower the shock and grab the shock from the centre of the shock, which was a problem as it would tend to bind a little bit.

THE 1982 GP SEASON

Argentina

From the first GP in Argentina, it was clear that the Honda race team's coffers were full and money would be spent whenever or wherever necessary. Each rider had two machines and there were three separate teams being co-ordinated by Oguma acting as race team manager. The paddock suddenly seemed to have been swamped by Honda personnel.

At the first GP of 1982, Miyakoshi's theory on the competitiveness of a small compact three-cylinder machine was fully vindicated. Power had been raised to 120 bhp by the time the GP season started, and this seemed to be enough to close the gap on the disc-valved fours. Spencer qualified less that 0.1 seconds behind Kenny Roberts and in the race duelled for the lead with Yamaha team-mate Roberts, and Barry Sheene. Only during the last three laps did he drop too far behind to be able to go for the win, which went to Roberts, from Sheene, with Spencer 20 yards behind. Lucchinelli and Katayama came in fifth and sixth respectively, demonstrating a perfect reliability record in hot temperatures. Kanemoto remembers,

> After the race in Argentina, Freddie and I looked at each other, and he said, 'What do you think?' and I said, 'I'm really surprised.' The machine was a very good machine for the amount of time that had been put into it, but Freddie was a big credit to the thing.

For the riders it had been a tough start to the season, especially for Katayama, who had not run at the head of the field for a couple of years. As he recalls, 'I realized my riding skills were less than they used to be. When I finished the race at Argentina, I was so tired I couldn't walk. When I returned to Europe I did a lot of physical and mental exercise to regain my fighting spirit.'

Austria

Five weeks later, the first European GP kicked off, with snow falling during practice for the Austrian GP. Spencer crashed during practice and could only qualify in twelfth place, behind Marco Lucchinelli. Race day was a little warmer and dry, and for a time Spencer led the race from a bunch of eight riders at the phenomenally fast circuit. The NS seemed to lose very little on speed at the circuit and pundits who had predicted that the triple would flop were beginning to feel rather foolish.

Unfortunately, Spencer's bike seized mid-race, but Lucchinelli had a fantastic race for the win, until he crashed out on the last lap, breaking his foot, and leaving Uncini to take the win on his RG500 Suzuki.

Spain and Italy

In Spain, Spencer took pole position, but had to pull out of the race as he was leading and going away, when the ignition to one cylinder failed. In Italy, Spencer finished second to Uncini, but it was surely just a matter of time before Honda's first GP victory would come.

Problems with the NS

The results seemed to be spectacularly good for a new machine with a new rider racing on unknown circuits. Not everything was

By the Dutch TT in June 1982, square-section aluminium had replaced the steel frame. Erv Kanemoto is busy patching up Spencer's bike after the practice crash.

going as smoothly as it appeared, however. According to Kanazawa,

> We had a big problem with engine seizures. With the motocross heritage of the NS we had decided to use chromed cylinder walls, just like contemporary motocross machines. When we got seizures, we thought that there must be something wrong with the chroming process. In the end we sent some cylinders to Mahle in Germany for a Nikasil coating and these cylinders were a lot better. We never actually identified the cause of the failures, but in the end we assumed that the chroming could not withstand extended periods of maximum engine speed on an open throttle.

Assen

At Assen, the last version of the NR500, the NR4, was wheeled out for Ron Haslam to ride and he benefited from some varied weather conditions to claim a creditable twelfth place. The race had started dry, only to be interrupted by a downpour of rain which forced a second leg. Spencer had crashed on the wet circuit and could not repair his bike in time for the restart. He had been running some of the new Nikasil cylinders, with slightly altered port timing, which brought the power up to a claimed 125 bhp. With the arrival of the NR500, new aluminium frames also appeared for the NS500. Weight was now 265lb (120kg), and the magical ratio of power to weight moved for the first time above 1.

Belgium

At the Belgian GP at Spa Francorchamps it all came together for Honda and Freddie Spencer; appropriately for the American rider, the GP took place on 4 July, American Independence Day. It was one of the classic races of the 1980s, with the Suzuki RG500 of Middelburg, the OW60 Yamaha square four of Crosby, and the OW61 V4 Yamaha of Roberts all taking turns at the front of the field. From lap nine of the twenty-lap race, it was Freddie Spencer who led, Roberts slipping back through the field on shredded tyres. Spencer took his first 500 GP by a

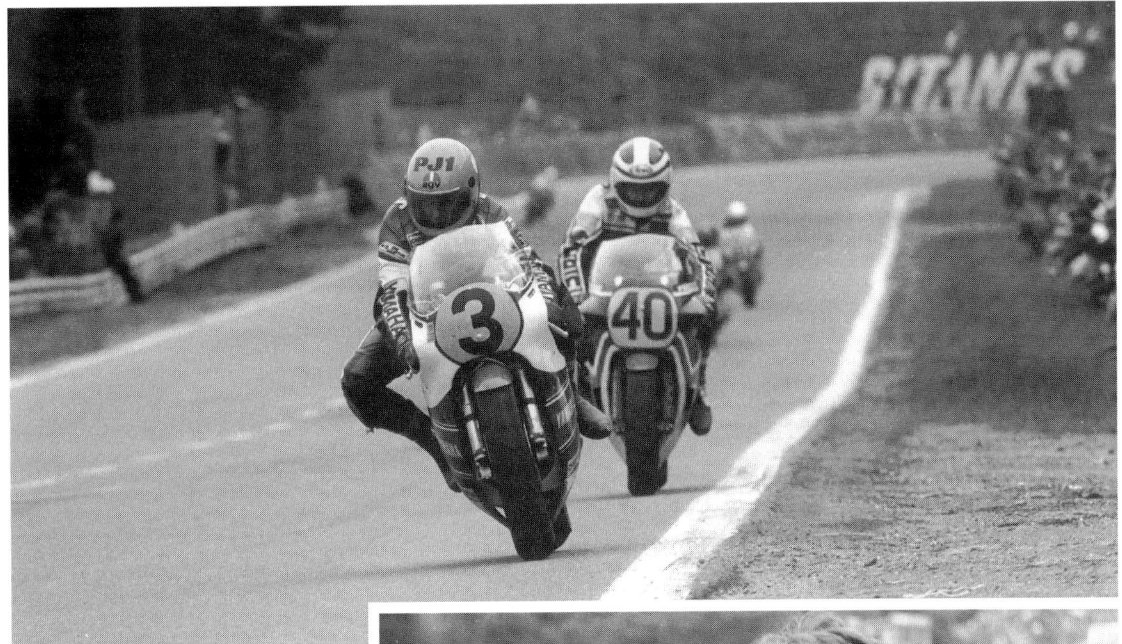

Roberts was in superb form at the 1982 Belgian Spa, but his tyres were torn up by the Yamaha; Spencer passed to take Honda's first 500 win for fifteen years.

(Right) *The face of exhausted exhilaration. Spencer's first GP win on US Independence Day 1982.*

margin of four seconds, and Honda had won their first 500 GP since the great days of Hailwood and Honda fifteen years before.

The GP team on the spot was ecstatic; back in Japan, however, the atmosphere, especially at management level, was more subdued. Kanazawa felt that Miyakoshi had expected the team to win a GP much earlier in the year, and was disappointed that it had taken them so long to take a victory. According to Kanazawa, Miyakoshi was 'quite an optimistic person'.

The win at Spa motivated the people in Japan working on the NS enormously. As Oguma recalls,

> Before the win in Belgium, up to Assen, all the riders were getting the same parts, but from Assen, we concentrated on Spencer. The strategy was to beat Yamaha and Roberts, although we respected him very much. The communication and assistance from Japan got a lot better and we started winning races regularly.

Ron Haslam's eleventh place on the NR (that could easily have been a tenth) went unnoticed in the jubilation surrounding the race win on the NS. Haslam felt that he should have got a point at Spa: 'Kork Ballington on the Kawasaki cut the chicane and should have been penalized but wasn't. I think it was the best GP result of the NR ever.'

Yugoslavia, Silverstone and Sweden

The next race, in Yugoslavia, saw Spencer finish in fourth place when he suffered a partial seizure on the last lap. At Silverstone, Katayama showed that he had recovered much of the form he seemed to have lost during his NR days, and briefly led the race. He might have been able to take third place, but for a broken crankshaft late in the race. Spencer was second behind Uncini, who was heading to a safe world championship after Roberts crashed and broke his hand on the first lap of the race.

Ron Haslam took the last version of the NR – fully developed and now totally eclipsed by its successful two-stroke cousin – to a disappointing fifteenth place in its last GP. Although it was never again seen at a GP race, the NR remained close to the hearts of many of the engineers at Honda R&D. The technology that was developed during the project was resurrected for the abortive development of a 250 turbo-charged four-stroke twin that was to be used for the 500 class, and for the NR750 that was developed for the Bol d'Or endurance race and the ultimate street bike that Honda constructed at the end of the 1980s.

In Sweden, Katayama claimed Honda's second GP of the season and the first of his own 500 class career. Spencer's bike had been unable to start, as it came back from the warm-up lap firing on just two cylinders.

San Marino

Tension within the team had risen as Spencer got the best parts, despite a return to form for Katayama. At the San Marino GP at Mugello, the penultimate race of the year, Katayama decided to tweak the team-manager's tail. Katayama remembers,

> They tried to produce the same bhp from each engine, but that year there was 5 bhp between the best and worst engine. The best was 126 bhp and the worst was 121 bhp. At Mugello I asked the team manager whether my bike was maybe not as fast as Freddie's. He assured me it was the same. I asked them to show me the engines, so I could pick up the one I wanted to use. He said, 'But they are all the same.' I said, 'OK. I'll tell you which one is good.' I had a very special

> pendulum, which would move in a certain way and indicate how powerful the engine was. We went to the engines and checked them all and pointed out the powerful and less powerful engines. I said, 'I'll take these two engines this time, as you said they are all the same', pointing to the most powerful ones. They wouldn't let me have them. I was already regaining my confidence and the GP went well. Despite an engine down on power and a poor tyre, I set the fastest lap, although I crashed when I caught Freddie.

Spencer won the race, making it GP win number three of the season.

Hockenheim

Finally, the GP riders travelled to Hockenheim in Germany for the last race of the year. Spencer was well in the lead until his ignition started playing up with just two laps to go; then, peeling into one of the corners, he touched Franco Uncini, who had caught up with the slowing machine, and both riders went down. Katayama was fourth and Lucchinelli fifth.

At the end of the season, Spencer had managed two GP wins and was placed third in the championship table behind Uncini and Graeme Crosby on the Agostini Yamaha.

Spencer's Success

Spencer's championship third place in 1982 was an incredible achievement for both man and machine. Spencer had quickly adapted to riding in Europe, building an international reputation as someone in possession of super-human riding skills. As Kanemoto recalls,

> We were at Silverstone and he was going to London with his girlfriend. I said, 'Don't forget you have to be in Sweden for Thursday practice.' He arrived there after practice, and when I said, 'Freddie, practice is over', he said, 'No one told me.' I said, 'Don't tell me that. This is Erv you're talking to.' The next day he went out and, by the second practice, he was at the lap record. I remember overhearing Graeme Crosby say, 'There goes that theory of having to come here for years to learn the circuits.' Freddie could learn circuits so quickly. If he wasn't close to the lap record within twelve laps, you thought there was something wrong.

UPDATING THE NS FOR 1983

Recurring Problems

Despite Honda's successes in 1982, there was still some room for improvement in the NS. It was still a little under-powered. Even the most powerful of the engines was 15 bhp down on the OW61 Yamaha (in which the major weakness was the chassis featuring a rear shock mounted in a horizontal plane behind the engine, and compressed via a complex arrangement of rocker arms. Roberts spent all season wrestling with it and the tyre problems it created.)

There were too many problems with the NS ignition that required the use of a heavy battery. It had a tendency to over-heat. According to Katayama, 'It would over-heat a little sometimes, running at 80 or 85 degrees, and would start to lose bhp over 75 degrees. The throttle response was also a little slow and worse when it was over-heating. Then you'd have to open the throttle three seconds before you needed it.' The 1982 version also had the engine set a little too far back in the chassis, and had a tendency to lose the front end, as had happened to Katayama at Misano. All these issues, as well as the need to lower the weight, were addressed in the updates that were made for the 1983 season.

Testing

Different bikes were constructed for back-to-back tests and Ron Haslam was asked to go out to Brazil to test them in December 1982. Freddie Spencer didn't like testing much, and Haslam was quickly identified in the eyes of Honda as an excellent test rider. In Oguma's view,

> It was possible to distinguish which riders were best at which tests, depending on their personality. If there were three versions of something to test, Katayama was best. If there was only A or B, then Spencer was best at testing. Lucchinelli was not a very good tester. We used whatever Katayama or Spencer chose for Lucchinelli. Ron Haslam was the best tester for endurance aspects of the bikes. For instance, the short NGK spark plugs were developed by Ron Haslam. He could ride consistent fast laps and that is what we needed. Later, he did a lot of development work for us.

Haslam recalls,

> I was sent to Brazil for three to four weeks to test the NS, but actually to test three different models. One had an engine set back, one set forward, and the third had a different steering geometry. I had to find the best

Katayama's 1983 machine appears little different from the 1982 bike, but ATAC chambers are hidden in there somewhere.

bike. The bikes also had some carbon-fibre front forks, but they didn't work. There was too much stiction. They were very strong, but you couldn't stop them flexing. When they flexed, they stuck. They did continue into the GPs with them a little bit, but they gradually disappeared.

Changes to the Bike

The use of carbon fibre helped reduce the weight of the bike to under 265lb (120kg). The rear and front wheels were 16in. The ignition was changed, doing away with the heavy battery pack, and the engine was fitted with a special new valve that was given the epithet ATAC, standing for 'Automatic Torque Amplification Control'. This was Honda's equivalent of the Yamaha powervalve, intended to raise the power level at lower engine speeds by increasing the total volume of the exhaust pipe. It was marginally effective, but less elegant than the powervalve and much more bulky and tricky to operate. Simply because of a lack of space, the ATAC system was initially fitted to just two of the exhaust pipes.

THE 1983 SEASON

Having made the necessary changes to the bike, Honda went into the 1983 season with four factory riders – Freddie Spencer, Takazumi Katayama, Marco Lucchinelli and Ron Haslam – equipped with 255lb (115kg) machines that generated 130 bhp.

RS500 Production Racer

These were not the only three-cylinder Hondas to be seen on the GP starting grid. One of the bikes Haslam had been testing was a prototype of the RS500 production replica of the 1982 NS500s. The RS500 was a very close replica of the NS500, with slightly less magnesium and no carbon fibre, but with an aluminium chassis. It was a little bit heavier (275lb/125kg dry) and a little less powerful (120 bhp at 11,500 rpm), but was a very competitive machine for the GPs as Raymond Roche, one of the owners of the six RS500s that had been produced, was to show.

Suspension was relatively sophisticated, with bump and rebound adjustable at the front and rear as well as ride height adjustment at the rear. The bike's weakest point was the engine position, which was not far enough forward, causing the same light front end that the 1982 NS had displayed. Priced at $30,000 in Europe, it was 40 per cent more expensive than the only other 500 production racer, the Suzuki RG500. A comprehensive set of spares was included with the Honda, including cylinders, heads, pistons, sprockets, carburettor jets, spark plugs, and so on. However, the factory equivalent of the RG, the XR71, had just taken the world championship, so there was a lot more interest in the cheaper, race-proven RG over the unknown RS.

South Africa

Nobody could have known it at the time, but the 1983 GP season was set to become legendary as the King and the Prince fought for the supremacy of the track. Whatever else happened was just a distraction from the battle of the Titans – Spencer and Roberts, Honda and Yamaha, three-cylinder and four-cylinder, reed-valve and disc-valve, Michelin and Dunlop, Showa and Ohlins.

Just after shipping to Europe, a production fault was discovered in the RS500 gearbox and new parts were shipped to the first GP in South Africa for replacement.

At the South African GP, Spencer lead from the second lap to the flag, beating Roberts by seven seconds, with Ron Haslam in third on his NS500 debut. Raymond Roche brought the RS500 home in seventh place, beating Roberts' new team-mate Eddie Lawson in the process.

The European GPs

The first European GP, at a very cold Le Mans in France, was the scene of both triumph and tragedy. Honda filled the podium, after Roberts' Yamaha split an expansion pipe and he dropped to fourth. The tragic death of Swiss rider Michel Frutschi, who crashed his RS500 and hit an exposed catch fence pole, dampened the celebrations.

At the next race in Italy, Spencer won again. Roberts slid off into a gravel pit when fighting with Spencer, re-started, but ran out of fuel on the last lap. Three races gone, three wins for Spencer.

At Hockenheim in Germany, it was Spencer's turn for trouble as a split exhaust caused him to drop down to fourth place before the race was stopped due to a heavy rain shower. Despite his win, Roberts was still 18 points behind Spencer. In Spain it was a race-long duel between the two, the win going to Spencer by 0.5 seconds. A week later, in Austria, it was Yamaha's day and Honda's nightmare as the machines of both Haslam and Spencer broke their cranks. Now Roberts was back in the running, just 6 points behind, with half the season's racing behind him.

The first-ever all-Honda podium in the 500 class. Spencer won, with Lucchinelli and Haslam second and third at the 1983 French GP.

Ron Haslam's riding style was always exciting to watch and his 1983 debut year on the NS brought him the 'Rocket' epithet for his fast starts.

Haslam had been unable to sustain his fantastic start to the season, and a crash in Spain left him with a fractured hand that plagued him for the rest of the year. With all the attention on Spencer, Haslam's GP effort was getting less support from Honda. Haslam's recollection is that,

> Freddie would get the newer cases and cranks and everything, as he was leading the championship. Every meeting he had a new engine, and that was needed because he was super hard on engines. He revved the engines so hard that after two races the crankshaft and crankcases had worn so much they'd gone oval. That's why they were changed so often. I used to take his old cases and Loctite the bearings in them and they'd be very good, like new. I was using his replaced kit as I would otherwise have been running the cases for half a season.

Honda clearly had no intention of dumping Haslam, it was just a question of their priorities. As Haslam says,

> I was Freddie's team-mate and I'd tailed off a little bit and was a bit frustrated, and I

> wasn't sure if it was me or the bike. Honda were so helpful on that side. There was a big International race at Donnington, and I asked about Freddie's bike. They went straight outside to get it for me. This was just after the last GP of the year. When I first got on it, I wasn't keen on it. It wasn't a nice bike to ride, the suspension was hard. I decided not to change it because I was trying to decide if I had a problem or the bike. I actually got used to it and then I preferred it. Although the suspension was harder, it was much more predictable. The engine was quicker as well. It felt newer and sharper.

That bike was the ultimate NS500. It had just taken the world championship in Spencer's hands.

Second Half of the 1983 Season

Spencer almost lost the world championship in the second half of the season. Yamaha's link-up with Ohlins began to pay dividends and Kenny Roberts was at last able to get the suspension dialled in to his requirements. Race by race, Roberts became stronger as Spencer faded a little.

Spencer really won the world championship at the seventh GP of the year in Yugoslavia. Roberts couldn't get the Yamaha started and was dead last at the end of the first lap. In a display of riding at its most aggressive, Roberts managed to claw his way up to fourth place, and it was expected that he would be given third place on a plate, as it was held by his team-mate Eddie Lawson. As the last laps went by, Lawson kept race pace and received no signs that he should slow, so Roberts lost another two points to Spencer; those points could have given him the title at the end of the year.

Team orders were not well planned in either camp, as Katayama took second place at Assen from Spencer, whose tyres turned out to be too soft on the baking hot Dutch circuit. Both the Honda riders were following home Kenny Roberts, although Katayama came within a bike's length of catching Roberts as he took it easy on the last lap and wheelied over the line. Spencer had a repeat of the tyre problems at Spa and was overtaken by Roberts for the lead at mid-race distance. Roberts had closed the championship lead to just five points.

Spencer and the NS on their way to the 1983 world championship.

At Silverstone, Roberts was in magnificent form, taking the win from Spencer. Spencer had been struggling a little during practice, having a lot of trouble getting on to the back straight. He complained to Kanemoto, 'Kenny's getting away from me', and Kanemoto helped him, with advice on working with the bike's characteristics:

> Kenny was on the side of the bike, coming out of the corner leaning over, and accelerating

A year after Spencer's first GP win, and the King and Kid are at it again. Spencer's tyres have gone off and he has just been caught by Roberts, who slides into him as he passes.

away. I was able to give Freddie a little bit of insight. Because the engine would rev so quickly, when you were leaned over you had to hook another gear. I said to Freddie, 'What if you turned the bike twice?' If you squared the corner, you could get the bike upright and fire it off down the straight. It worked. Freddie came back and said that he could run with Kenny in that corner now. It was a completely different line, but working with the characteristic of the bike to get the best performance. You don't want to change the bike as you may well lose the advantage that you have in the next two corners.

Sweden

At this stage, it looked as though the tide had changed in Yamaha's favour. With just two points advantage to Spencer and two races to run, the GP circus packed up and went to Sweden for what was to become one of the most renowned GPs of the 1980s.

Roberts shares a joke with Kanemoto and Spencer before the start of the 1983 Swedish GP. After he lost the race to Spencer, he wasn't talking to anyone.

Everybody realized that the Swedish GP was going to be critical. As Kanazawa says,

> We needed to win at Anderstorp because we knew that Imola was not a good circuit for the NS500. After Spa, we asked for something special for Sweden and we received new cylinders. We also fitted the ATAC to the middle exhaust, so all exhausts used this system. When I saw how fast the bike was, I really started to believe we would win the championship.

Spencer qualified almost two seconds ahead of Roberts. In the GP, Spencer led off the line, but was caught and passed by Roberts on lap seven of the thirty-lap race. The Honda rider eased the pace a little and a gap opened with Roberts, but after a few laps Spencer closed again on the Yamaha rider and shadowed him for the second half of the race. Going into the penultimate corner of the race, a right-hander, Spencer pulled out of Roberts' draft and they approached the corner side by side, with Spencer on the better inside line, determined to brake as late as Roberts. In attempting to get ahead of Spencer so he could cut across, Roberts eased the brakes a little, but entered the corner too fast and ran wide into the dirt. Spencer also barely made the corner, but recovered fastest to take the race by half a bike's length.

Roberts was incandescent with rage; he was mostly angry with himself for getting caught out, but initially he blamed Spencer for riding him off the track. Later he was to say, 'I was upset more with myself. I underestimated him completely. I should never have allowed him to do it.' Kanemoto recalls,

> In the straight we were having trouble. The back straight was entered via a slow corner, and both the triple and the four were slow through there, and then it was just hooking gears down the straight. It was just like a hairpin – you had to turn it and then accelerate. We knew that the Yamaha was quicker; it hadn't been in practice, but we could see that Kenny was getting quicker and quicker as practice progressed. We were doing section times and we could see that the place that Freddie might have an advantage was at the end of the back straight, as he was riding a smaller and lighter bike. Kenny felt that he got the wrong end of the deal, but if he had blocked out that area Freddie wouldn't have been able to pass.

San Marino

Spencer and Honda went into the last GP of the season – and the last GP of Kenny Roberts' career – with a five-point cushion; Spencer needed just to follow Roberts home to take his and Honda's first 500cc world title. The San Marino GP was run at Imola and all Roberts could do was hope that his team-mate Lawson could steal second place thus giving Roberts the title.

Lawson started poorly, but was in third place by lap seventeen of the twenty-five laps. Roberts was leading Spencer, riding as slowly as possible, making his bike as wide as possible, to help Lawson catch up, but Spencer passed as soon as his advantage over Lawson dropped under five seconds. It stayed that way to the flag, with Roberts, one of motorcycling's greatest riders, winning his last GP, and Spencer and Honda taking their first world title. It was the end of a truly extraordinary season. For Katayama,

> It was incredible. I could feel what Spencer and Roberts were doing during the racing, even though I could not see them. They would go a lot quicker than me, maybe three seconds a lap. Roberts was a very strong fighting rider. He became a little bit older, and couldn't win as easily as he had before Freddie came. The 1983 season burned him out. He rode so well and did an incredible job and he could be proud of what he achieved. He was able to stop, knowing he would not be able to ride a season at that pace again. The lap records they set in 1983 were unbroken for three years. It was one of the best seasons ever in 500cc racing.

THE FATE OF THE NS500 THREE-CYLINDER RACER

The year 1983 was to mark the high spot in the history of the NS500 three-cylinder racer. It had proven to be a devastatingly effective tool in the hands of Freddie Spencer, but it seemed clear, both to the race team and to the engineers in Japan, that it would be very difficult to develop the engine further. It was not clear at the time that the success had largely been due to the right balance of power and agility. One problem in approaches to design was a tendency to concentrate on deficiencies rather than to analyse what worked and what didn't. At some GPs, such as Silverstone, the lower power of the NS had made it impossible for Spencer to keep up with OW Yamaha. As Yamaha got to grips with the handling problems experienced by OW riders from the inception of the V4s, it seemed certain that the NS would not be competitive. By the middle of the 1983 season, Honda had started to work on their answer to the OW Yamahas, the NSR500.

The NS500 was to live on in the GPs throughout 1984 and 1985, and the genius of the original design became increasingly clear as the NSR experienced teething troubles and the NS continued to run at the front of the field.

The last official year of production of the RS500 production racer was 1988. Some minor changes were made to the engine, but the single substantial alteration was a completely new rolling chassis for the 1986 season. The tube frame made way for a full beam frame, still using aluminium alloy as the source material. The engine was mounted in three places. At the back of the engine, there were two engine-mounting locations above and below the gearbox. A V-shaped aluminium strut hung down from the front of the frame, to bolt to the engine crankcase just under the two vertical cylinders. The Comstar wheels were replaced by six-spoke magnesium wheels that were to become the trademark of all of Honda's race models. The front wheel was 16in and the rear 18in. The weight had dropped closer to 265lb (120kg), from the 275lb (125kg) dry weight of the original RS500, and power was closer to 130 bhp.

It was with this tool that privateer riders continued to compete in GPs, through to the end of the 1980s and into the 1990s. It was only with the arrival of the ROC and Harris Yamahas in 1992 that it became possible for the last of the RS500s to be put out to pasture for a well-earned retirement.

According to Ron Haslam, the three-cylinder was a fantastic bike, a true classic of the modern era:

> The three-cylinder hadn't got the sheer power or pull of the fours, which would run away from it. It compensated for this by pulling off-power and with its lower weight. It was one of the best bikes I've ever ridden for handling, close even to today's bikes. You always felt that you were totally in control.

This was not something that could be said of the fearsome fours that were to replace it.

The RS500 was to remain the mainstay of the private GP racers well into the 1990s. Dutchman Cees Doorakkers was still picking up championship points with it in 1991.

5 Changing of the Guard

The Conception and Initial Development of the NSR500 Two-stroke V4 (1984–86)

HONDA RACE SHOP

Design Practices

Surprisingly, the Honda race shop (from 1982 officially entitled Honda Racing Corporation, or HRC), was not so different in 1983 from the way it had been in 1978 when the NR500 was being designed. Many of the design practices that had been applied then were still valid five years later, despite the problems they had caused. One of these practices, in particular, would result in the production of Honda factory racers that were innovative, but flawed. The first of these racers was the 1984 NSR500.

Within HRC, the design of a new bike was entrusted to an engineer who was given the title of 'project leader'. This engineer was responsible for the total product, in turn relying on project leaders for the chassis and the engine. The project leader had total control of the design, usually as a result of his proposal having been selected at an early stage of the development cycle. In principle, the project leader could choose to run square wheels and there would be a very good chance that such a bike would be built. In addition, every four years there would be extensive re-assignment of staff, HRC engineers going back to the business and new engineers, with little or no exposure to racing, joining HRC. The combination of the unquestionable authority of the project leader and the influx of new inexperienced engineers, was a recipe for trouble. And so it was for the first NSR500.

The Competition

Another maxim that heavily influenced design choices was the insistence that a problem should be tackled in a different way from the competition. The Suzuki RG500 was a spent force; attempts to build a more and more compact version of the square-four had resulted in inadequate crankcase volumes and a breathless engine. It was, therefore, the Yamaha V4 against which the new Honda four-cylinder would need to compete.

PLANS FOR A NEW BIKE

Chassis

Having to compete against the Yamaha V4 made Honda's position tricky, as the V4 had exactly the configuration Honda needed to use, assuming the continued use of reed-valves and a single crankshaft. It was important that there should be a significant difference between the Honda and the Yamaha, so the Honda design team decided to make radical changes to the chassis. It was decided to move the fuel tank to a position under the engine. A small diaphragm pump drove the fuel to a very small header tank behind the steering head, with lines leading off to the carburettors. With this tank location, the exhaust pipes needed to be re-routed and it was decided to route them up and over the engine, exiting at the back of the seat unit, with a dummy tank protecting the rider from the searing heat.

It is unclear whether Honda were in any way influenced by work within the Elf project in France, in which ultra-innovative chassis designs were being developed for use in endurance racing, with some backing from Honda. During 1982 and 1983, the ELFe racer, with factory Honda RSC1000 engine, had been run with the fuel tank under the engine.

The theory behind Elf's design choice was the perceived need to lower the centre of gravity of the bike as far as possible to improve the handling. A fully loaded fuel tank high in the frame is a significant factor in the resultant position of the centre of gravity. It was not understood at the time that the heavy weight underneath the centre of gravity (CoG) would seriously impair the ability of the rider to turn the bike around the axle formed by the CoG. This increased roll polar moment resulted in the rider having to exert much more force to get the bike to change direction. In addition, fuel surge under braking and acceleration would stress the mounting lugs, which would crack and needed to be welded up frequently.

The position of the exhaust pipes above the engine enabled the correct dimension of pipe to be used, but, despite extensive insulation material, the rider would receive a lot of heat into the upper torso. Worst of all, the carburettors at the back of the engine were bathed in pre-heated air trapped underneath the dummy tank. The result was an engine for which the carburation was difficult to set up and which would not remain consistent for the extended period of a race.

The chassis moved on from the aluminium tubing of the NS towards the twin-beam frames that Yamaha had started to use in 1983. Beams ran along the top of the engine from steering head to the swing-arm pivot behind the engine. The engine was caged within loops of aluminium that were used to provide extra engine-mounting points.

Suspension and Wheels

Rear suspension geometry was essentially Pro-Link as before, but the wheel it supported carried a quite different tyre from those previously seen in GPs. They were round and black, but Michelin proudly embossed on the wall the fact that they were no longer cross-ply tyres but radials. This construction would open up the possibility of greater contact patches for the rubber and far cooler running temperatures. Both front and rear radials were available. To prevent the sticky black surface picking up too much dirt, the first rear-wheel hugger was found attached to the rear swing-arm.

Testing

The new bike was developed during 1983 and the 140 bhp that was shown on the dyno suggested that the bike would go a long way to accomplishing its mission of hanging on to the 500 crown. By December 1983, two bikes were ready for testing at Surfers' Paradise in Australia. Freddie Spencer never enjoyed testing or running qualification laps at the GP, usually doing the absolute minimum to set a fast time or make a decision on the settings of a bike. Perhaps this was why the testing failed to turn up the shortcomings of the bike that were to surface later. The transition was clearly not going to be easy for Spencer. Back-to-back tests between the NS and the NSR led Spencer to express a preference for the NS, but there was no choice available to him. The NSR had been built to win the 500 title again and this would be the bike that would be used.

The first and worst NSR500. The exotica extended to reversed positions of exhaust pipes and fuel tanks as well as carbon-fibre wheels and front forks.

Ron Haslam was also at the tests. He remembers experiencing,

> ...the funny NSR; a complete failure. First impression was the acceleration. It was like a rocketship. It was a lot more power-bandish, but off-power it didn't pull. On-power it would come in with such a rush that it wasn't that good. Compared with the three-cylinder, it didn't want to stop. Hit the brake and it would push you forward like a car, as if you had locked the wheels. The weight of the fuel in the tank was too low. The pull on the arms and the acceleration felt ten times better.
>
> With the NS being lighter, the bikes were covering the distance in the same time. When it came to getting lap times down, you just couldn't do it. You had to push so hard and the bike felt in command of the rider. The best thing was sliding the bike out of the corners, in very predictable controlled slides. It wouldn't snap away from you. You could just spin it and take it to the edge of the track. It would rather spin like a car than hook up. The four made you feel that you were riding very hard, whereas the three gave you a relaxed ride for the same performance.

Jerry Burgess was one of Ron Haslam's mechanics at the time, and was later to become Mick Doohan's team leader and right-hand man. He recalls,

> The first comment most of the riders had was about the engine characteristic. Raymond Roche said it was like an electric mixer. It was very smooth, but you had no feeling from it. It revved, but it created no

> feeling. It didn't have any torque compared to the triple, it just had rpm. Maybe it needed a bigger crankshaft or some other work.

THE 1984 SEASON

Daytona

The season started early for Freddie Spencer, with a ride on the NSR at the Daytona 200. The NSR500 was up against Yamaha's mighty OW69, the 680cc bored-out version of the OW60 square-four engine that had been run by Sheene and Crosby during the 1982 GP season. This brutal machine had won the 1983 Daytona 200 in the hands of Kenny Roberts, and it was wheeled out again for a repeat performance, with a power valve and other mods to tame the 150-plus bhp power delivery.

The 1984 Daytona would have been the NSR's race, but for an exhaust pipe that started to split on lap thirty, with Spencer holding a slight lead over Roberts. Gradually, Spencer slipped back, unable to challenge the King, the drone from the pipes announcing their disintegration. Roberts went on to win the race, taking his last win

Winter at Surfers' Paradise and Spencer gets to ride the first NSR. He was impressed by the amount of wheelspin the bike produced; he overlooked its lack of torque.

at a circuit that had seemed to be jinxed for him during his glory years.

Both front and rear radial tyres were used by Honda at Daytona, but the front tyres showed themselves to be prone to front wheel patter and were not used in the GPs.

A Bad Fall for Spencer

Two weeks later, during training for the South African GP, the first mishap of the season befell Spencer. He recalls that, as he went into the corner, 'the front end went light and the back collapsed, and the next thing I knew I was sliding into the straw bales'. The spokes supporting the rear wheel had broken as Spencer entered a corner at 70mph (110kph). Honda had been using a large amount of light material on their bikes since the first days of the NR500 and carbon-fibre wheels had become a standard fitting on the factory machines.

Honda would not reveal the cause of the accident, or admit that carbon fibre had been the material that had failed. Spencer had badly hurt both feet and was ruled out of competing in the first GP of the season.

Italy

Spencer had recovered from his fall by the time the next GP was run at Misano in Italy, and he cruised to an easy victory from Eddie Lawson. He felt that, of all the tracks used in the championship, Misano was the best for the V4: 'We found out later that the machine lacked torque, but at Misano you run really close gearbox ratios and the engine is always revving hard, so it was no problem.'

Donnington Park

A week later, Spencer was running away with the six-race Trans-Atlantic Trophy series at Donnington Park. Pulling away at the head of the field during the fifth race, Spencer crashed at Redgate and broke bones in his left foot. He explained later what had happened:

> The crash was partly my fault. The NSR has really different handling characteristics from the NS500 and they really showed up at Donnington and, quite frankly, just caught me out. Redgate Corner is one where you accelerate really hard all the way through and the crash happened because the front end of the bike turned in. On the NS500, when this begins to happen, you simply have to give it more throttle so that it picks up the front wheel and straightens itself out. The V4 is very different because of the totally changed weight distribution. With the fuel tank under the engine, the weight of the fuel is transferred forward under braking and tends to push the front wheel. Therefore, if the bike does turn in, you can't compensate with a burst of throttle. You have to use some muscle and actually pick the bike up. I used too much muscle too quickly, and the bike reacted faster than I thought. It got some grip and pitched me over the high side.

Austria

Spencer was not fit to run in Spain and the next GP in which he competed was the Austrian at the super-fast Salzburgring. At last it was clear that there was a major problem with the bike, as Spencer was more than a second slower than he had been the previous year on the NS, in similar weather conditions. He only managed second place after Mamola, on the NS, slowed dramatically to let Spencer close the fifteen-second gap between them. The jeers from the crowd struck deep in the heart of the Honda team. Honda were clearly in deep crisis.

Honda Team in Crisis

To make Honda's problems worse, the next GP was at another circuit that was not expected to favour the NSR – the new closed circuit at the Nürburgring. After the first day of practice, the fears of the Honda team were confirmed – they were in ninth place, and one second down on Lawson. The de-briefing session dragged on as the team looked at the options open to them. Spencer and Kanemoto were anxious to go back to the NS, arguing that it would be possible to get the best of both worlds by using the NS for slow twisty circuits and the NSR for the faster tracks with fast corners. Showing a surprising open-mindedness, Oguma agreed to send Stuart Shenton, Katayama's mechanic, and Kanazawa back to the HRC headquarters in Belgium to collect the only spare NS in Europe. Oguma recalls,

> After the Austrian GP I was on the telephone all night discussing the problems with Japan. I actually had two positions in the company – I was both team manager and chief engineer within HRC – so I understood the pressures to continue with the NSR. At the Nürburgring, the NSR was clearly not well suited to the circuit and we needed to win the race. I decided to use the NS, but they were not happy back in Japan.

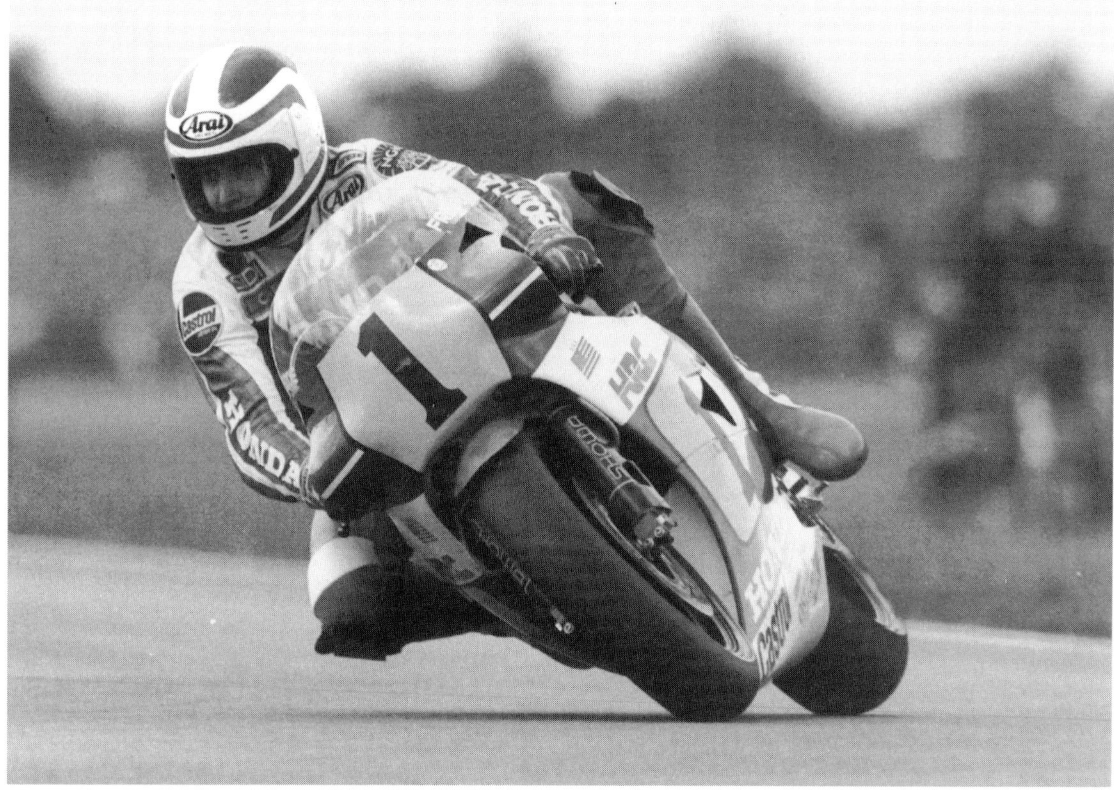

Only someone of Spencer's prodigious natural talent could get such a flawed bike to perform as well as it did.

The Next GPs

At the Nürburgring, the team were to use Marco Lucchinelli's 1983 NS, unraced since the end of the previous year. By the end of Saturday practice on the NS, Spencer had claimed pole position, 1.5 seconds faster than Lawson. He won the race by sixteen seconds from Lawson. Back on the NSR, Spencer won at Paul Ricard, a circuit better suited to the characteristics of the NSR, and again on the NSR in Yugoslavia.

Mamola and Haslam, regular NS riders, were also given NSRs to try during practice in France and Holland respectively, but both used the three-cylinder machine during the races. Haslam's comments were less than flattering. As Kanemoto remembers,

> Haslam rode the NSR at Assen, and we were trying different carb settings. Keihin was there. I remember having a meeting with Oguma and Haga [from Keihin], and we were trying to use Haslam's experience to produce a better bike. I remember Ron saying to Oguma, 'If it weren't for Freddie, this bike would never ever win a GP.' It was a real compliment to Freddie.

Maintenance of the NSR

The NSR wasn't getting any more popular with the mechanics. According to Burgess,

> The maintenance side of the bike was disastrous. You physically couldn't get to the spark plugs through the top exhaust pipes. You couldn't leave the motorcycle overnight because the carbon would dry in the exhaust and fall back on to the piston face. With a normal exhaust the pipe is away from the piston face; with this bike the exhaust was above the piston face. We could not get in there through the side access to change the main jets easily. They developed a circular main jet which was an eccentric and you could get in underneath and turn it, so you had four options for the jet size. This was not a solution to the problem, just a quick fix to the setting during the practices. You only had two sizes either way, but it saved us taking the carburettor bank out, which is what George and I always used to do – take the seat off, pull the carbs through the side with the throttle cables still hanging, and change the main jets. From a mechanic's perspective it was a nightmare. It was too difficult. A racing motorcycle has to be built outside of the track and set up at the track. It is not a case of building the thing at the race track.

Ishii was the carburettor engineer for the team. In his opinion, 'The eccentric main jet was a clever idea to help us out at the race track, but I never used it. It was always difficult to feel the clicks as you turned the adjuster and I never wanted to gamble that it was right. We always removed the carbs.'

Dutch TT and Belgium

It was unclear to Honda which bike to use at the Dutch TT, so they stuck to the NSR, especially as Lawson also seemed to be struggling. Suddenly, in the final session, Lawson cut through to take pole position, while Spencer was still fifth. Attempts by the Honda team to swap to the NS on race day were thwarted by the Yamaha team manager Agostini, who drew their attention to a regulation stating that the race bike must have been used in practice.

Despite a good start on the NSR, it was a disappointing race, with Spencer retiring when a plug cap came loose and could not easily be replaced, due to the problems of access through the exhaust pipes.

In Belgium, Spencer rode both the NS and NSR during practice, but chose the NSR to take a convincing win, with fellow

Spoilt for choice at the 1984 Belgian GP, Spencer chose the NS triple and won by six seconds.

(Below) *No one believed the NSR could be a bad bike and all the Honda guys wanted a ride. Mamola was given it for the British GP and won.*

Honda riders Mamola and Roche pushing Lawson back into fourth place.

The End of Spencer's Season

Spencer was still looking at a twenty-point deficit on the Yamaha rider, but the tide seemed to have turned. However, during practice for an International race at Laguna Seca, Spencer crashed and broke his collarbone when the brakes failed. His season was over. Mamola took the NSR to victory over Lawson at Silverstone and then it was whisked away back to Japan, never to appear again.

A NEW VERSION OF THE NSR

Improvements

It was obvious to HRC in Japan what needed to be done to improve the performance of the NSR. Engineers such as Kanazawa, who returned to Japan after the Dutch TT, explained the problems that the NSR was giving the riders and work started immediately on a conventional version of the bike. The firing order of the cylinders was changed. On the 1984 NSR the firing order had been back-left, front-right, back-right, front-left, at 90-degree intervals. For the 1985 NSR the order became, back-left, front-left, back-right, front-right.

The jackshaft at the back of the crankshaft was removed, power take-off now being at the right-hand end of the crankshaft via the clutch to the main transmission shaft. Otherwise, the engine was not changed significantly, but a new full-beam frame was produced, with sheet aluminium gussetting around the headstock and a large diameter cross-tube at the point where the beams completed their flare out from the headstock. The cross-braced triangulation of the rear swing-arm was also gone, leaving a regular box-section aluminium unit connected to a Showa suspension unit using a layout broadly similar to the Pro-Link system. The biggest problems came with the exhaust pipes. Oguma recalls,

> The chassis engineer stated that it would be 100 per cent impossible for the exhaust pipes to be fitted. For a time it looked like he might be right. For a month, NakajimaSan was searching for a layout that would give us the right volume pipes and fit behind the fairing. Eventually he succeeded. It was a masterpiece of design, with the pipes winding back and forth under the engine, to exit as two low pipes on either side of the rear wheel.

Testing

Final weight distribution on the NSR was determined with the assistance of a test session in Surfers' Paradise, Australia, at the end of 1984. According to Kanemoto, 'They wanted to get the weight distribution right, so the tank was underneath, but the engine was run on gravity from a small tank on the top. Then, weights were added to simulate the normal weight distribution on the bike, and it was a lot better.'

THE NEW SEASON

Daytona

The first opportunity to see if the engineers had got it right again came at Daytona, now a 100 mile (160km) Formula One event, and without serious competition from an equivalent Yamaha two-stroke. The NSR was much better than it had been the previous year, the only failure coming from the exhaust pipes that split during practice. Spencer won the race in controversial circumstances; he was assisted in getting his bike re-started while the one-minute board was displayed. Some thought he should have been docked a lap, but he wasn't.

Spencer thought the bike was vastly improved, explaining,

> It's much easier to get it from one side to the other; it feels completely different. It seemed on the old bike that it was like having a heavy rock on a long stick. It was very difficult to control. Now I have the weight of the petrol much closer to me. You can't stop the weight of the petrol sloshing about completely and, with it all down low, it just seemed to push the front wheel away.

Competing in Two Classes

The next race was the first of the GPs in South Africa, but this was not just a regular GP meeting. Spencer had agreed to compete in both the 250 and 500 classes, going for a unique double world championship that had never before been achieved. It was a heroic undertaking, which had been given consideration since the middle of the 1983 season.

Oguma's explanation was as follows:

> We wanted to give Mr Honda a special present in 1985. He was not involved in the daily running of the business any more – he was the Supreme Advisor – but he was very interested in the racing activities. I wanted to ask him to come to the races but I was not allowed to, because management were worried that we might not win. During 1983, I was spending a lot of time watching the performance of the 250 class and preparing a report to be sent to Japan. Towards the end of 1984, I had a meeting with Freddie [Spencer] and Erv [Kanemoto] and told them I wanted to go for both classes, and that I would guarantee perfect back-up for both. Freddie was happy to race in both classes, but Erv was not so happy.

Erv Kanemoto remembers it a little differently:

> After Freddie was hurt in South Africa in 1984, Oguma and Fukui and I came to his room at the hotel. Prior to coming to Europe, Freddie and I had discussed what he would be able to achieve – how many world championships he could win. I said three would be pretty good. When he crashed, Fukui and Oguma were talking about building a works 250 and Freddie said something about wanting to ride the thing and I said, 'If you could pull this off, it would put you back on track.' HRC's idea was to do selected races where they drew a lot of crowds, but I said, 'Let's do the first group of them, and we could drop out at any time.' There was a chance that Freddie could do something special. If something went wrong, we could re-evaluate it all. But Honda's initial idea was just to do the big races like Hockenheim. He started off doing well and continued doing well.

Chassis Change

It was going to be a tough season. Although the NSR was a lot better, it still wasn't perfect, and still had a tendency to push the front wheel. Spencer was unable to prevent Lawson from taking the South African GP win by five seconds. During the four weeks before the first European GP at Jarama, Spain, the team went to Rijeka in Yugoslavia. They were there ostensibly for tyre tests, but these were tyres mounted on a new bike with the weight further forward.

Jerry Burgess was now looking after Spencer's NSR with George Vukmanovich,

A place for everything and everything in its place. The conventional layout of the 1985 NSR was all that Spencer needed to re-take the title. Stuart Shenton (centre) and George Vukmanovich (right) help prepare the bike.

and recalls how they had had some handling problems with the bikes in South Africa: 'We did some extensive testing in Yugoslavia and made some big changes to the chassis before we started the European season. That seemed to be a step in the right direction. We shortened the steering head by approximately ¾in (20mm).'

The European GPs

Although Spencer crashed the bike, losing the front end, during practice for the Spanish GP, he won the race by a comfortable fourteen seconds, under the satisfied eye of Soichiro Honda, at last present at a GP. The handling was so much better that Spencer was able to use the 16in Michelin radial tyres for the first time at a GP, and set a pole position time at the German GP that was four seconds faster than his own lap record set on thc NS three years before. During the wet race, his new Michelin rain tyres were not as effective as the older Michelin full wet tyre used by Christian Sarron, who won the race, taking the lead from Spencer mid-race.

A week later, it all came together with the first 250 and 500 double win of the season at the tight Italian circuit at Mugello. This was repeated in Austria.

Behind the Scenes

Spencer seemed able to race desperately hard twice a day, apparently without suffering any ill-effects. However, there was another side to the racing of which few people were aware. Kanemoto recalls,

> In those days, you had to take the victory lap; so many times, we just pushed the second bike to the start line, while he changed his leathers, grabbed a new helmet, and tried to dry himself off a little bit. He was always late. Psychologically, that was so tough. You run the race on a psychological high and, as soon as the race is over, there is a big let-down. He had to get back up again in a very short time for a new race. I really appreciate what he did.
>
> In Mugello, Freddie lost a contact lens. He came in and his eyes were red. He said he had a really bad headache, and he rode with one contact lens. He said, 'I don't know if I can concentrate enough to ride.' I said, Make a lap, see where you are, don't take any chances, see how comfortable you feel and, if you pull in, at least you know that you gave it your best shot.'

Although much better than the 1984 model, the 1985 NSR could still get badly crossed up, as Spencer demonstrates coming out of La Source at the Belgian GP.

With only Spencer getting the NSR in 1985, Mamola had to make do with the NS, and rode it to take sixth place in the championship.

For 1985, Spencer was the greatest road racer of his generation. It wasn't all plain sailing; he damaged his knee when he clipped a straw bale during the race in Yugoslavia, falling from the bike when coming home behind Lawson. At Assen in Holland, he was skittled out of the race by Christian Sarron, determined to show he was the best rain-rider in the world by overtaking everyone on the first lap.

Spa and Le Mans

It was back in the double groove at Spa, one of Spencer's favourite tracks. Then it was on to Le Mans in France. The track was not a favourite of Spencer's, and the pressure was getting to him, despite the ten-point lead he held over Lawson. Jerry Burgess understood the problems:

> Le Mans was a very rough race track and the NSR was not working well at all. Freddie wanted to run the triple that we had been carting around in the back of the truck all season and had never used. When things are going bad, you generally don't want to introduce a third problem. We persevered with the four-cylinder, but finally we got the triple out. Because it hadn't been used for four months, the acid from the oils had probably got to the crankshaft a bit, and he did only two laps before the crank broke. But it was enough to realize it was the machine to use at that race track.

We were all in a bit of a spin, because we had a bike that Freddie said was better and it had a broken crankshaft. We had a pretty serious problem to work out and the bottom line is not to give the rider too many choices. We needed the help of the 250 guys to rebuild the triple and put together two four-cylinders that were better. It was a nightmare really. In the end, Freddie used the four-cylinder in the race and he won. Wayne Gardner ran it up to him in the beginning, but Wayne was on the Dunlop tyres, and used a very soft one, which didn't run the distance. Wayne stopped after blowing the side out of the tyre. Qualifying and racing are two different things and Freddie was threatened in the qualifying; he felt that the bike was not adequate and experience teaches you that you have to balance the race over thirty laps, not one or two.

The partnership that made the unique 1985 double title possible – Freddie Spencer and Erv Kanemoto.

Achieving the Double

At a cold, wet, miserable GP at Silverstone, Spencer tied up the 250 world championship, and stretched his lead on Lawson to twenty points by winning the 500. Using their years of experience of working together to take crucial informed decisions for race set-up and tyre choices, Erv Kanemoto and Freddie Spencer were able to make the correct choice of tyre for the chilly damp Anderstorp circuit in Sweden. The unique achievement of winning the 250 and 500 world championships in the same single year was claimed. It was a super-human performance, but achieved at what price?

THE 1986 SEASON

Work on an NSR for 1986

Based on Spencer's mid-season experiences with the NSR, most of the work on an NSR for 1986 went into curing the tendency that the V4 had to push the front wheel. The engine was moved forward in the chassis, and the swing-arm lengthened, to put more weight on the front wheel to reduce its tendency to lift as the bike accelerated out of the corner. The fabricated aluminium brace that supported the top of the rear shock absorber, as well as the rear sub-frame, was far larger than on the 1985 NSR. Access to the carburettors was improved by allowing a section of the sub-frame to be unbolted.

Both 16in and 17in front wheels were tried, the preference going to the latter,

The official portrait of the 1979 X0 NR500, Honda's hope after eleven years away from GP racing.

Paul Dallas wheels out the NR500 to the embarrassment of practice for the 1979 GP at Silverstone.

By 1981, the NR500 looked like it could win races; it won the 200km race at Suzuka.

Freddie Spencer astounded friend and foe at the 1981 British GP by revving the guts out of the NR500 and holding fifth place, until the engine blew.

(Below) *The deathly hush before the start of the 1982 Belgian GP, won by Spencer (40) on the NS500 2-stroke triple.*

(Below) *Spencer on the RS250R-W on his way to the second win of the day at Mugello in 1985, the first of his amazing double wins.*

(Above) *The climax of one of GP racing's most exciting seasons came with Kenny Roberts' win at the 1983 San Marino GP. The title went to Spencer and Honda, while KR went on to manage son Junior, sandwiched between the two heroes.*

Sito Pons wrestles with the 1986 NSR Honda at the Spanish GP, his Campsa-sponsored machine mixing it with the HB and Rothmans riders all season.

(Below) *By the end of the 1987 race in Spain, Gardner had a 23-second lead and went on to win a deserved title.*

Yatsushiro was supported with a 1986 NSR500 for the 1987 season and showed himself a capable if not spectacular rider.

The blue and white Rothmans NSR250s didn't have it all their own way. Reinhold Roth was a continuous threat on the HB Hondas, until his tragic crash in 1990.

Gardner leading the race of the decade, the 1988 French GP.

In 1989, Sito Pons was the absolute king of the 250 class on his Campsa NSR250.

(Above) *Pier-Francesco Chili found the 1989 NSR500 a bit of a handful, as did all the Honda riders that year.*

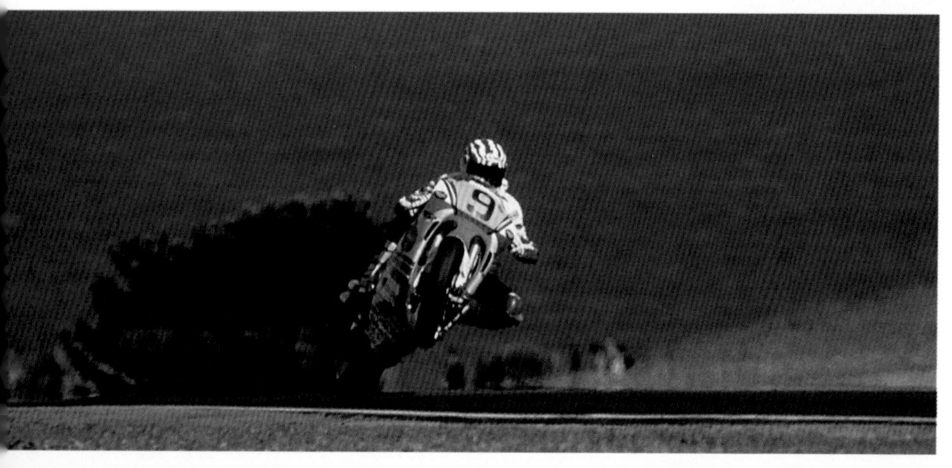

A spectacular new force arrived in the Rothmans Honda team in 1989; at his home GP in 1990, Mick Doohan was only beaten by team-mate Gardner.

The all-season all-Honda needle match between Bradl and Cadalora resulted in a spectacular 1991 season.

Last lap of the 1991 Japanese GP; Doohan is set to take the first of seven second places that year, finishing a very close runner-up to Rainey in the title.

(Above) *Gardner streaking away to his last win at the 1992 British GP, having just announced his retirement after a career fighting the NSR500.*

(Left) *It's wet on the grid for the 1992 Japanese GP and Jerry Burgess makes the last adjustments to the NSR that is about to set the competition reeling.*

Alex Criville won a GP in his very first year in the class, but it was to be a couple of years before he was challenging for class domination.

The talent was clear but not on Michelin tyres. Max Biaggi (5) only managed to win the European GP at Barcelona during 1993, but greater things were to come.

(Left) *Loris Capirossi seemed doomed to being the almost-but-not-quite NSR250 rider, with his second place in 1993 and third in 1994.*

(Above) *Although 1994 was Biaggi's and Aprilia's year, there was plenty of good racing from NSR250 riders such as Romboni (5) and Okada (8).*

Honda's Japanese riders in 1995 were Shinichi Itoh on the NSR500 and Tadayuki Okada on the NSR250.

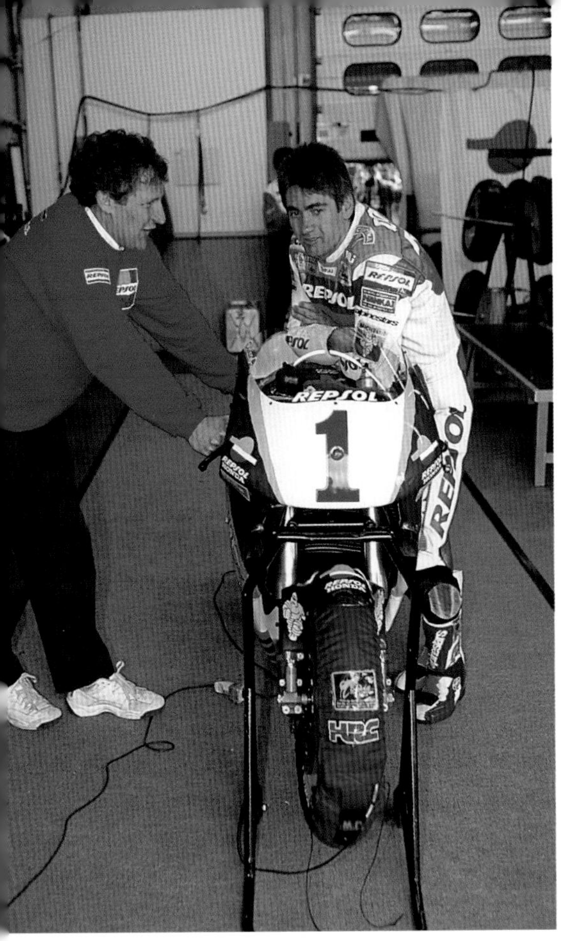

(Left) *The partnership of Jerry Burgess and Mick Doohan has been vital to the four successive titles they have achieved.*

Olivier Jacque burst into the 250 GPs in 1995 and by 1996 was battling for GP wins. His first came here in Brazil.

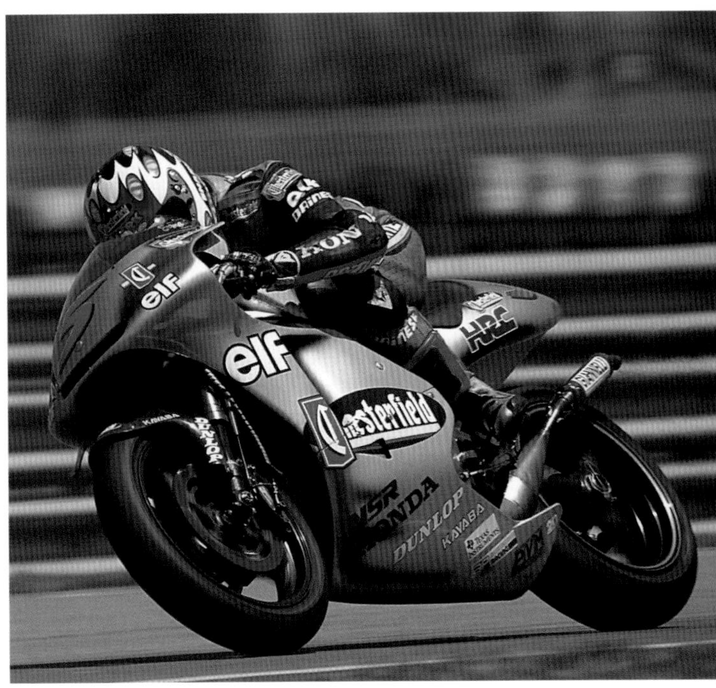

(Below) *The end of a tense 1996 season for the Repsol Honda team came at the Australian GP; they were hardly talking after the race.*

(Above) *Repsol Honda crushed the other teams in the 500 class in 1997, with Mick Doohan only occasionally being bested by Okada (7) or Criville (2).*

A happy sight for Honda. Doohan has clinched his fourth title, Japanese rider Okada is second and Alex Barros has taken a private production NSR500V to a third place at the 1997 British GP.

(Below) *The most dominant team in the history of the 500 GP class – Mick Doohan, Alex Criville, Tadayuki Okada and Takuma Aoki.*

which necessitated a curved radiator to prevent the wheel crushing the radiator under heavy braking. Some work on the cylinders and exhausts pushed the power up to around 150 bhp, with the power tailing off more slowly above 11,800 rpm to improve the engine's ability to over-rev. There were different sets of pipes available. One set was tuned for maximum power at the cost of mid-range tractability, but with an ability to over-rev the engine to 12,500 rpm. The reworked cylinders and crankcases were narrower than those on the 1985 NSR. Again, it was a problem finding room for the fatter exhaust pipes, but a chamfer on the lower edge of the box-section swing-arm gave the pipe designer just enough room to squeeze in the exhausts.

Changes in the Team

Although the bikes did not change much, there were some big changes in Team Honda. Spencer now received a team-mate in the form of Australian Wayne Gardner, who had been nurtured for this position for the previous four years by Honda Britain.

Gardner had run a full GP season in 1985 on an NS500 and had finished in fourth place, tied on points with team-mate Ron Haslam, also on an NS500. More importantly, Gardner had won the Suzuka Eight Hours race in 1985, riding the RVF750 V4 four-stroke; he had also survived almost being crushed to death by a large part of the 250,000 crowd that surged on to the track after the race. Wins at the unofficial Japanese and Selangor GPs, beating Eddie Lawson at the latter, confirmed his value to Honda. During the European winter season he had competed in the Swann series in his home country and taken the 1985 NSR to four wins from six races.

Gardner was clearly ready for a full works GP ride, but he wasn't too happy with the bike he would be riding. He was given the four-cylinder NSR by Honda to run in the Swann series in Australia, while Malcolm Campbell was given the three-cylinder. As he recalls,

> Everyone thought I would just clear off on the four, but the three was still a pretty good bike. The four-cylinder I thought was a piece of crap. I was using Dunlops and just tearing them up on the four. At Surfers' Paradise I was getting full-lock sideways, with smoke coming off the tyres. Then I was eventually high-sided and slid into the ditch. When we got back into the pits, we found that the side-wall of the tyre had split. The NSR was big and heavy and cumbersome. It made good power, but it would all disappear in wheel spin; there was no traction. It shook its head all the time.

Gardner was provided with a small experienced support team, including Jerry Burgess, who remembers the story thus:

> At the end of 1985 we did a race in Japan, for Honda to show off their machines and riders to their dealers and the Japanese public. Freddie crashed and broke his collarbone; he had been contracted to ride at Malaysia the week after and of course he couldn't make it. I was sent there with Wayne and he won that race. The first I ever heard of working with Wayne was when Erv rang me at the end of 1985 and asked me what I thought. I said I was really happy where I was – we had just won the world championship, we all got on really well – and Erv said it would be good for me. When I talked to the Honda management, it was clear that they had talked to Erv. They indicated that I could do more and I felt that if I didn't take on more they would think I was slacking. I looked at it with a certain amount of trepidation. We had done the Swann series together at the end of 1985

> and Wayne had won, so some foundation was laid. The team was his Honda Britain mechanic, Wilf Needham, Stuart Shenton, and myself. Basically I was the leader as I had worked on the four-cylinder all year. It was pretty logical. It was good experience for Wayne. I don't think it was set in concrete that I would be leading the operation the following year.

Although Gardner was a full team member, Spencer was still the undisputed team leader, so the 1986 NSR was developed to match his riding style. It was Gardner's job to learn to adapt his riding style to get the best performance from the bike. There was no question of it being modified to match Gardner's requirements. As Jerry Burgess puts it,

> We assumed that this was a better bike than the one that Freddie had used to win the 1985 championship, so Wayne had to adapt. It was a bit of a learning thing. Wayne was a young rider, first time in a factory team, and the emphasis was more on giving him a lot of miles and time to get to understand the bike.

Serious Problems for Spencer

There was no pre-GP season shake-down at Daytona. The two Honda teams assembled at Jarama for the Spanish GP, and in practice it was as if Freddie Spencer would carry on from where he left off the previous season. He was half a second faster than Gardner in practice and almost a full second ahead of Lawson. The flag dropped on the race and he disappeared, building a lead of five seconds by lap seven. The end of Spencer's GP career can be traced to lap nine of the 1986 Spanish GP. He started to slow and was caught by Gardner within a couple of laps, pulling in to the pits on lap fourteen, suffering from a tendinitis that caused him to lose the feeling in his right hand. He was never to ride competitively in a GP again. Gardner took the win in Spain; it was a fantastic start to the year, the full drama of which had yet to become clear.

Kanemoto remembers the trouble Spencer had with his wrist:

> He said, 'That's the first time I've stopped in a race. My hand stopped working, then I start pulling hard and locking up the front brake, as I had no feeling. I decided to ride with the rear brake and had no control over the bike.' Then he pulled out. The injury was one part of the story, but the other part of it was almost like burn-out. He had been extending himself way too much.

For the rest of the season, the motorcycle media focused on the 'will he/won't he' escapades of Spencer, who several times left his team guessing as to whether he would or would not appear at a GP. After missing two GPs while undergoing physiotherapy for the problem, he had an abortive ride in Austria when the steering damper mounting bolt pulled out of the frame. He returned home and underwent a carpal tunnel operation to ease the pressure that built up in his arms when riding. Recovery from this operation caused him to miss all the remaining GPs, despite some intermediate announcements of an imminent return. Throughout his career he had been averse to riding unless one hundred per cent fit, and physically and mentally he seemed less than that. Any other rider might have been dismissed under such circumstances, but Spencer had built up some credit with Honda, frustrating though it was for them.

According to Oguma,

> When Spencer became unreliable, he quickly went from being the good guy to being the

The first GP of 1986 in Spain, with Spencer streaking away from the field. Minutes later he would pull into the pits, his GP career over.

> bad guy. I felt this was unfair. People so quickly forgot what he had achieved for Honda in 1985. I also felt largely responsible for what had happened to Spencer, as I was the person who had asked him to run both classes in 1985. It was a very difficult year.

Kanemoto had his own feelings of guilt: 'I guess it's easy to be smart after the fact, but I could see that it was taking a toll on him in 1985. I believed he was able to do something special and that he was able to recover from anything.'

Gardner's Season

Wayne Gardner found himself in the vacuum left by the Honda's number one rider. He tried not to let the situation cause him problems, but he felt the pressure keenly. Jerry Burgess felt the need to give some mental as well as technical support to his rider:

> It was difficult for Wayne, as all the attention was focused on him. There was a lot of hype when he was leading the championship for a short time, with some people telling him he could do it, and others saying it was only the first year. As well as all that, there were the publicity responsibilities for Rothmans. I think it was quite a tough year for him. I tried to tell him, 'You're not doing this for anyone else but Wayne Gardner. If you do it for yourself and you do well, everyone else will be happy; they're just along for the ride.'

Gardner had hoped for a low-profile first year as a full factory rider, but things turned out differently.

To make matters worse, Gardner suffered an injury at the second GP of the year in Italy during a freak starting grid accident. Burgess remembers,

> He was hit on the back of the leg and the leg was pushed into the footpeg – it was a push start in those days. The gear lever was bent round and prevented him from shifting gear. He had to make one lap in first gear, which at Monza is ridiculous. He came in and asked what he should do and I replied that it was his choice. We straightened the gear lever and he went back out. He had done some quite serious damage to his knee. In those heated moments, he and I were not aware of this. He was certainly not fit for some time after that. At a fast track like Monza, it wasn't really worth going back out, but that was typical Wayne Gardner determination.

Gardner managed second places in Germany and Austria, third in Yugoslavia, and then another win in Holland. His results were remarkable – not only was he injured, but the 1986 bike handled very badly. He seemed to be fighting the bike all the way around the circuits:

> It would always under-steer on the corners, under-power in and out of the corner. That was Honda's problem for many years. Their theory was to push the bike down into the chassis and forward. It's unbelievable that a company like Honda could have made such a major mistake. The only way to make this bike go round corners was to get it sideways and get on the throttle and wheelspin the tyres. The braking was good, which was one of my strong points and I would make up a lot of time there.

According to Burgess,

> Wayne's aggressive riding caused the dramatic movement of the bike. The tyres were OK as such. The engine did produce a power that was tough on the tyres. It was part of the Honda philosophy that lasted up to 1992 – to produce peak power that made the bike difficult to ride. The rear wheel broke traction as the throttle was opened, and the bike snapped back. The biggest problem, as you can see in video footage showing Wayne's feet off the footpegs, was that when the bike broke traction it would throw all that energy back into the front of the bike and upset it diabolically. I wouldn't say that it was a suspension problem; the chassis geometry wasn't as good as it should have been.

Gardner under intense pressure from Mike Baldwin, Christian Sarron and Rob McElnea at the 1986 French GP.

(Right) *After finally getting an NSR to ride, Raymond Roche found the bike a handful in the wet at the 1986 Belgian GP.*

The End of the Season

The year 1986 was to be Lawson and Yamaha's year and, after the Dutch TT, the gap of just eight points was never closed, despite Gardner's win at a soaking British GP at Silverstone. There had been some experimentation with different cylinders and pipes, but at Silverstone, the ATAC chambers on the exhaust pipes were replaced for the first time by Honda's equivalent of the Yamaha Powervalve. Rather than the guillotine valves that Yamaha used to lower or raise the upper roof of the exhaust port at certain engine speeds, the Honda system worked with a drawbridge that would be lowered or raised for the same effect. It was more compact than the ATAC chambers, with space on the new NSRs at a premium.

With just two GPs of the year remaining and a sixteen-point advantage, Lawson was looking good for reclaiming the 500 title. Gardner had to beat Lawson in Sweden or the title would go to Yamaha. It was an impossible task; the balanced package of the OW81 was clearly superior to the bucking and twisting NSR. Gardner managed to keep close to Lawson for the first half of the race. Mid-race, Lawson pulled out a five-second lead that he extended to fifteen seconds at the flag, and he was again the world champion. Gardner was very disappointed, but he had performed magnificently in his first full season, on a new bike, and in the glare of publicity surrounding the Honda team. He believed in himself, his team believed in him and the Honda company believed in him. The prospects for 1987 looked good.

In a world of Rothmans Honda, the factory Moriwaki NSR in the hands of Yatsushiro was a welcome sight.

6 Blood, Sweat and Tears

Development of the NSR500 Two-stroke V4 (1987–91)

COMPARISONS WITH YAMAHA

The loss of the 500cc title in 1986 was a bitter pill for Honda to swallow. Fate had dealt them a cruel blow by incapacitating their world champion, making it almost impossible to mount an effective defence of the title, but they did not wallow in self pity. Instead, they decided to look at the shortcomings of the bike and their own strategy, and to learn from the correct decisions rivals Yamaha had made in developing the OW81.

Although they had managed to extract an additional 10 bhp from the NSR during the winter of 1985, Honda were convinced that the Yamaha was more powerful. The Yamaha may have been marginally more powerful, but Yamaha's main advantage had come from the better match between the new Michelin radial front tyres and the chassis geometry of the Yamaha. Yamaha had spent several sessions testing with Michelin before the 1986 season, whereas Spencer had been unable to do any tests due to sickness and Gardner had his hands full getting to grips with the new bike. Gardner had also struggled with the top-end power characteristics of the Honda engine and it was decided that the new design would have to have a better mid-range, even at the expense of top-end power. Fatter exhausts were needed, as long as the chassis would provide enough room for them to be tucked out of the way.

DESIGN DECISIONS

Carburettors

The first design decision that was taken was to move the carburettors from behind the rear cylinder bank to a position in the V of the cylinder banks. On the first NSR, it had been decided that the V4 should have a 90-degree angle between the cylinder banks, to ensure a mechanically balanced engine. With so little room between the cylinder banks, the carburettors had to be mounted at the back of the engine. This compromised the flow characteristics of the inlet tracts, especially for the front cylinder pair, with a long passage between the reed-valves and the primary compression space under the piston. Also, the flow of cool fresh air was poor at best, despite the use of ducts and baffles to channel air to the back of the engine. The angle of the V was opened up to 112 degrees and it was possible to mount 36mm twin-choke Keihin carburettors at the front of the engine.

Since the 1985 NSR, the reed cages had been mounted vertically, minimizing the width needed for the reeds and giving a better charge flow to the crankcases, according to Honda. The new cylinder angle on the NSR forced the introduction of a balance shaft behind the crankshaft, to cancel the secondary vibrations produced by the engine configuration.

Under the skirt of the NSR, the new location of the carburettors on the bike could be clearly seen.

Crankshaft and Cylinders

There was another change made within the engine that had nothing to do with the engine itself. During 1986, Wayne Gardner had been fighting the NSR, the bike pushing the front wheel as it came out of corners. It was determined that the gyroscopic effect of the single crankshaft running anti-clockwise was contributing to this effect by unloading the front wheel as the bike accelerated out of the corner. Putting an extra jackshaft in the engine, to act as balance shaft, meant that the engine could run forward and the gyroscopic effect would help keep the front wheel glued to the track on exiting corners. The jackshaft was driven off the right-hand end of the crankshaft. The very first NSR of 1984 had used exactly the same configuration, but this had changed in 1985 and been retained in 1986. The engine kept a 90-degree firing angle, but the sequence of cylinders changed. Now the order was left rear-front right-right rear-front left, a diagonal firing sequence.

Exhaust Pipes

The space freed up by the relocation of the carburettors made it possible for the exhaust pipes to be fitted more easily. The pipes from the rear cylinder bank could sweep straight back under the seat and sub-frame to exit from the tail unit. A single pipe from each of the front cylinders swept back under the engine and alongside the swing-arm, up over the rear wheel. The freedom this gave the pipe designers would have liberated a handful of mid-range horsepower from the engine. It was not a lightweight bike, however, weighing in at 275lb (125kg) and producing just under 160 bhp at 12,000 rpm.

TESTS IN AUSTRALIA

The bikes were ready for the traditional winter tests at Surfers' Paradise and Gardner's times were significantly better. According to Jerry Burgess,

Honda were still secretive in 1987 and only a half-naked bike was displayed for the all-seeing eye of the camera.

The 1987 bike was dramatically changed. They came up with a bike that was faster, handled better and was reliable, although the 1986 bike had also been reliable. They believed that they could argue the case for the investment and the costs of building a completely new bike, because of the effort that Wayne had put in. He was ready to take on the challenge. They knew what the Yamaha had, what we had, and what we didn't have. They put together a good package. It corrected all the major design errors of the earlier bikes.

THE HONDA TEAMS

There were to be three teams running the new NSR, with Rothmans sponsoring Wayne Gardner and Freddie Spencer, and HB, another tobacco company, switching allegiance from Suzuki to back Niall Mackenzie on an NSR.

Spencer's tale of woe continued. He had set fastest time in qualification at Daytona, but a rider crashed in front of him, taking him out and leaving him with a broken collarbone and fractured shoulder blade. Bad luck seemed to be following him around the world. Initially, it was thought that his injuries would heal before the GP season started, but, after a single practice session for the first Japanese GP in twenty years, he withdrew.

THE 1987 SEASON

Japanese GP

Niall Mackenzie impressed everyone by claiming pole position in only his second race on the NSR. A couple of weeks earlier he had won an international race held at Suzuka, easily beating the new Suzuki V4 ridden by Kenny Irons. Race day dawned wet and cold, and rain specialist Randy Mamola got his new relationship with Yamaha off to a good start by winning the race by thirty seconds. Wayne Gardner was second and Niall Mackenzie was holding third on the last lap, when he slid off, thinking he was still under pressure from Ron Haslam. In fact, Haslam had also fallen a couple of corners before, and third place went to Takumi Ito on the Suzuki. Lawson had pulled out of the race after his choice of intermediate tyres was shown to be a mistake in the very wet conditions. It wasn't a win for Honda but they had scared Lawson.

Jerry Burgess recalls,

> Eddie Lawson had pulled out of that race, and during the course of the week, the word was out that Eddie couldn't believe how

Niall Mackenzie moved up to ride factory NSRs in 1987 after several years on 250s. He startled the class by setting pole position at the first GP of the year.

quick the Honda was. He was already down in the mouth, which is just what we wanted to hear. Since we were chasing Eddie, the result was a springboard to us, even though Randy [Mamola] had won the race. Then we won by twenty-three seconds in Spain from Eddie. That was the sort of result that made us think it was really possible. It made Eddie feel much more doom and gloom. It was only at Austria, later in the season, where Randy caught and stayed with Wayne, that Yamaha began to think that their bikes could beat Wayne.

Spanish GP

Mackenzie was also riding well for HB Honda, although he was finding it tricky to adapt his style to the use of the Michelin radial tyres. While at the Spanish GP, he explained,

> In the corner the radial offers good grip and stability, but because of my riding style, I have a problem going in. I like to brake deep and, when I do, the front end starts to judder. I prefer to use the cross-ply, but I know that will not last the distance here and I am going to have to get on with the radial.

Spencer was not at the Spanish GP and the frustration within the company was barely suppressed, with team manager Oguma commenting that the transporter carrying Spencer's NSRs was 'just a spares truck at the moment'.

German GP

At the German GP, Gardner was pulling away from the field at a second per lap, when his machine suddenly faltered and he was reeled in by Lawson. One of the power-valves had stuck closed and the loss of power was dramatic. Gardner finished in tenth place, claiming a single point under the scoring of the day. Spencer had also been briefly present at Hockenheim, but cut his knee badly on a knee-slider and was ruled out of the race.

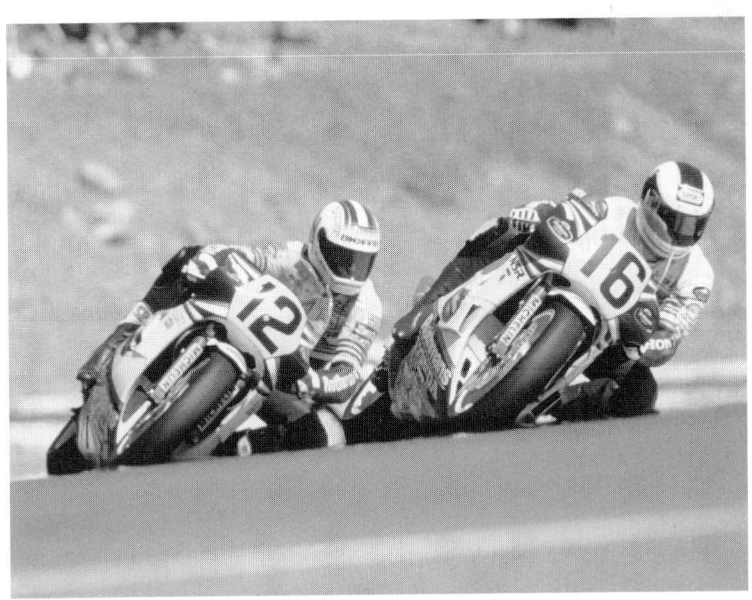

Rothmans was still willing to fund the Honda effort generously, enabling Yatsushiro (16) and Roger Burnett (12) to run a few GPs on 1986 NSRs.

The Season Continues

Now Gardner raised the stakes a notch higher by winning three GPs in a row and opening a seventeen-point lead over Randy Mamola, with Eddie Lawson another seven points behind. Gardner's fellow NSR riders were having a harder time.

Poor races in Germany and Italy led Mackenzie to spend a couple of days testing in Yugoslavia with Erv Kanemoto. They discovered that a narrower rim on the front wheel suited his riding style far better, enabling him to get the power on early as he exited the corner. Previously that had not been possible, as the bike ran wide on the exit. He took another third place in Austria very close to the Gardner/Mamola battle at the front. Then he fell during practice for the Yugoslavian GP and broke his ankle. Spencer returned at Yugoslavia, set fourth practice time, crashed re-breaking the collarbone he had broken at Daytona, and returned to the USA. It was astonishingly bad luck.

The next two wet races in Holland and France were Yamaha benefits, the Dunlop rain tyres clearly superior to the Michelin tyres. Lawson won at Assen and then crashed at Le Mans. The British GP had been moved to Donnington, which was expected to give Niall Mackenzie and Wayne Gardner an advantage as far as track knowledge was concerned. In fact, it was Freddie Spencer, back again, who led the first few laps, before running wide at one corner and missing the chicane a couple of laps later. He pulled in to the pits and retired, claiming that the bike had seized, but the problem remained a mystery. Lawson inherited the lead and was challenged by Gardner, who was unable to pass, having chosen too soft a tyre.

In Sweden, Gardner ran away with the race and eased off to win quite comfortably. Having set third-fastest time in practice, Spencer found the race tiring, but managed to hold on to seventh place. The Czechoslovakian GP was a repeat of the Swedish, with Gardner running away from the start. Spencer lost a contact lens on the warm-up lap and could only manage eleventh place after a run up a slip road.

At this stage, Gardner had an advantage of twenty-six points over Mamola, with just four more GPs to go.

San Marino

The Grand Prix of San Marino, at the Italian circuit of Misano, turned out to be unsuitable for the NSRs and all the riders struggled. Spencer complained that the power band was too wide; he could not control the rear tyre by getting it loose in the power band, and controlling the slide with the over-rev. Mackenzie was slower than he had been the previous year on the last version of the Suzuki RG Gamma. He complained that the Honda had too much power and was less stable under braking.

Gardner got on with the racing, but finished third, a long way behind the Yamahas of Mamola and Lawson. Spencer crashed when Pier Francesco Chili ran into him and the unlucky American was knocked unconscious for a few minutes, but escaped any further injury. Gardner could only manage fourth place at the Portuguese GP, run in Spain at Jarama. His bike seized when it lost all its coolant, and he finished the race limping in on two cylinders.

Burgess remembers the Portuguese GP:

> It was a very very hot day and the Hondas had a tendency to run hotter than the Yamahas. Wayne came in during practice complaining how his forearms were getting hot when he was tucked in under the fairing. The heat had been coming up from the engine and the radiator. We did make some

shields for it, but obviously the heat that built up caused a water loss, probably just pumping it out. We took the engine apart but couldn't really find anything wrong.

The End of the Season

With two GPs to go, in South America, Gardner almost had the title sown up, but his was not the kind of character that would let him ease up on himself. Burgess enjoyed the Brazilian race, because everyone had expected Gardner to ride reasonably conservatively, but

> … he adopted the philosophy of 'Why go through another week of pain if I can get the job done here?' He caught everybody napping when he went out and took off. By the time they realized what was going on, it was too late. By this stage of the year, Randy was still just ahead of Eddie in the championship. The final positions were a little bit orchestrated by Wayne in the last GP in Argentina. He arranged where he finished, knowing that if he let Randy win or finish in front of him, he would keep Eddie back in third place in the championship. He more or less let Randy finish second – just a twist of the knife.

Honda's Second World Championship

Honda had regained the world championship and Wayne Gardner and Jerry Burgess had done it in their second year as a GP team. It was an achievement of which all three parties could be proud. Burgess explains,

> There was no needle between us and Eddie Lawson. There was just an enemy to be beaten. We *had* to beat them. Wayne felt the same way. We were fairly desperate, never having won one of these championship things. We were stepping into the unknown all the time. Everyone held it together. The pressure was really on the mechanics to give Wayne a reliable bike and a bike that could finish. He had already proved that he could win races if the bike held together. Everyone says that towards the end of the year the pressure goes on to the rider, but it also goes on to the guys preparing the bike. We were pretty tense. It was a good race in Brazil when it was all over.

Gardner now says Honda fluked it in 1987, but he was at the peak of his career and the bike was good enough not to prevent him taking the championship.

Gardner's belief, however, is that Honda 'fluked it' in 1987. He says, 'It was never a good bike, believe me. You should look at the film footage of that time and you'll see how much more road I used than the Yamaha guys.'

WINTER DEVELOPMENT

Changing the Engine and the Chassis

With the world championship back with Honda, and a bike that had been superior to the competition in the first half of the season, one might expect only an evolutionary update to be made during the winter development cycle. Gardner had asked for the engine to be given another 1,000 revs, pointedly making no suggestions for improvements to the chassis. He got the 1,000 revs, as well as a slightly more compact engine, and another 5 bhp – and a new chassis that was a disaster, making the bike totally uncompetitive in the early GPs of 1988.

How could this have happened? Quite simply, it was musical chairs time again at HRC, and 50 per cent of the engineers were moved out of racing into other areas of R&D. A new set of engineers took their place, brimming with ideas on how to improve the NSR, but lacking experience with racing bikes.

Lowering the Bike

The weakest aspect of the handling on the 1987 NSR had been the stability of the bike on exiting slow corners. The gyroscopic effect of the engine seemed to make it more difficult to pull up straight for the blast down to the next corner. It was thought that this would be improved by significantly lowering the bike, but the changes resulted in a bike with a swing-arm pivot position that would cause the bike to squat down under acceleration, overwhelming the rear suspension. As had happened twice in the past, an engineer lobbying strongly for a design choice had succeeded in selling the idea, and had been given free rein to implement it. Burgess remembers,

> We tested the bike in 1988 at a race track we normally never used, Corder in Melbourne, for PR reasons. Wayne said to me, 'Jeez, this bike spins the rear tyre easy.' We all thought that meant it had good power, but it was basically the chassis causing the problems. When I questioned HoriikeSan about the 1988 bike later in the year, I said, 'You must have known it wasn't going to work; a lot of that stuff had been tried years before.' He said, 'Yes, I didn't think it would work, but the engineers had convinced the necessary people.' When the designers are given the job of designing, under the Japanese system the guys from years before, who are out of the picture, have to stay out of it. HoriikeSan explained to me that he would have been very surprised if the new idea had contributed very much to what we were trying to achieve. He was right.

According to Gardner, 'The bike got worse in 1988. The combination of lowered swing-arm pivot and lower engine position meant that the bike just sat on the road surface and wheelspun. I was falling off the thing, trying to stay on it; it was terrible.'

THE 1988 SEASON

Looking for a Solution

The way the situation was handled was the Honda way; people close to the company had come to accept this, discouraging as it could be. The really bad news was that it was too late to do much about the bike. There were too many consecutive races to allow the team to work out and execute modifications, and to test the results. It was up to Jerry Burgess to find a solution as soon as possible, with the GP season turning into a nightmare.

After the first four GPs, run in the first five weeks of the season, Gardner had a

The highs of 1987 turned into the lows of 1988 for Gardner, when his prayers for a better bike went unanswered.

twelve-point deficit on Eddie Lawson. At last, there was a chance to try some of the changes that might do something about the squat. In the opinion of Jerry Burgess,

> We had to consider the front. What we did in the end was re-machine the steering heads so that we could create something more like the 1987 bike, and then we were able to push the rear swing-arm down with the shock absorber. We were able to lengthen the mount-point at the top, effectively lifting the bike higher off the ground. Had we done that without machining the steering heads, we would have just made the steering-head angle steeper, which would have made our problem worse. Wayne went on to win three or four in a row.

An Improved Bike

The bike was a big improvement, but the test session at Rijeka in Yugoslavia also resulted in Gardner lining up for the Italian GP with a broken foot, sustained when he high-sided at the start of the tests. Niall Mackenzie continued the tests and was able to lap half a second faster than Gardner's pole position time of 1987: 'Initially, it didn't seem to be very different at all, but after we got the suspension on the new bike sorted out, I went back and tried the old machine. By comparison, it was unrideable.'

Gardner rode to second place in Italy, with his foot broken and in considerable pain. A bad choice of wet tyres for the race in Germany saw him slump to ninth place. He would have won in Austria, but for the fact that the bike seized on one cylinder mid-race, while he was dicing with Lawson for the lead. Burgess recalls,

> They had sent over some bigger bore carbs from Japan and some other stuff and we put them on the bike. Wayne was very pleased and wanted to ride the bike. It had the power and everything, but we didn't have enough time to put the laps on the new parts to check what damage it might have been doing to the engine. Those carbs with the settings we had tended to run a little lean in one area; we detonated a piston, and eventually it broke and seized.

The Honda team started to see more success, with wins in Assen, Spa and Yugoslavia showing how much the bike had been improved.

French GP

After a number of consecutive wins, the Honda team arrived at Paul Ricard for the French GP, later claimed by many to be one of the best races of the decade, with a three-make four-rider tussle for the victory. Gardner broke away, from Sarron and Lawson on the Yamahas and Schwantz on the Suzuki, with two laps to go and started the last lap with a two-second advantage. Then, at the end of the Mistral straight, the Honda seized – 'the most disappointing moment of (Gardner's) life' – and Gardner limped home on three cylinders to take fourth place.

Mechanic Wilf Needham has his hands on the culprit responsible for the poor handling of the 1988 NSR. The swing-arm pivot was incorrectly located, causing the bike to squat under hard acceleration.

(Left) *Yamaha guy meets Honda guy, and Honda win the championship. It took Eddie Lawson a lot of work to get the ride and a lot more to win the title.*

The End of the Season

With a deficit of twenty-seven points, and the season drawing to a close, it looked unlikely that Gardner would be able to retain the title, but he was determined to go down fighting. He came second to Wayne Rainey at the British GP, slicing seven points off Lawson's lead. Lawson won in Sweden and Gardner was second, and in Czechoslovakia the positions were reversed. At the last GP of the season, Gardner had to win, with Lawson retiring. In fact, Lawson claimed the last race in front of Gardner and the title was back with him and Yamaha.

In the middle of the season no one would have predicted that Gardner would still be challenging for the championship at the last race of the year. But for the disastrous initial chassis, Gardner and the NSR would have been able to retain the title. Gardner's bravery in trying to tame the NSR during the early races of the 1988 season earned him everyone's respect. With hindsight, he was probably at the absolute peak of his form that year; fate denied him the chance to prove this with a world title.

CHANGES TO THE BIKE FOR 1989

The Chassis

The pioneering spirit that had seen the pro-squat chassis design of the 1988 NSR was still alive within the design offices of HRC. Another theory was being developed that promised to provide new insights into frame design and offer long-term benefits. It was the right idea, but flawed in its initial implementation on the 1989 NSR500. For the first time since the monocoque chassis of the NR500, the chassis had been intentionally weakened in certain areas, rather than strengthened. Hattori explained,

> During 1988, we learnt about squat ratio and anti-squat ratio, and prospect ratio and the relationship between front grip and rear grip. In 1988, it was trial and error, but we gathered all the information and made a concept for 1989. Until the late-1980s, we thought that the frame rigidity should be increased as the power increases. This was wrong. The correct rigidity is a sum of the forces acting in the three planes of the motorcycle. In the past we concentrated on the overall rigidity, and not on the sub-components.

Kanemoto knew that 'the 1989 bike did not handle well', but felt that 'most of that was due to the engine characteristics'. In his opinion, 'When the engine is peaky, the front is up and down; when it is smooth, you can open the throttle earlier. All the changes to improve handling that year were to the chassis.'

Suspension, Forks and Swing-arm

Although the chassis had been designed in terms of the required stiffness in each of the three planes of the bike, the front and rear suspension was strengthened considerably. During 1988, Yamaha had started to use Ohlin OUT front forks, otherwise known as 'upside-down forks'. With the slider tubes holding the front axle and the outer stanchions passing through the headstock and triple clamps, it was claimed that rigidity was significantly improved. At the rear of the bike, the swing-arm seemed totally different. The right-hand side of the arm was now 'banana-shaped', sweeping up and over the two exhaust pipes that exited to the back of the bike on the right-hand side. The left-hand side of the swing-arm was horizontal, but with massive bracing and triangulation along its length.

The Engine

The engine had undergone relatively subtle changes to widen the power band at the expense of the top end. Movement of the exhaust powervalve was made more sophisticated by coupling throttle position as well as engine speed to the servo motor operating the linkages. Whereas the 1988 NSR could be revved out to 13,500 rpm, the limit was about 12,800 on the 1989 NSR, but decent power started pumping at 8,000 rpm, giving riders a luxuriously wide power band. During the winter, perhaps to satisfy their curiosity, HRC engineers had committed heresy and built a twin-crank engine. Any advantages brought by the different layout were not felt to be significant enough for 'the Honda way' to be changed.

HONDA TEAM FOR 1988

The riders charged with seizing the title back from Yamaha looked, on paper, to be a dream team. The 1987 world champion Wayne Gardner was once again heading up the Honda effort, and could have expected to be treated as their number one rider. This expectation was compromised by the sensational defection of Eddie Lawson from the Yamaha camp to Honda, working with Erv Kanemoto. Honda would be riding with the number one plate, earned by a rival factory. It had taken some quite hard pushing from Lawson for Honda to sign him.

Oguma's recollection of the situation is as follows:

> In principle, I did not want to have Lawson on the team. When he asked I said, 'No, thank you'. He had such a strong association with Yamaha, and was really a Yamaha person. We preferred to have riders who understood the Honda way, who talked our language. He said that we should look at him as just another motorcycle racer, who had ridden Kawasaki and Yamaha, and now wanted to ride Honda to see what type of bike they were. I was worried, as he did not speak the Honda code, but together with Erv Kanemoto it could be OK.

There was also a bit of a shake-up in the composition of the team. Jerry Burgess recalls being asked by Honda 'to take care of this new kid and do with him what I had done with Wayne'. Their opinion was that Gardner could tell his team what he wanted, and that the young riders needed to have that information squeezed out of them. Burgess says,

> I was happy to stay with Wayne, but I also looked forward to working with this guy called Mick Doohan. I saw him ride in Japan at the end of 1988. He came to the HRC factory at the end of 1988, they asked me to take him out to lunch, and we got talking.

Doohan had been riding for Yamaha in Australia, but he was lured away by Honda with the offer of a no-pressure start in GPs as a low-profile back-up to the Lawson and Gardner 'dream team'. He figured he would be able to learn the circuits and develop his GP riding style in the shadow of the two great contemporary riders, one of whom it was felt would win the 1989 title. The reality turned out a little differently. Doohan remembers that, at the time,

> Yamaha were very strong, with so many young guys, probably six or seven riders on factory Yamahas, whereas Honda only had Wayne Gardner and Niall Mackenzie. Basically, it was a three-rider factory team, I was much younger than the other guys, so

The new face at Rothmans Honda – Mick Doohan; he spent the first season worrying he might have made the biggest mistake of his life.

> it seemed the best for my future. I did a two-year deal with them and, after riding the bike for the first time, I wondered if it was a smart move. I rode the 1988 bike and I couldn't get any feel from it whatsoever. I rode the Yamaha briefly just before and I felt quite comfortable on it. Then I went to the Honda; the second day on it, it threw me down the road and it didn't stop throwing me down the road for some time.

PROBLEMS WITH THE BIKES

Pre-season testing had shown that there were some problems with the new bikes; Eddie Lawson crashed during testing, and even the rookie suspected that something was wrong. Burgess remembers Doohan saying to him at an early test session, 'This thing wobbles'. Burgess said, 'Welcome to 500 racing,' to which Doohan's reply was, 'I don't care if it's a 500 or a mini-bike, it shouldn't wobble.' According to Burgess,

> He was quite right. Geometrically, it certainly wasn't as stable as a rider would like. I wasn't working with Eddie, but Eddie was probably saying to Erv that the bike did not have the stability of the Yamaha. The feeling at the time was that the lack of stability came from the lack of stiffness, and we worked round the stiffness area. Through that year, and into the next year, though, we also made some terrific geometrical changes to Mick's bike, and it has been pretty much that way ever since.

Prior to moving to the 500 class in 1990, Sito Pons was allowed to ride one of the 1989 NSR500 bikes in Brazil. It was a sobering experience. His opinion was that it was 'terrible, unrideable'. He remembers, 'Along the straight, I had to fight the bike as it would not steer in a straight line. This was Wayne Gardner's machine, not Eddie Lawson's. I think Lawson's was better. Maybe they gave me the worst machine they had.'

The most important piece of equipment on this shot of the 1989 NSR is the steering damper. Even wound totally closed, the NSR would weave and wobble.

THE 1989 SEASON

First Half of the Season

The start of the season saw Gardner once again fighting the writhing mass of machinery that was the NSR Honda. At the Japanese GP, he ran off the track twice and, surviving a heart-stopping high-side, could only manage fourth place; Lawson took third, a long way behind the superb fight between Kevin Schwantz and Wayne Rainey, and hurting from yet another crash during qualification. Doohan was running well in fourth place when the NSR holed a piston and he was out. At his home GP, Gardner triumphed over his wayward bike and took the win in glorious style, leading home an express train of riders – Rainey, Sarron and Magee.

Burgess admired his performance:

> Wayne was the sort of guy who rose to an occasion like that. He certainly performed well in front of his home crowd. People like Mick and Eddie didn't get that extra boost. They knew that there are twenty-five points available at each race and no more for the home GP, and didn't stick their neck out. Wayne seemed to ride at the home GPs a little above what you would get away with over long periods of time.

The teams scrambled to get to the USA a week later for the US GP and for Wayne Gardner, it marked the end of his season. Honda were experiencing serious brake problems and were no longer exclusively using Nissin products as they had in 1988. Lockhead carbon brakes were also available and being tested. During one practice session, Gardner ran out of brakes and T-boned Mick Doohan; later, he ran off the track twice, all while running Nissin steel discs. He crashed again on the spare bike, with carbon discs, when he locked up the front wheel. During the race, he misjudged a corner while duelling with Kevin Magee for third place, and crashed, breaking his leg badly. He was out for five GPs, returning only for the mid-season Dutch.

Doohan was having a tough time. Not only had he been taken off by a brake-less Wayne Gardner, he had also done some crashing of his own. As Burgess recalls,

> He crashed in practice at the Australian GP and ground two of his fingers on his left hand well down to the bone. The tendon was exposed on his ring finger. The problem was

> to be a thorn in our side for a good couple of months after that. It didn't come good until we got to Misano. He had a rubber glove, with some sort of cream to help the healing process, but it couldn't be hurried. At Jerez, he crashed without further injury. Just slipped off, mainly in frustration at not running at the front. The fingers were still a horrible mess.

European GPs

In Europe for the first GP, and now solely responsible for de-bugging the NSR, Lawson received the first of many updated frames. It had a reinforcing crossbar above the engine between the frame spars, something that had been removed the year before in the search for the right balance of stiffness in the chassis. Many revised frames were tested during 1989. Lawson won in Spain after Schwantz slid off while comfortably in the lead.

There was no race in Italy, after the riders called a strike when occasional rain turned the slippery Misano track into an ice rink. Lawson had hoped to win at the German race, where he expected the superior top speed of the NSR to give him the advantage. Instead, he was dealt a psychological blow by Wayne Rainey, who slipped past him on the entry to the stadium and took the win. Third place went to Mick Doohan, an incredible achievement in his first GP season.

Mid-season, with the GP teams assembled for the French GP, there was an opportunity for Honda to see how the other teams were taming the 170 bhp engines. According to Gardner,

> It was during the 1989 season that Honda realized they had been developing the chassis in the wrong direction. The turning point was Le Mans in France. My motorhome was parked across from the Suzuki pit, and in the very warm weather, they had the flaps of the tent open. I could see them working on Schwantz's bike, side on. I was very interested in the bike as I was amazed that Schwantz had been able to go so fast on it so quickly. I told the team, and someone came back to my motorhome with a long lens and spent the whole afternoon shooting pictures of the bikes. The films were taken back to Japan, blown up full size, and projected on to the wall, and everything was measured off it. This led to the changes that were tried in 1989 and became more permanent in 1990 – the higher engine, and swing-arm pivot.

By now, the bike was beginning to become more rideable and Lawson had worked on modifying his style to get the most out of the flawed design. In Kanemoto's words:

> All riders want to change the bike to make it ride like the bike they rode before. At the beginning of the season, we went through that with Eddie. I told him that the bike had totally different characteristics. We could improve some of the stuff that he wanted but it would cancel out the benefits of the original Honda design. You always have to give something to get something and the worst case is that you trade even, or trade in more than you get. Mid-way through the season, Eddie changed and learned to live with the problems that we still had.

The End of the Season

The championship was a balanced battle between Rainey and Lawson, with Schwantz occasionally spoiling the fun on his Suzuki. Lawson seemed to be gaining a slight edge as the season moved into the closing stages. By round twelve, the British GP, Lawson had cut Rainey's advantage to just six points. On the penultimate lap of the Swedish GP,

The team behind the 1989 world championship, headed up by Erv Kanemoto.

Rainey high-sided out of the race, while shadowing Lawson and setting him up for a last-lap pass. The six-point deficit was suddenly a fourteen-point advantage. By finishing ahead of Rainey at the last two GPs of the year, Lawson managed to salvage the title, something that had seemed impossible at the start of the year.

Gardner had never been able to get tuned in to a bike that required so much change from its rider. He managed a third place at Sweden, but crashed or retired at many of the other races.

Mick Doohan was also out of several of the mid-season GPs after the Suzuka Eight Hours race, where he clipped someone's exhaust, passing on the outside of a corner, and crashed, taking off the top of the little finger. Burgess says,

> We had set a goal of finishing seventh that first year. He missed a couple of GPs after crashing at Suzuka, then returned to the Brazilian GP and rode to a genuine fourth place there. After four weeks' recovery from the Suzuka race, he was physically changed. He'd been doing an enormous amount of running and was fit. In the race he was sliding the bike perfectly through the corners and it was magic stuff. It was

> terrific for him to finish the season on such a high.

All the Honda riders had made a heroic effort during the 1989 season, struggling to run competitively with a bike that was always less than perfect. Having proved himself capable of taking the title on both Yamaha and Honda, Lawson returned to the balanced package that Yamaha's YZR500 had become and left the way open for Gardner and Doohan. Lawson was never a Honda guy. He had won a title riding a Honda, by bringing the NSR as close to the YZR as was possible, and making up the deficit by changing his own style. In heart and body, though, he remained a Yamaha man.

CHANGES TO THE BIKE FOR 1990

The Chassis and the Weight

It was clear what needed to be done for the 1990 NSR. Honda decided not only to have another go at the chassis, but also to engage in a serious weight-saving exercise in an effort to lose around 20lb (10kg) and get down to the FIM minimum of 250lb (115kg).

They used the information gained from the 1989 season, which enabled them to map the rigidity and produce a better bike, in Hattori's opinion, 'one of the best NSRs we ever produced'. The 1990 NSR was very light, weighing just 255lb (116kg). The frame weight was 15–18lb (7–8kg), and was reduced as much as possible, to enable Honda to put other extras on the bike, such as traction control or fuel injection. In Hattori's view, 'The chassis is just a supporter of the engine. Of course, the chassis has a role suspending the bike, like the forks and shock, but basically we don't need it. We could use the space taken by the frame for better things.' Carbon fibre was also considered as a possibility, to reduce the weight of the chassis by 2½lb (2kg), but they were not certain that the rigidity was correct. It would have been difficult, and very expensive, to make changes.

The Engine

The engine became a magnesium and titanium special, although the design did not change all that significantly. Firing angle did change, with the use of a 180-degree crank for the first time, the left-hand cylinders firing together and then the right-hand cylinders. There was also a version of the engine built with diagonal synchronous firing, but this was not used in the GPs.

The carburettors changed a little as well. In 1989, both 35mm and 36mm cylindrical slide Keihin carburettors had been used, but for 1990 the PJ flat-slide carburettor was introduced for the first time, with a throat diameter of 38mm. Ducts were also mounted in the front of the fairing to channel cool air down to the bank of carburettors nestling underneath the radiator. Some more work on the engine porting had the power up to close to 170 bhp at 12,500 rpm, but the lower weight seemed to help the bike enormously in the drive out of the corner. Honda had got this one exactly right. Burgess says,

> It was a terrific bike. That year we had carbon silencers instead of aluminium. Every effort had been made to reduce the weight. The chassis was designed to be strong and not heavy and it worked. Although the designers had not been able to change direction in 1989, they had enough information to get their heads together and come up with something better the next year. They concentrated more on the centre of mass rather than the centre of gravity.

They put the weight in the right place. The weight was all around the engine.

The Riders

Although the bike was in good shape, the riders were less than one hundred per cent. Wayne Gardner was suffering from a loss of self-confidence, worried that he might not be able to re-capture the form he had shown early in the 1989 season. Mick Doohan had crashed at Suzuka during testing in December of 1989 and had not been able to contribute significantly to pre-season tests. There was one other team running NSRs – Serge Rosset's ROC team, providing Italian Pier Francesco Chili with one, after several years riding the NS500 triple.

THE 1990 SEASON

Beginning of the Season

The GP teams came together at Suzuka at the end of March for the first of fifteen GPs and it wasn't a good start for Doohan. As Burgess recalls, 'He had a lot of brake problems. After a few laps, the brake lever came back to the handlebar and he clipped the back of Eddie's bike. It must have been a very light touch as Eddie apologized to Mick for bringing him down. Mick had to say, "No, I ran into the back of you".'

Gardner took second place, but crashed out of the next race in Laguna Seca. Doohan managed to take second place in a field depleted by Lawson's 160mph (250 kph) practice crash, when his brake pads fell out, and Gardner and Schwantz's race crashes. It was a bit of a lucky result. Burgess recounts the story:

Mick took a long time to get past Chili. He knew that he was not going to catch Rainey, but it took him a lot longer than it would do today. Chili was pretty much public enemy number one, as he was the other Honda 'B' rider. Mick had set his sights on Chili for that year, feeling that he could beat him after racing him in 1989. Wayne Gardner had a lot of experience, which Mick respected; it helped him accept that it might not be possible to beat Wayne.

European GPs

For the Spanish GP, Doohan had grabbed the first of what was later to be many pole positions, despite crashing during practice. He remembers, when he crashed, 'the people around were more interested in telling others to come over and look at this guy with his foot stuck in the wheel. I said, "Can someone please come with a spanner to get this wheel off, so I can get my foot out."'

Gardner won the race and Doohan was fourth. The combinations of bike and rider were capable of winning races, but were inconsistent. Then it started to go wrong for Gardner, when he chipped two ribs during a test session in Italy. He could race, but it was painful and, at the first corner, going in too fast, he slammed into Chili and knocked him off into the dirt. Doohan finished third behind Rainey and Schwantz, with Gardner just behind him.

Still hurting from the rib injury, Gardner crashed again during untimed practice at the German GP and broke his foot very badly. He described the break thus: 'It seemed as though the bike was running over a pack of Cornflakes.' He decided to race again only when he was really fit, expecting to miss at least two GPs. Doohan was running well at Hockenheim, but on the second lap he crashed out on water that had spilled from another bike, performing an identical handstand to Chili, who crashed at the same time on the same water. Mid-season was a

By 1990, Gardner was struggling as Doohan slowly became the focus of the Rothmans team, but he could still beat Rainey and Schwantz on a good day, as at the Spanish GP.

series of fourth places, except for the wet race in Belgium, in which he finished in sixth place.

Burgess had tipped Doohan to win his first GP at Spa, but it was a wet race:

> The NSR was a great dry-weather bike and has never been a good wet-weather racer. There were ABC couplers but they didn't fix the problem. They just cut the power that you had rather than move it down the curve. You don't want the power to come on quickly, like it does with a peaky engine. Suzuki had the Honda problem at Spa, but worse.

At least one of the factors limiting Doohan's performance was the infamous 'B' tyres that Michelin were allocating to the second rider in each team. Gardner was getting the 'A' tyres whilst Chili and Doohan had to make do with the lower-spec 'Bs'.

Different Brakes

Braking had also been an issue and a change of supplier seemed to help. Burgess remembers,

> Just after Spa we started using Brembo brakes. At the Dutch TT we had approached Brembo to supply us with the brakes and we had to send them off to Japan for testing. It wasn't really necessary as Yamaha had been running them for years, but that is the way Honda do things.

Rainey Takes the Title

Gardner was back in France and took second place while Doohan struggled with his tyres. At the British GP, he was allocated 'A' tyres, but did not have enough time to set the bike up and learn a circuit that he was riding for the first time, and with which he was not too happy. Gardner was sidelined by a broken piston on the warm-up lap, something that had happened to him a couple of times earlier that season.

In Sweden, it was Gardner third and Doohan fourth. Wayne Rainey claimed the 1990 world title, a staggering 67 points ahead of Kevin Schwantz, with just two more GPs to run. Gardner was second at Czechoslovakia, and Doohan was ninth after crashing and re-mounting.

Chassis Changes

The chassis had changed quite significantly through the season. As Hattori recalls,

> At the start of 1990, the bikes were the same but, by the end of 1990, Gardner and Doohan had completely different types of chassis. We decided that we should build frames with the chassis geometry that was most suitable for the rider. At Le Mans we prepared a frame with the engine a little bit higher. Mick liked the new geometry of the chassis very much and he used it to win in Hungary. Wayne did not like it and went back to the standard frame. We could also change the trail and castor by off-set holes in the headstock plates.

Gardner agrees:

> There was a slight difference between the bike set-up for Mick and me. I liked the bike to have the engine about 5mm lower, which gave me a stronger bike under braking, while his was a little bit stronger in the middle of the corner. I had just a slight bit of under-steer mid-corner, but the brakes were stronger. They had spacers underneath the steering pivot head that they would use to move the engine up and down to get the correct position.

Hungary

Although they had lost the title, the Rothmans Honda team kept on fighting and in Hungary it came together for Doohan. According to Burgess,

> He had been knocking on the door all season, so it was no surprise, but we were jubilant all the same. The GP was chaos, as the circuit was so bumpy no one wanted to ride. Taking nothing away from Mick, no one really had the enthusiasm for a hard race. No one liked the place and the atmosphere was very down. In some places the kerbs were a foot high. You couldn't drag your knee over them. You had to ride in the traditional European style, and keep your knees up and not necessarily take the racing line. Mick sorted this out very early and got off the line. If you looked at the engine data, there were a thousand different ways to improve the bike, but it was just wheelspinning over the bumps. We just had a set-up that worked very well from the beginning and Mick was getting better all the time.

Doohan had been feeling that Gardner was enjoying favouritism during 1990, and had almost decided to leave Honda again. They offered to give him the same support, and the team went on to win the next race and get pole positions: 'We felt we had got on top of something that we had been struggling with.'

Australia

At the last GP, in Australia, Gardner pulled out all the stops and took the win, with Doohan taking a very close second. It was an excellent way to end the season, with Doohan claiming third place in the world championship, just nine points behind Kevin Schwantz. Honda were happy with the way their investment for the future was developing.

CHANGES FOR 1991

The Weight of the Bike

All the engineers' efforts to produce a bike that matched the minimum weight allowed by the FIM for the 500 class were nullified by a change in regulations that raised the minimum up to 285lb (130kg). Malicious

The lightest NSR ever built was the 1990 unobtainable special at 115kg on the nail.

tongues claimed that Yamaha had heavily influenced the decision, as their bikes were traditionally heavier than the NSRs, or the RGV from Suzuki. It was immediately decided by Honda that the weight would be put back into the engine. This meant that the chassis designers had to re-design the whole chassis, taking into account a heavier engine. Hattori recalls,

> We decided to add 15kg to the engine to increase the reliability, by using aluminium rather than magnesium for crankcases, for instance. We calculated the correct position for the new heavier engine, to maintain the same CoG as in 1990. The biggest problem was the tyres. We could not use the tyre experience of 1990 as the bike was so much heavier. Michelin were only involved just before the start of the season. All manufacturers had the same problem, but we had the biggest problem. It would take Michelin two or three months to get a new tyre, so we had to try and modify the chassis to make it work as well as possible.

In Doohan's view,

> The extra weight stopped us from progressing forward at the rate we were before, because it was harder to stop. You can't carry the same corner speed, because the momentum wants to throw the bike sideways if you carry more speed. You introduce more wheelspin as you have to launch that extra 15kg off the corner.

The Chassis

Off-season testing had also laid the foundations for the chassis dimensions that Honda were to adopt throughout the next decade.

In the off-season, Gardner and Doohan went to Japan to do some testing. Doohan's feeling was that the feedback they were getting from him was perhaps a bit better:

> They asked me to stay and they let Wayne go. We stayed there for a few extra days and we tried various different chassis configurations and engine heights and positions and so on. This is October 1990. We got basically to the point that today's chassis is. We started testing again in January. Wayne was initially quite happy with it, but then didn't really feel at home with it, so he modified his chassis and he dropped his engine down about 15mm to give him the turn-in easy aspect of it. I persisted along the way I went. For me, it was spinning too much, especially in the wet.

Tyres or Geometry?

Michelin had announced towards the end of the 1990 season that they were to withdraw from GP racing, just offering a standard 'off the shelf' racing tyre. They reconsidered this decision during the off-season, but six GPs had been run in 1991 before Michelin returned in full strength to the GPs. In the mean time, Honda had been using the last of the development tyres from 1990, which had been designed for a lighter machine. Other than the increase in weight, there were very few changes to the engine. The lack of suitable tyres seriously affected the initial performance of the bikes.

According to Hattori,

> At the start of the year we could not identify the problem as being with the tyres. Coming out of the corner, there would be under-steer. Mick had a tyre problem, and Wayne had a tyre and geometry problem. For the first two GPs, we did not know that the geometry was wrong for Wayne. We tried many different suspension settings and different pistons within the shock and different leverage ratios on the rocker arms. Finally, at Jerez, YoshimuraSan discovered that the geometry was wrong. After three GPs, we created a new frame and the complaints were gone.

Complaints about the frame might have gone, but complaints about the tyres were to last all season, especially from Mick Doohan. Michelin's commitment to the season was compromised by the late decision to support the GP teams, and Doohan had problems with the front tyre for most of the season. Burgess recalls,

> Yamaha and Suzuki were having trouble with their tyres early in the season, but Dunlop got them working. We were not altogether happy with the front tyre. Mick was probably the first guy to ride the bike like a 250 and use the front more, compared to Lawson or Gardner. His style is to carry much more corner speed and that puts a lot of load on the front tyre. Michelin were not able to get the right tyre to Mick that year. It was good for eight laps and then Mick would start pushing the front. We had a lot of problems at Paul Ricard. There is one corner where the front was just falling on to his knee. This corner is really tough on front tyres, even to this day. The problems were a lot greater in 1991 than now, though.

According to Doohan,

> Dunlop had the majority of the riders; they were building quite good tyres. We were spinning quite a lot, but pushing the front everywhere. I think it was more a tyre problem than my riding style. The Dunlop riders were running a completely different tyre and we were wheelspinning everywhere. When Michelin did decide to come back to

racing, the other riders decided to come back to Michelin and started complaining about the front everywhere. The improvements we had made were so substantial to me that I thought they were fantastic. It wasn't only that we had changed the motor around; we had so much more confidence with tyres, we were leaving these guys behind and winning by up to half a minute in some places from Schwantz and Rainey.

RAINEY WINS THE CHAMPIONSHIP

Mick Doohan came as close as it was possible to come to winning without actually taking the world championship title. In the end, Rainey held on to the title by a single point, in a system complicated by the fact that riders were allowed to discard their two worst scores. Rainey discarded a no-show in Malaysia after he had already taken the title, and a ninth place in Italy, where he had stopped to swap a shredded rear tyre. Doohan discarded his DNF in Holland, when he crashed out when the front tyre folded under him, and one of the string of third places he had taken. Rainey's advantage lay in his six victories that season against Doohan's three. Both riders finished in the top three, except in those races mentioned.

END OF AN ERA

The 1991 season was full of frustrations for Wayne Gardner, as he struggled to get to the front of the pack, while his younger teammate went after the world title. After the

Mick Doohan was capable of beating anyone in 1991 and came very close to stealing the championship from Wayne Rainey.

By 1991, Honda and Doohan had found the optimum chassis geometry which they claim to have continued to use through to 1997.

first three non-European GPs, in Japan, Australia and USA, Gardner decided that he wanted to revert to the older-style chassis that had been used in 1990, with the engine lower than Doohan liked it. In Burgess' opinion, this set-up offered 'much more stable braking; but when you lean it over to turn, it doesn't turn it, just goes straight on.'

Lowering the engine didn't seem to help Gardner's fortunes. In Italy he was high-sided and broke a bone in his foot, missing the GP. He continued to experiment with a lower-placed engine and, from round seven in Austria, found a setting that he could use, with the engine 10mm lower in the chassis. A string of third and fourth places was spoiled by chaos at the French GP, when he had to call into the pits to have his drive chain tightened, and then had to call in again for a new rear tyre after the first one chunked. He still managed to take tenth place. The rest of the season was marked by the continuing search for the correct chassis set-up, but finally, at the last GP of the year, it was close enough for him to beat his team-mate Doohan, and take second place behind Kevin Schwantz.

The Gardner era seemed to be drawing to a close at Honda. The company was grateful for all that he had done for them, and were happy for him to stay on for another year, but a process of renewal was in place and Mick Doohan was to lead it. There had been much discussion between the HRC communicators and Jerry Burgess on the direction to be taken with engine development. Burgess reminded them of the early days of Honda's two-stroke effort, reminding them that,

> … in 1983, when Freddie won the world championship against Kenny on the Yamaha, ours was not the fastest bike and not the most powerful bike. We knew we were at least 10 to 15 bhp down on the Yamaha. The thing still won. It won because it accelerated on the short straights and, even if it was down on speed on the long straights, most circuits have more short straights.

Doohan agreed, and they built into the 1992 bike the ability to open the throttle early. Doohan described it not as a setting problem, but as a problem with the character of the motor.

These words were to lead to a new-generation engine that originated within HRC, but was soon to become universal to all of the manufacturers – the Big Bang engine.

7 From Despair to Domination

Development of the NSR500 Two-stroke V4 and V2 (1992–97)

DEVELOPMENT OF THE NSR

New Ideas for the NSR Engine

In the late summer of 1991, there was a meeting of the engineering staff at HRC. It was intended to be a brainstorming session during which ideas could be freely generated and discussed – a collective effort to solve those power delivery problems of the NSR that had lead to years of high-sided, banged and bruised riders. The engineers felt able to concentrate on the engine – the chassis development with Doohan and Gardner during 1991 had led to two different, but satisfactory designs. It was felt that the engine should be developed in such a way that its power delivery characteristics would enable the chassis to perform at its optimum level. According to Hattori,

> The linearity of throttle control and the rear traction were not good. Of course, part of the problem came from the tyre, but we also thought there was an engine problem. We held a big meeting to discuss solutions and we finally had a list of about six ideas that we felt were worth trying.

Revising the Firing

One of the six ideas introduced by the engineers at HRC was to reduce the firing interval of the cylinder pairs. They claimed that this would significantly improve throttle control. The theory behind the design was that the revised firing order would result in the tyre breaking grip and spinning at the moment of ignition, causing it to move outwards, but then recover grip before the next cycle of paired ignition events. In this way, the rear tyre would be less likely to break away into the kind of uncontrolled spin that would stop abruptly and high-side the rider.

The engineers' idea underwent HRC's stringent evaluation procedure; Hattori describes that procedure:

> First step is to choose the idea, then we get the opinion of our Japanese test riders at the proving ground and Suzuka, and finally we give the idea to the GP riders. We built several engines with different intervals between the cylinder ignition and let the Japanese riders test them. We chose the best firing interval for the engine, based on the following characteristics: rider feeling; fastest lap times; consistency of lap times; total lap times.

To this day, the exact value of the firing interval of the engine is considered to be proprietary information and Hattori will go no further than state that it was 'very close to 70 degrees'. Wayne Gardner claimed that it was 62 degrees, but Jerry Burgess considers Hattori's statement to be more accurate. By the time the GP riders got to ride the new

What a difference a firing angle can make. Externally almost identical to the 1991 NSR, functionally in a totally different league – the 1992 NSR500.

bikes, a decision had been taken on the value for the firing interval, and a bike had been produced that was to revolutionize GPs.

REACTIONS TO THE NEW BIKE

Initial reactions were mixed. Burgess recalls,

> There was not a significant improvement in lap times and to the riders the bike felt very slow. It was almost like a street bike for them, because they could open the throttle so much earlier in the corners, which made them feel like they were going slower. We had to do a lot of analytical work on short sections of the track, checking data, to establish how the bike should be used. We had to do an enormous amount of testing, and each time we tested the bike it got better, with different components, so that it was a good bike by the start of the season. Because we were making such a major change, and the riders were initially a little sceptical, we had to do more testing to prove that our theory really was correct.

Gardner's recollection is that it,

> ... felt strange, as if a plug lead was loose. It felt slow, but the laps times were consistent and fast. I kept saying that there was something good in it. I kept saying that this was the way to go, but Mick wanted the older engine with more revs and a sharper engine delivery. We had a lot of discussions and we finally all agreed to develop the 62-degree engine.

In Doohan's view,

> It didn't feel any quicker. It was more consistent and it was better on tyres and we back-to-backed it at a few places. We had been having trouble keeping the tyre temperature down on the 180-degree engine and this seemed to help. People were misled into thinking that it was just a crank, but it wasn't; it was new cylinders, exhaust pipe and ignition. It made everything a lot different.

THE 1992 SEASON

Suzuka

The first GP of the season was held at a soaking wet Suzuka circuit in Japan, and the paddock was electrified by the weird sounds coming from the new NSRs. There was immediate speculation about the firing interval of the engine, many pundits explaining that all cylinders were now firing simultaneously. The training times of Gardner and Doohan did not underline the revolution that had taken place, but when the race started, for twenty-two laps of rain-swept Suzuka, Doohan ran away from the field to win by almost thirty seconds. The reduction in wheelspin was a godsend in the slippery conditions and he exploited it fully.

The End of Gardner's Career

Gardner wasn't so lucky at Suzuka. His recollection of that day is as follows:

> The engine and chassis felt perfect; during the race I fell, got back on the bike and went after the leaders. I was really angry with myself and was cutting back through the field. I was up to about fourth place when I lost the front wheel and slid between the cushions feet first into the Armco. I broke my right leg in the same place I had broken the left leg before. I could see that the leg was badly broken and I laid it down on the ground and decided that was the end of my career.

Gardner won the 1992 British GP; the day before, he had announced his retirement from the sport – a perfect way to quit.

Gardner did recover and race again that year, but he decided that he'd been hurt enough. He announced his intention to retire at the British GP that year and went out and won the race. It was a fitting end to a great racer's career.

Continued Success for Doohan

Doohan's win in Japan was initially put down to the wet conditions, but wins at the dry

Australian and Malaysian rounds had the racing world in turmoil; everyone was trying to figure out the secret of the new engine and its success. The margins of the wins – ten seconds or more – were much bigger than had previously been usual. Doohan seemed to be set to dominate the whole season; the wins continued in Europe, although he was pushed into second place by Schwantz in Italy and Rainey at Barcelona for the European GP. At Hockenheim, he beat the field by a staggering twenty-five seconds.

Maintenance by the Team

Out on the track, everything seemed to be going perfectly, but there were problems with the engines. A more stringent regime of preventive maintenance needed to be introduced, in order to guarantee race reliability. Hattori recalls:

> Until the middle of the season we had crankcase problems, and the magnesium crankcases needed to be checked after every race. The close firing system increased the weight of the engine as the crankshaft needed to be stronger. We made two types of crankcase, a magnesium one, and an aluminium one, just in case it was needed. The aluminium crankcases were very strong, but the magnesium crankcases would not last much more than 600 miles (1,000km), so the total mileage of the crankcase was kept to that. Crankcase rigidity is very important for movement of the crankshaft, and small-end and big-end bearing longevity. We increased the diameter of the clutch and changed the shape of the teeth of the transmission to ensure durability. From the outside it may have looked like a reliable engine, but after every practice session the whole engine needed to be inspected, and some parts possibly replaced. It was a high-maintenance engine.

Serious Injury for Doohan

There is little doubt that Mick Doohan would have won the first of his world titles in 1992, but for his catastrophic crash during practice for the Dutch TT at Assen. He had fallen off the bike, and his leg was trapped under it as he slid over the tarmac and grass. He flipped his body over, trying to get out from under the bike, and, doing this, snapped the fibula low in his right leg. Complications developed as he recovered in a Dutch hospital; a slow reaction to the treatment turned a nasty break into a potential amputation as circulation problems occurred. The GP race doctor, Dr Costa, spirited the patient out of the country for a long period of recuperation.

Despite a valiant attempt to race at the last two GPs of the year, in Brazil and South Africa, Doohan lost his title fight to Wayne Rainey by four points. As Burgess remembers, it wasn't certain he would be allowed to race in Brazil:

> Nothing was clear when he travelled down to Brazil with Dr Costa, as it was Dr Richards who had the final say. Mick had to sit on the bike and then physically lift himself up and down twenty times, which he did with one leg rather than the other. He told me afterwards how difficult that had been, but it was enough to convince Dr Richards that he wouldn't put himself or anyone else at risk. I think it was the right decision, for Mick's peace of mind. If he wants to do something, you'd better let him do it. No one was putting pressure on him to ride, but, as long as there was a faint chance, he wanted to go for it. He was quite upset when he finished in twelfth place. Something that he had worked for was slipping out of his grasp.

The sting in the tail of Doohan's accident had yet to be fully realized. He spent almost

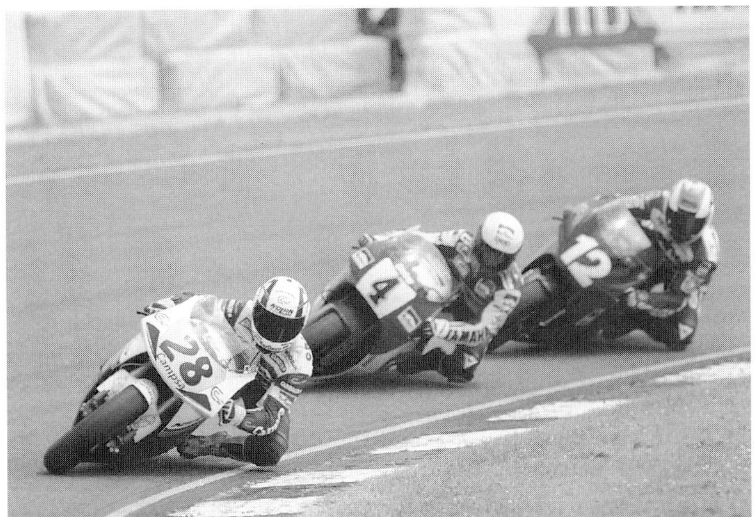

With the big boys out for the count, the new generation were left to go for glory. Alex Criville (28) won the 1992 Dutch TT from Kocinski (4) and Barros (12).

(Below) *The one he didn't win – Mick Doohan was almost invincible in 1992, until that crash. Wayne Rainey got the better of him in Spain.*

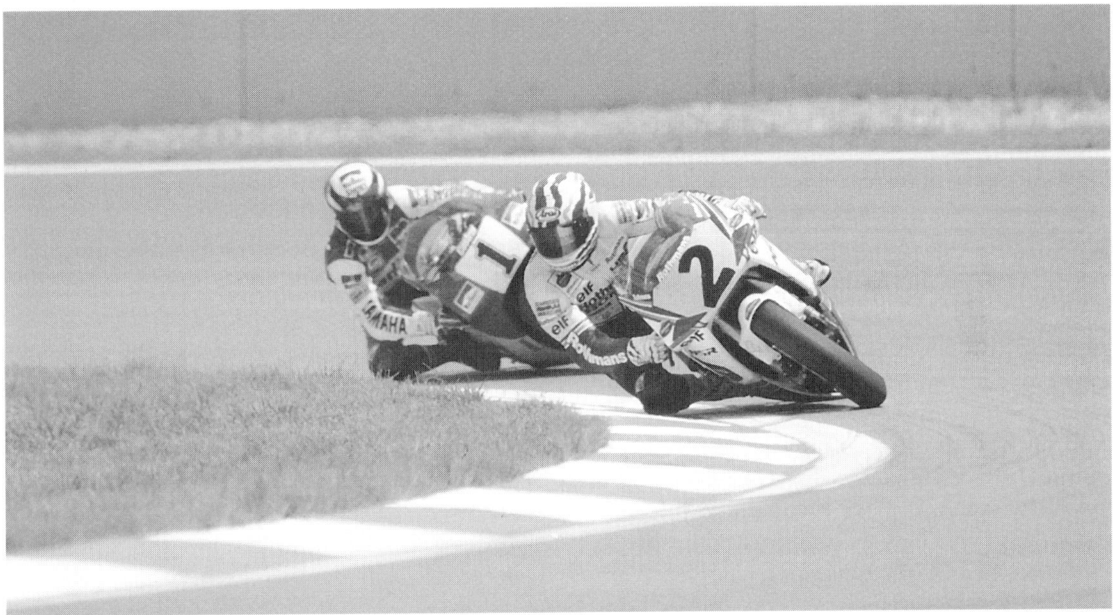

all the winter season recuperating from the accident and trying to get some strength and movement in his leg. This relative inactivity contrasted significantly with the rigorous testing schedule the year before, which had resulted in the team dominating the early GP races.

FUEL INJECTION FOR THE NEW SEASON?

HRC delegated the testing schedule to the other two riders in the Rothmans Honda team, Shinichi Itoh and newcomer Daryl Beattie. There was some significant testing to be done, as HRC had implemented another of the ideas that had been come up at the brainstorming session in autumn 1991. They had decided to run fuel injection on the NSR.

Purpose

According to Hattori, the main purpose for the development of the fuel injection (FI) was 'a cleaner exhaust, better control of the mixture, and better fuel consumption, resulting in a fuel tank that was 5 per cent smaller'. As he explains, 'You cannot control the mix of air and fuel in a carb, but with FI you can and this enables you to map out air and fuel mixtures that can help eliminate detonation at certain engine speeds.'

Implementation

FI systems had previously been raced on the NSR250 in the all-Japanese championship of 1990, and the NSR500 system built on the lessons learnt from that technological adventure. A flat-slide was found to provide better control of the airflow than the butterfly valve used on the 250. A main and an auxiliary injector was used, located adjacent to each other, the auxiliary injector only becoming active as the engine approached the maximum speed of 13,000 rpm. The NSR500 was bristling with sensors where monitoring was needed in order to provide the correct amount of fuel into the inlet tracts. In total, data was fed from eight different sensors into the PGM-FI onboard computer. They monitored: engine speed; throttle position; inlet manifold pressure; combustion pressure; exhaust gas temperature; air pressure; air temperature; engine coolant temperature.

A small mechanical pump was needed to raise the fuel pressure to 10kg/cm^2 at the injectors and this was driven off the end of the crankshaft. If the theory were to work

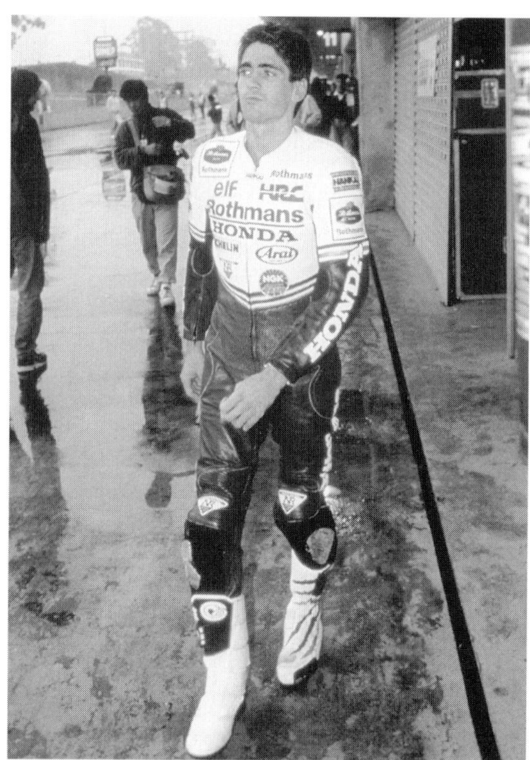

Emaciated, drawn and haggard, Mick Doohan limps through the drenched pits at a miserable 1992 Brazilian GP. A small matter of an S-shaped left leg wasn't going to stop racing for the title that should have been his.

out, the engine would be more fuel-efficient, provide absolutely correct fuel delivery, automatically corrected for any changes in ambient air temperatures, and eliminate detonation.

Testing

HRC considered it was worth testing and developing and, as with previous innovations, it was felt necessary to do this during the GPs. Hattori explains:

> We decided that the best way to learn about FI was to race it. In testing outside of a

> race, the rider is less fired up for trying to get maximum performance from the bike. In the race he will be riding very hard and only then, with faster lap times, will problems turn up.

Problems turned up long before the GPs. A few weeks before the start of the season, Doohan felt fit enough to participate in the Honda tests organized at the Malaysian circuit of Shah Alam. He took a heavy tumble and broke his right wrist when a leak in the plumbing of the PGM-FI system sprayed fuel on to his rear tyre. And there were other things about the bike he didn't like:

> I didn't do any off-season testing and when I returned the bike had changed quite significantly. It had different cylinders. It had gone completely off in the wrong direction. Admittedly, they had young guys on it. Itoh wasn't new to it, but was just part of the Japanese system and telling them whatever they wanted to hear. Daryl [Beattie] didn't have the experience, so he was using whatever they threw at him. I came back and the bike just felt wrong from the beginning.

Burgess explains,

> While Mick was away, Itoh had been developing the bike in Japan, and the engine was becoming very like the older engines, with lots of top end. Mick standing at the side of the track was able to point out that Beattie and Itoh were not able to open the throttle until a metre past the point where he was able to open it on the 1992 machine. He felt that the 1992 bike was better.

GP in Australia

HRC were determined that the fuel injection system would be race-developed, so, when the three Rothmans Honda NSRs lined up for the first GP of the season at Eastern Creek in Australia, they were all running the new fuel delivery system. Daryl Beattie took fourth place, but Doohan pulled out of the race on the seventeenth lap. Doohan explains,

> During the first race in Australia it was running between two and four cylinders. I pulled in as I didn't want it to spit me off. I was already injured and running between two and four wasn't really confidence-inspiring. I came in and said to Mr Oguma, 'Are we here to race or here to test? This obviously isn't working properly. There

Air-box design was beginning to receive more attention at HRC, as demonstrated by the spectacular carbon-fibre air ducts on the 1992 NSR500.

seems to be no significant improvement from the FI. I'm going to look elsewhere unless I can have carburettors.'

Beattie and I showed up at Malaysia with carburettors and Itoh completed the development programme of the Fuel Injection. Really there was no improvement over the carburettors, so that's why we still run them now. Had I been there for the off-season testing, I don't think we would ever have got to the stage where it would have been run as much as it was.

Abandoning the System

Itoh did continue to develop the system for Honda in 1993, and used it to claim the first measured 200mph (320 kph) at Hockenheim in mid-season. After a couple more outings during 1994, however, the system was quietly dropped. Hattori recalls,

Throttle linearity proved to be worse than with a carb, so we moved the programme back to a fundamental research level, to look at fuel atomization, and flows into the crankcase and around the reed-valve. Understanding these factors is essential to obtaining good throttle control.

Creating a 'Hybrid'

Pressurized Air-box

Doohan continued to work to get the bike back to a spec similar to the one he had used to smash the opposition at the start of the 1992 season. There was one significant change that had been made to the NSR that they decided to work to keep. Since the beginning of the 1990s, all the manufacturers of 500cc GP machines had been experimenting with the design of air-flow systems to the carburettors, initially concentrating on getting a supply of consistently cool, turbulence-free air to the mouth of the carburettors. For the 1993 season, Honda were running a pressurized air-box for the first time. Rectangular air scoops could be observed let into the fairing on either side of the bike, just above the front mudguard. At high speeds, the air flow would result in an increase in pressure in the air-box of about 0.2 psi, and this seemed to help the top end a little. There was also a

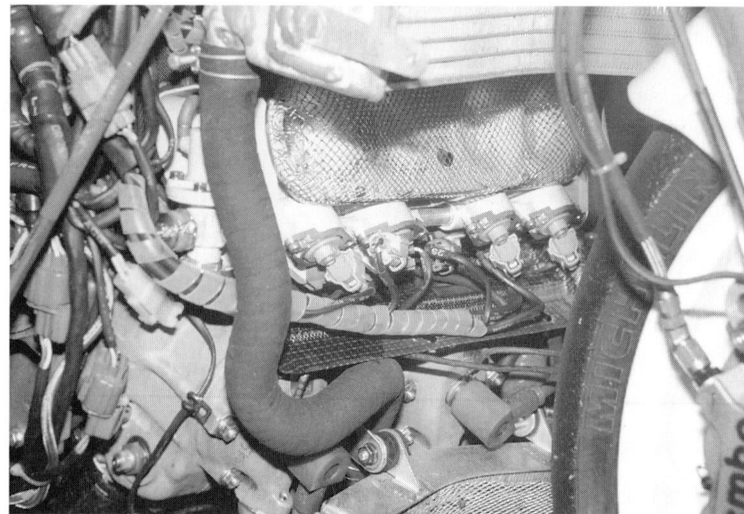

After the fuel injection issue almost broke up the team at the start of the 1993 season, Itoh was left to complete its development programme that season.

small pump fitted to the bike to pressurize the flow of fuel to the carburettor float chambers, but this was removed mid-season.

Efforts were being made to produce a hybrid bike, combining the best of the 1992 and 1993 models. Burgess remembers,

> By Assen that year, we had swung back to a 1992 set-up after some work that I did with the engineers still to run the pressurized air-box. We used the 1992 cylinders, exhausts and ignition, but realized we were giving away top-end speed. We worked out that the advantage we had given away did come from the pressurized air-box. In 1992, the air-box had not been pressurized, just a open ducting system to the carbs, with the pressure bleeding off at the back. At Assen, Mick qualified on pole and finished a close second to Kevin Schwantz, and we realized we had got back on track. After Assen, we had a package that we could use; he was second at Catalunya, and then won in Mugello.

A More Satisfactory Bike

Doohan remembers,

> By mid-season in 1993, we had the bike back very similar to how it was in 1992. Everyone was a lot happier with it, not just me. It was much easier to open the throttle. It didn't have the top speed that it had at the start of the year, but that was not so important. A straight is perhaps ten seconds of a two-minute lap time, so you want to get around the twisty bits; that's always been my point with the Japanese.

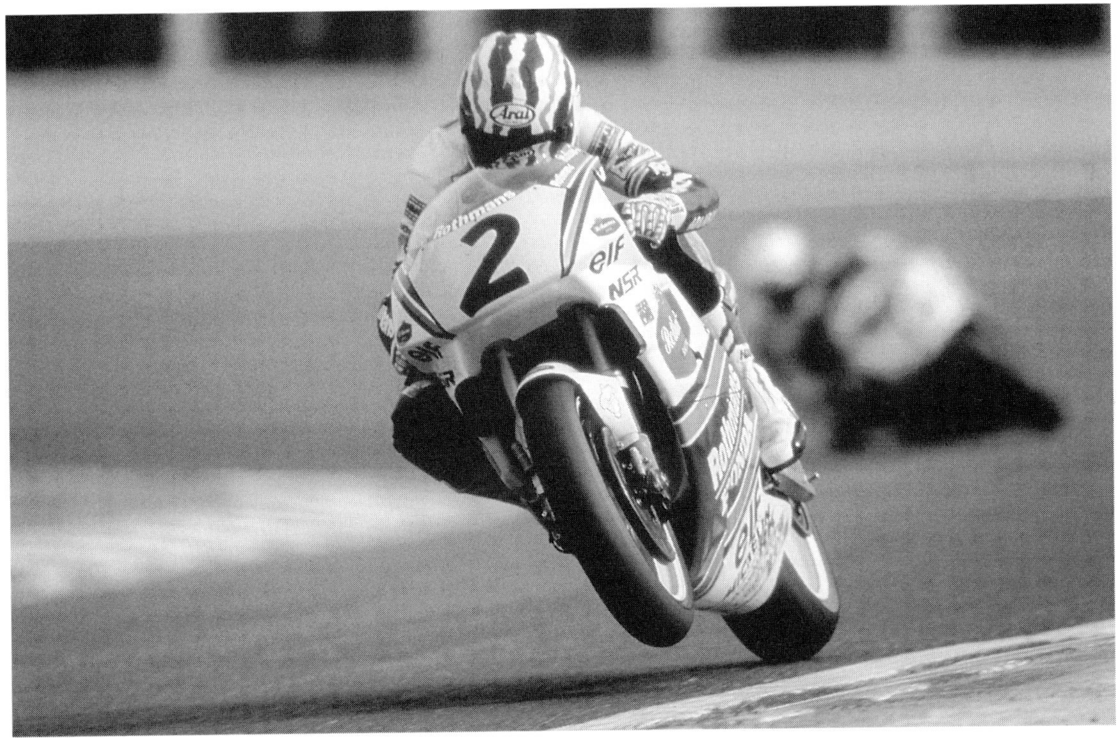

Still barely strong enough to ride the bike, Doohan struggled in 1993 to re-capture his 1992 form.

Doohan's race-long battle with Team Lucky Strike Suzuki at the 1993 Dutch TT saw Doohan's return to form, even though Schwantz won.

(Left) *Beattie (4) and Itoh (6) had occasional good rides during 1993, but were eclipsed by the recovery of Doohan.*

THE END OF THE 1993 SEASON

The Honda bikes had been sorted out too late to stop Kevin Schwantz taking his first and only 500 title. Sadly, this achievement was over-shadowed by Wayne Rainey's tragic crash in Mugello, which left him paralysed from the waist down.

Doohan, who had undergone a year of agonizingly slow recovery from his crash in Assen, was still scarcely strong enough to ride a GP bike on the limit. At the next GP after Rainey's crash, he clipped a kerb and went tumbling and sliding down the track at Laguna Seca. Unable to pull himself up on his injured leg, he flopped around on the circuit as bikes sped past to his left and right before finally dragging himself off the race line. He decided to end his season then and there, in order to undergo intensive treatment to improve the leg, which still had little movement in the ankle and a pronounced outward bow. Before he left for the treatment, he had one last meeting with HRC.

He asked them to keep the bike exactly the same, so that when he came back, he'd be on a familiar motorcycle, and they could work from there: 'I thought the bike was pretty good at the end of 1993, but I wasn't strong enough to ride it. They listened to me and that worked out as a great advantage for us.'

THE 1994 SEASON

From Good to Perfect

HRC honoured their promise to Doohan, and the bike that was tested just prior to the start of the 1994 season was unchanged from the end of 1993. That was not to say that HRC were not developing any new ideas, but these were to appear later in the season. The 1993/1994 NSR still did not entirely meet Doohan's expectations, but the early GP schedule in Asia did not provide enough time to test some front suspension changes that Jerry Burgess felt could improve the bikes. On arrival in Europe for the Spanish GP, a crucial test session turned a good machine into an excellent machine. Burgess recalls,

> We always had some nagging problems with the suspension in 1993. Mick was never really happy with it. Again, it was not until we went back to a set-up close to the 1992 suspension at a private test at Jarama in 1994, prior to Jerez, that we actually got some joy. We tried some stuff that had been rejected in Mick's absence during 1993, and it was a new motorbike. The changes were to internals on the front suspension. We also changed the rear suspension a little, but it was the front that had been the bigger problem. We were able to run softer front tyres after that.

The result of these changes was that Doohan was virtually unbeatable, winning the next six races to run up a total of nine wins from fourteen GPs, and take his first world championship by 143 points. The blend of excellent racing technology and outstanding rider skills had crushed the Suzuki and Yamaha efforts; Yamaha were certainly struggling after losing Rainey's analytical and development skills.

Trying out Other Ideas

With the title well and truly sown up by the last GP of the year, the race team and HRC agreed that it was acceptable to wheel out the prototypes of a couple of the other ideas conceived late in 1991.

At the European GP at Catalunya, Mick Doohan's engine was fitted with a system that injected water into the exhaust pipe at

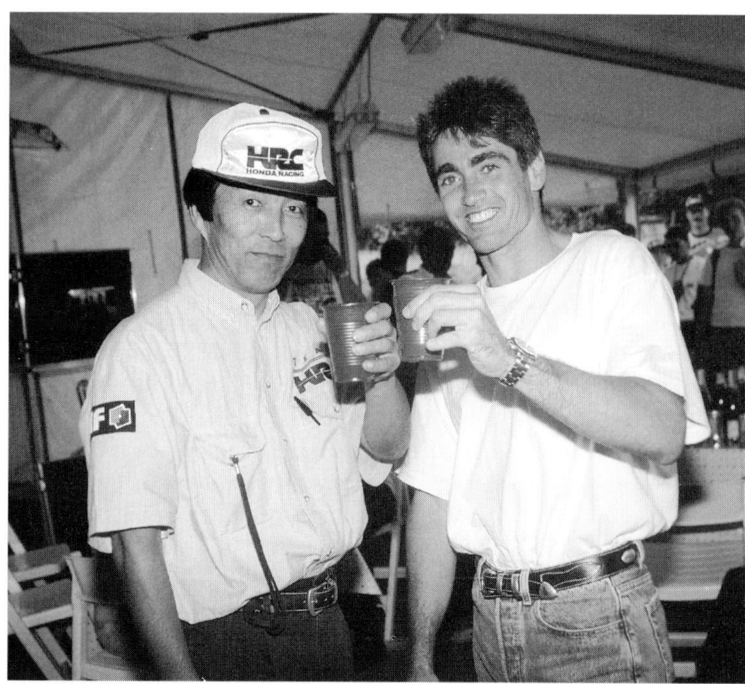

(Left) *Champagne with the boss, Oguma…*

…'Tinnies' with the lads (Doohan's support team); 1994 was the first of many championship titles (below).

low engine speeds. The theory behind the design was that the mist of water would cool the exhaust gasses down, changing the wave dynamics of the pipe in such a way that it would have the effect of a lengthened pipe. In this way, a pipe designed for optimum top-end power could also be tricked into producing better low- and mid-range power. This is the high-tech opposite of the asbestos strips that riders would wrap around the header pipe of the exhausts to raise the temperature of the exhaust gasses, adding a few hundred revs to the top end of the engine. Doohan wasn't too enthusiastic about it, but ran it in the race, finishing second. Burgess remembers,

> It added 15lb (7kg) to the weight of the bike and Mick had trouble steering the bike. The water tank was in the fuel tank and it made everything heavy. It was really just in its prototype stage. Had the championship not been wrapped up, we wouldn't have seen it.

In Hattori's opinion, 'the advantage of the system lay in the mid-range and we were able to achieve the same effect through changes to the cylinder and crankcases'. The idea was shelved.

During practice for the same GP, Alex Criville ran a new semi-active rear suspension unit jointly developed by Honda and Showa. The compression and rebound damping of the unit were controlled by electronics, monitoring a number of aspects of the bike's performance. Tiny motors within the unit would select the optimum choice from twelve needle positions for the compression and rebound damping. Criville's

It was a nice idea, but not what Doohan needed. The water injectors in the special 1994 NSR can be seen here, mounted to the exhaust manifold.

initial reaction was quite positive, but as he came to learn to get the most out of the NSR by adopting Doohan's riding style, the PGM suspension, as it was called, was no longer found to be needed.

Work on the Cylinders

Having had such a successful year in 1994, there was little that HRC needed to do as far as Mick Doohan was concerned. HRC themselves felt the need to work on the NSR cylinders in an effort to regain some or all of the power that had been lost when the technical regulations governing the GPs had stipulated the use of a lower-octane fuel in 1994. HRC had been shocked to see the loss of power on the dynamometer when they first ran with the new fuel at the start of 1994. For Doohan, it was not such a big deal.

Burgess recalls testing at Philip Island, where,

> ... entering the last corner after a number of slowish corners, you tip the bike on to its side to go on to the straight. Mick's reaction was that the bike was actually better through this corner as the rear wheel no longer spun up. It really didn't bother him, and hardly seemed to affect his performance.

Patient work by the HRC engineers at the end of 1994 resulted in new cylinders with some improvement in top-end power and a fatter mid-range.

Other Developments

Air-box development had also been continuous since the introduction of the first

After four years of struggle for rider, team and engineers, the 1994 NSR was again the best 500cc racer in the world.

pressurized version in 1993, but it took until the end of 1994 before the HRC engineers were satisfied with the linearity of the throttle response.

The one new feature of the NSR that was a direct development specifically for Doohan was the introduction of a hydraulic clutch to replace the throttle. From his return to racing in 1993, Doohan had been forced to use a rear brake operated by a lever on the handlebar, due to the weakness in his leg. He continued to use this even after the strength returned to his leg, but it meant that his left hand, scarred from the many crashes in the past, would tire during the race, making clutch operation difficult. The lighter operation of the hydraulic clutch made his life a little easier.

The chassis was not significantly changed, although HRC did fit a slightly less stiff rear swing-arm in the spirit of their insights into the components of torsional rigidity. Doohan felt that it was no real improvement, but it was no worse either, so it stayed on the bike.

New material was used on the Brembo carbon brakes and this had a lower operating temperature, permitting the shrouds that had previously graced the fronts of most GP machines to be removed. The team had actually been using these brakes since the 1994 American GP.

With this evo-version of the mighty NSR, Doohan went out into the 1995 season to defend his title.

The last mistake Doohan made at a GP for more than two years. He crashed out of the 1995 German GP, but managed to avoid a repeat until the last GP of 1997.

THE 1995 SEASON

It was a good year again, with seven wins and three seconds out of the thirteen races that season, but there had been a sticky patch early in the series when it looked like Doohan might have a real battle on his hands with Daryl Beattie and the Suzuki. After wins in Australia and Malaysia, Doohan had a narrow lead over Beattie on the last lap of a wet Japanese GP, when he lost the rear end and sliced through the mud and debris trackside, while Beattie rode past for the win.

At the next GP, in Spain, Doohan was leading comfortably when he high-sided and crashed, fortunately without injury. Two weeks later in Germany, he was not so lucky, breaking the ring finger on his left hand in practice and crashing again during the race. This one Beattie won, taking his championship lead up to twenty-nine points. Then Doohan clicked back into the dominating form of the previous year, with four straight wins, while Beattie broke his collarbone in a fall at the Dutch GP. From that point on, Doohan was only to be beaten twice, by Luca Cadalora on the Yamaha. By the penultimate GP, Doohan was again world champion.

Doohan was not the only NSR rider to win a GP that year. Albert Puig won the Spanish GP after Doohan had crashed, and his fellow Spaniard Alex Criville won the last GP of the year in Barcelona. These riders seemed to realize that the NSR had been developed by Doohan, and Doohan's riding style and the NSR's design characteristics were an almost unbeatable combination. Criville in particular altered his riding style to match closely that of his team-mate at Repsol Honda, and the improvement was dramatic.

CHANGES FOR 1996

There was no pressure from the NSR riders for massive changes to the bike for 1996; once again, only minor evolutionary changes were made. Again, there was some work on the cylinders and, although absolute power was not something with which Doohan concerned himself, for the engineers it was a challenge to be met.

According to Hattori, 'The lower-octane fuel we were obliged to use from 1994 caused us a lot of problems. The best power year was 1993, but in 1996 we were almost at the level of 1993.'

Doohan was more interested in improving the front suspension of the bike and worked closely with Showa to achieve this:

> We tried some different forks at the start of 1996 and they seemed quite good; essentially, they remained the same into 1997. Since 1996, my main aim was to make the NSR go across the bumps a little better and handle better. I believe the other guys' suspension was working better than ours. They were able to hold lines better, they got across the bumps better, while we were having a lot of chatter, rather like the 250s in 1997. That was my priority.
>
> We tried a couple of different chassis setups and these did not have the dominant character change that the suspension did; that's why we left the chassis alone. It seems that the character of the bike can be changed significantly – how it turns, and so on – just by changing the suspension. I think the 1997 chassis is quite good; no one seems to complain about it. If they did, then perhaps there might be a problem.

The only other changes were to the air-box, 320mm discs for the front brakes replacing the 290mm units, and a more aerodynamically efficient fairing. There wasn't much for a hungry young HRC to get stuck into, but fortunately there was another bike that needed designing and development – the NSR500 V-twin.

BUILDING A V-TWIN

Bikes for Non-works Riders

Honda had decided at the end of 1994 that it was their turn to contribute to the sport, by producing a small batch of over-the-counter 500 race bikes that could be used by the non-works riders in the GP class. It had always been a struggle for these riders to find competitive machinery – the highlights for them had been the RG500 Suzuki and the RS500 Honda. Both these bikes found their way on to starting grids long after they had lost any chance of competing with the factory riders.

The crisis that developed at the end of the 1980s and in the early 1990s had been partially defused by the batch of engines that Yamaha produced, modelled on the world championship-winning 1991 YZR500. Housed in Harris and ROC frames, these bikes were effective enough for riders to manage top ten finishes, but only when prepared by mechanics versed in the strengths and weaknesses of the reed-valve V4 engine. Many riders struggled to get the bikes set up correctly.

Honda decided to do it differently. Hattori recalls,

> It was decided to build a V-twin, when it became clear that the all-Japan 500 class would stop if we didn't. We needed to build more bikes for the 500cc class, but of course the NSR would be far too expensive. It was most important to reduce the cost of the bike and the running cost. The two-cylinder bikes seemed to offer the best options. Other alternatives were a V4 and a V3, using an RS125 cylinder as base. Developing an RS125-based V3 would not be so expensive. The alternatives were ranked, based on development costs, initial costs, running costs and performance. The power of the V3 would be close to a V4, but so would its weight. It would be a bike that was trying to be a V4, but wasn't.

But there was one other factor that was perhaps the most important one of all when the decision was taken to build a twin. As Hattori explains, 'We had tried a V3 already, ten years before. It would be no fun for us engineers. For us it was a new challenge to make a V-twin successful.'

Configuration

In preparation for general availability of the machine for the 1997 season, a factory version was produced. Tadayuki Okada, the 1995 vice-champion in the 250 class, was contracted to help develop it in the GP races, along with long-time Honda GP rider Shinichi Itoh.

The machine that they started testing in the winter of 1995 was true to some of Honda's ideals but different in other ways. Inevitably, the engine had a single crankshaft, with the ignition and water pump driven off the left-hand end of the crank. The right-hand end of the crank drove the clutch and balancer shaft located at the front of the engine under the crank as on the NSR250. Instead of the 75-degree included angle of the cylinders on the 250, the 500 was forced to widen the V between the cylinders to 100 degrees to provide enough offset to ensure that the cylinders did not foul each other.

The reed-valve cages were located at the back of the engine, within an air-box that was sealed by the bottom of the fuel tank once in place on the bike. The 40mm Powerjet Keihin carburettors fed the almost square 68 × 68.8mm cylinders; another Honda tradition – keeping the bore and stroke almost identical, rather than having a shorter stroke, as used by Yamaha in the past – was being followed.

Honda had also decided to build a maximum-capacity engine rather than the 400cc that had been initially adopted by Aprilia, who had two years of development of their twin before the Honda first appeared on the track. Aprilia's main problem had been a difficulty in keeping the front wheel on the ground when exiting corners, a problem compounded by the weight advantage of 65lb (30kg) permitted by the FIM. The NSR500V prototype was light but, at 225lb (103kg), still exceeded the minimum permitted by the regulations, despite the use of magnesium crankcases.

The chassis design followed the respected principles of the four-stroke and two-stroke racers in using the single-sided Pro-Arm swing-arm. The frame was a triple-section aluminium beam, with bracing at the upper and lower rear engine mounting points. Showa 43mm upside-down forks were used for the front suspension and a ProLink Showa design at the rear. Double 290mm Brembo carbon discs provided the main stopping power up front, with a single steel disc at the back.

THE 1996 SEASON

The Twin's Debut

The first race of the 1996 season turned out to be as dramatic as it could have been, with Okada on the new twin setting the best time in practice, a second faster than Doohan's pole time the previous year. Even though the venue was the Malaysian Shah Alam track, which was expected to favour the twins, no one had expected this sort of performance. In the race, Okada made up for a poor start and pulled through to head the race before running off the track as rain started to fall. On the re-start, he was again leading when he crashed on a tyre that was too cold to take the pace he was trying to set. In the end, the race went to Luca Cadalora, new convert to the Honda NSR, with Erv Kanemoto looking after it for him. A blistered rear tyre kept Doohan back in fifth place.

The twin had made a spectacular debut. Doohan was keeping his options open,

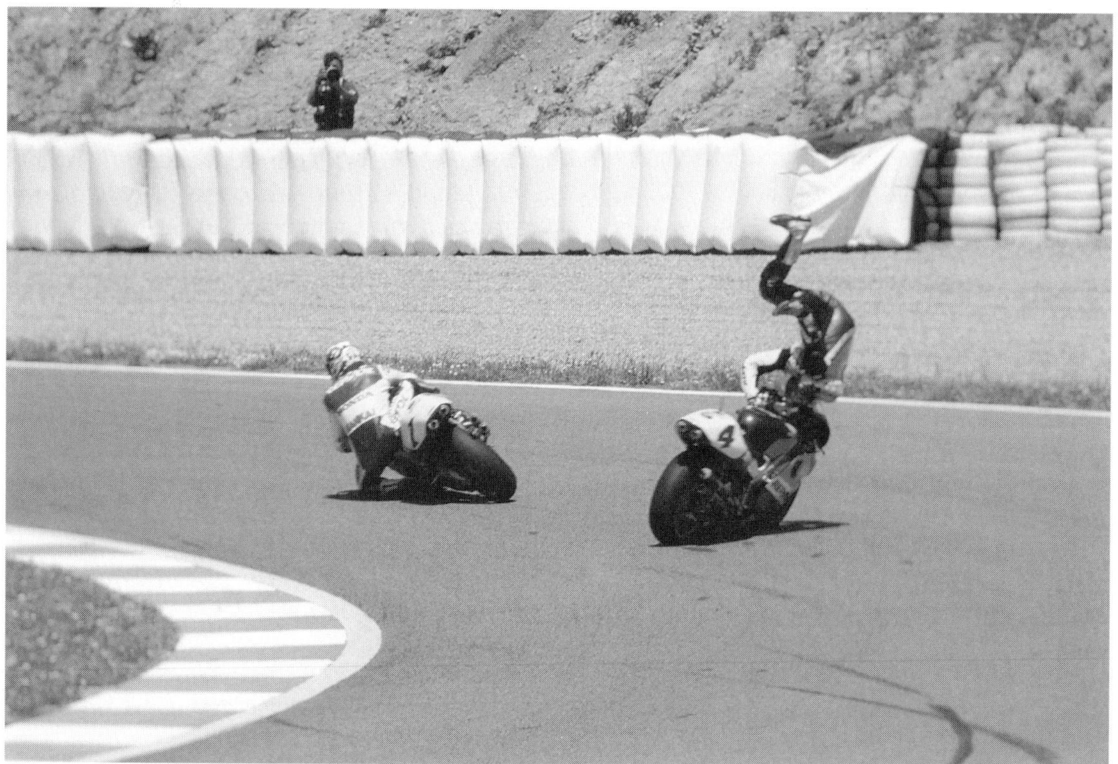

A high-sider happening to Alex Criville at the last corner of his home GP in 1996.

The closest 500cc finish ever? Criville wins the 1996 Czech GP by half a tyre width.

having ridden the bike for about ten laps in a private test session at the circuit before the season started. As he says,

> I didn't know if they were going to concentrate on the twin's development at the cost of the four. I was just keeping that door open, and they had said that, if I really wanted to, I could run it. In the end, the guy I was racing against was on a four-cylinder; even if the twin could beat me at some twisty race tracks, I was concerned about the guy I had to race with for the championship. So it made more sense to stay on the bike I knew.

Doohan Takes the Championship

Initially, it had been thought that Doohan's main competition would come from Daryl Beattie, but the Suzuki challenge had faded during the off-season development. Instead, it was team-mate Alex Criville who was to push Doohan at many GPs, and ended up beating the world's best motorcycle racer on two occasions. But Doohan did dominate the class, with eight season wins, on the way to his world championship hat-trick. The NSR itself was only beaten twice throughout the year, by an inspired Norifume Abe in Japan, and a fortunate Loris Capirossi in Australia, both on Yamaha YZRs. The bike was almost too good.

PRODUCTION OF THE NSR500 V-TWIN

The NSR500 V-twin had proved itself to be competitive enough for the production line to get cranked up and the production model was launched at the mid-season Dutch GP. With a spec very close to the bike ridden by Okada and Itoh, anyone with $100,000 could order a bike with an extensive set of spares. Honda were expecting to receive about twenty orders.

Okada went on to finish the season in seventh place in the championship, including a

A new force in 500cc racing was the V-twin campaigned by Tadayuki Okada in 1996. Those titanium exhausts didn't make it to the production version.

second place at the final GP of the season in Australia. Although the production machine was a little heavier, due to its aluminium crankcases, there was no doubting its competitiveness. As Hattori explains,

> In 1996, experience was our greatest problem. We had no data except for Suzuka and Shah Alam. For 1997, we have more data and the performance will be truly measured. For instance, the gear ratios are completely different from a V4 or an NSR250. If Okada had a lucky choice, then he went fast. During the season we had some durability and chatter problems with the tyres, but it was better at the end of the year.

Honda's expectations for twenty sales were torpedoed by the decision to limit grid sizes in the 500 class to just twenty-four in 1997. In the end, just eleven NSR500 Vs were built for the 1997 season.

CHANGES TO THE NSR

Returning to the 180-Degree Engine

There seemed to be little incentive to make significant changes to the NSR after such a dominating season; suggestions for change came, however, from a surprising quarter – Doohan. As he explains,

For 1997, I asked to try a new motor like the older 180-degree engines, because it was getting harder to open the throttle with the 'big bang' style of engine. I believed if we could take that bottom power away and get more back to a conventional two-stroke, it might be a bit more easy to ride. Straight away I felt that it was better, but the adverse side was that it was really hard to backshift and it launched in gear when you revved it because it was producing more torque. It's hard to unload that torque when you backshift.

The bike to me feels better. The other guys are not used to this style engine. They have grown up with the 'big bang' – a bike that is torquey all the way through. This is better for me, and I think the others have been scared off by the rumours of how the old ones used to be.

The bike that was produced combined the 180-degree firing angle of the 1991 NSR, with the advances made in ignition, pipe, cylinder and air-box design. While HRC engineers were happy to do some experimentation with Doohan, they were cautious, and not totally convinced it would work.

Results in Testing

Burgess remembers Doohan testing the bike at Eastern Creek after the GP in 1996:

No one had ever done a 29 at Eastern Creek and during that day Mick reeled off eight

Alex Barros showed how effective the NSR500 V-twin could be by taking third place at the 1997 British GP.

The 1997 NSR500 was an absolutely dominant machine, with Doohan taking twelve victories from fifteen starts on the model with the 180-degree firing order.

consecutive 29s, the last being a 29.1. This was absolutely phenomenal. The tyre condition, which was their main worry, was absolutely fine. We did some wet-weather testing during practice for a race at Sugo and there were no problems in the wet. We continued the off-season testing and had both a 180 and older firing order bike, but Mick still had a preference for the 180. We had a little bit of trouble with the shifting, which we cured by changing the lift of the clutch.

The final crunch came when we were preparing to go to Malaysia for the first GP and I asked him if he wanted one of each and he said, "No, make them both the same." All our data had been showing us that we were spinning less than Alex was spinning, that the torque of the standard engine used by Alex was greater, but that when it did break traction, it spun very quickly. Our engine had less torque and a little bit more feel. In Malaysia we didn't have a tyre problem and everyone else did. That convinced me; if we were ever going to have a tyre problem, it would have been there.

Although the bike had been developed at Doohan's request, it was also available to the other Repsol team members. Despite testing the bike twice, however, Criville rejected it in favour of the 'big bang' engine. Whether it suited other riders or not, Doohan became almost unbeatable on it in 1997, winning twelve races to take world championship number four, becoming, after Giacomo Agostini, the most successful 500cc racer of all time.

For the NSR, 1997 was a year of record-setting, as Honda passed Yamaha in the count of the most 500cc wins by a manufacturer. The NSR had contributed 109 of the 134 wins and had for the first time won all the season GPs, a feat only achieved by MV Agusta back in 1969 and 1970. This was achieved in a GP world, where huge investments of R&D money are made by three competing factories whose only aim is to knock Honda off the pinnacle of excellence they currently own. It is a remarkable tribute to the engineers, race teams and riders who brought the NSR into the late 1990s.

8 The Rest of the Family

Development of the NSR250, RS250 and RS125 (1984–97)

EXTENDING HONDA'S SCOPE

From the 1970s to 1983

Honda's return to GP racing in 1979 was seen as a means to an end and not an end in itself. The need to compete at the highest level of the sport stimulated the young engineers to conceive and implement innovative new designs, which breathed new life into a motorcycle R&D division that had grown a little stale during the 1970s. The challenge of building a competitive 500cc four-stroke was enough to occupy the R&D team fully, and no consideration was given to extend Honda's presence into other classes. As the NR project faltered, and the NS two-stroke project took over, all energy was spent on ensuring that the bike would be a racing success; again, there was no interest in expanding the scope of Honda's GP racing effort. By 1983, however, mission had been accomplished, and there was a base to be built on – a two-stroke base.

A Two-stroke Bike for the Street?

The success of the NS500 made it possible for Honda to contemplate building two-stroke motorcycles for the street. This would have been unthinkable in the 1970s, when the only two-strokes run by Honda were motocross bikes. The development of the NS had altered this blinkered view of the world and helped Honda understand that, although they had a preference for four-strokes, there were applications for which a two-stroke was simply the best choice. One example was the lightweight sports 250 road bikes that had been the domain of Suzuki, Kawasaki and Yamaha throughout the 1970s and into the 80s. Honda's CB250 twin simply could not compete with these bikes on performance, and Honda lost out on a potential sales in this sector of the market.

Early in 1983, the first changes in approach became visible, with the announcement of the MVX250, a two-stroke modelled closely on the NS500 that had been campaigned that single year in 1982. So anxious were Honda to get a presence in this market that they didn't even wait for the NS to prove itself completely. The MVX quickly evolved into the replica NS400 that was marketed beyond Japan to those wanting to share in the race-track legend that Spencer and Honda were building.

In the mean time, a street twin was developed during 1983, identified as the NS250 when it was announced to the press early in 1984. It was also decided to offer a production racer to the GP community, to compete directly with the Yamaha TZ racers that had ruled the roost for ten years, as well as the Rotax-engined hybrids that had sprung up since the start of the 1980s. The production racer would be called the RS250R, and it would be based on the NS250, to minimize costs and simplify production.

THE FIRST HONDA RS

Much had been made in the past of the link between Yamaha production racers and the RD series of street bikes. The commonality between the two had been extensive through to 1973, when the race bikes had been the air-cooled TD models. With the arrival of the water-cooled TZs in 1973, the models grew apart, and by 1984 they were completely different. Honda miscalculated the level of development that was needed to race a 250 bike at sub-top GP level, and the RS proved to be a costly failure for the few riders who purchased one at a price 60 per cent higher than a TZ.

It was a 90-degree V-twin measuring 56 × 50.6mm with the left-hand cylinder vertical and the right-hand cylinder horizontal. Reed-valve controlled induction fed into the base of the cylinder, and was thus controlled by the inlet skirt of the piston. The crankcases were identical to the street bike and consequently over-engineered. The 34mm Keihin carburettors seemed restrictive when compared to the 38mm units fitted to contemporary TZs. The ATAC chambers found on the RS500 were also present on the 250, with a mechanical linkage to open and close the chambers. A square-section aluminium frame was used to compensate for the heavy engine and the complete bike tipped the scales at around 220lb (100kg), a competitive weight. The bike was claimed to produce 66 bhp at 11,500 rpm, again around the same as the TZ250L of 1984.

On the track, the RS proved to be disastrous – slow and unreliable. In the GPs, it

The first Honda 250 two-stroke GP racer was the 1984 RS250R. Any half-decent TZ Yamaha could beat it.

was run by Roland Freymond and Jean-Louis Guignabodet, but seldom finished a race and never took a single GP point. By mid-season, HRC were rushing special parts over to Freymond in an attempt to improve the bike, but they didn't help.

THE 1985 RS250

Prototype and Plans

At the 1984 British GP at Silverstone, a prototype for the 1985 RS model was handed to Toni Mang for evaluation; after twenty laps he came back to the pits, commenting that it seemed down on top speed. Freymond found it significantly better than his 1984 model, with the engine speed increasing from 11,200 rpm to 12,500 rpm. The bike failed after eleven laps of the race.

The best races that the RS was to have all season were in the hands of Irish road-race star Joey Dunlop. At the Isle of Man races he was challenging for second place when the bike ran out of fuel, and he won the 250 race at the non-championship Ulster Grand Prix. At the last GP of the year at Mugello, the plans for the 1985 model were revealed; these included a full twin-beam spar frame and engine with at least 70 bhp available.

Three Different Types of 250 Racer

During 1985, three types of 250 GP racer were being supported by Honda. The over-the-counter RS250 was purchased by a significant number of riders who used the bike for both national, international and GP racing. The bike had a pure race version of the 1984 250 engine, with smaller crankcases, the vertical cylinder turned 180 degrees, ATAC exhausts as standard and revised cylinder porting, wrapped in the twin-spar beam frame that had been announced at the end of the previous year.

The second type of racer was the special versions of this bike that were made available to riders Toni Mang and Fausto Ricci. They were classified as semi-works riders, and provided with RS250s that were significantly faster than the standard bike, but they ran separate teams, with their own sponsorship arrangements.

Finally, there was a completely different bike for Freddie Spencer, the man who had been chosen to do the impossible – to win the 250 and 500 crown in a single year. His 250 was called an RS250R-W, and it was half of the NSR500 that he was using to go after the 500 title. Its major difference from the other RS models was the 54 × 54mm bore and stroke, and the fact that it used vertically-mounted reed-valves that flowed straight into the crankcase, with the 38mm carburettors positioned behind the engine above the gearbox. The gearbox was accessible via a cover that could be removed once the clutch had been dismounted. (The standard RS250 required the crankcases to be split for changes of gearbox ratios.) The frame was very similar to the standard bike in geometry, although made from a different aluminium alloy. The total weight of the machine was 198lb (90kg), the exact lower limit allowed by the FIM regulations.

Two Classes for Spencer

Confirmation that Spencer would compete in two classes in 1985 only came after he had won the 250 class at Daytona, using the RS250R-W. He had been considering the idea since 1983, but no one really expected him to go for it, with the pressure that was on him to regain the 500 title that he had lost in 1984. Having seen how capable the 250R-W was, he took the plunge and set himself up to run twenty-four GPs through 1985.

A chip off the old block. The 1985 RS250R-W was the first NSR250, despite the name, and Spencer was invincible on it during his famous double-title year.

(Below) *The RS250R-W was half of the NSR500, complete with magnesium crankcases and titanium exhausts. The ATAC chambers on the pipes are clearly visible.*

The general feeling at the time was that he would not be able to sustain such an intensive race programme and, just like Kenny Roberts in 1978, would be forced to drop the 250 as the fight for the 500 crown developed. Nothing could be further from the truth, as Spencer ran away with the title, the combination of machine and rider excellence proving almost invincible. The only hiccup came at the Spanish GP, when the bike slowed with a split exhaust pipe and Spencer limped home in ninth place, and a second place to Martin Wimmer at a wet German GP at Hockenheim. Spencer won seven of the first nine GPs, and the fourth place at Silverstone was all he needed to secure the title, with two more GPs left on the calendar.

Toni Mang proved to be the best of the semi-works Honda riders, finishing behind Spencer, but mixing it with the works Yamahas of Martin Wimmer and Carlos Lavado, and taking the runner-up spot in the title fight.

Wins for the RS250

The RS250 proved itself in 1985, with consistent finishes in GPs, to claim a score of points in the hands of riders such as Alan Carter, Dominique Sarron and Jacques Cornu. Massimo Matteoni won the European Championship using an RS and Joey Dunlop took the bike to victory in the Isle of Man and the Ulster Grand Prix.

THE 1986 SEASON

The Bike

With the 1985 TZ Yamaha production racers proving less than successful, mainly due to their use of reed-valve cages on the crankcase induction system that were too small, there was much interest in the 1986 Honda RS250 from national and international riders. The bike that was made available to them differed very little from the 1985 model. There was no change to the port timing, but the flat-slide carburettors grew to 38mm, and there were new exhaust pipes. The front-wheel diameter came down from 18in to 17in and twin discs were used up front to improve the braking. It was clearly a year of standing (almost) still for the RS, and this was reflected in the lack of results it achieved. There were isolated victories throughout Europe, but again it seemed to be the Rotax-powered bikes and the occasional Yamaha that seemed to have the upper hand.

Riders

As in 1985, a team of semi-works GP riders was provided with a bike very similar to that used by Freddie Spencer, but not identical. The bike was called the NSR250 and weighed about 10lb (5kg) more than the 1985 RS250R-W. The extra weight came from the aluminium crankcases and carburettors that replaced the magnesium ones that had been used by Spencer. Also, the upper mounting position of the rear shock was strengthened, through the use of two vestigial beams converging at the top of the shock to form a robust triangle of support. A flock of these bikes was entered in the GPs for 1986, with none of their riders getting a full works backing for the machines that they had received. The bikes remained the property of HRC, and had to be returned at the end of the season, but no leasing fee was required from the recipients.

Most successful of these riders were Sito Pons, Toni Mang, Dominique Sarron and Jean François Baldé. None of them, however, could compete consistently with Carlos Lavado on the new YZR250 V-twin, Yamaha's response to the Spencer special of 1985. Toni Mang started the season well,

NSRs seemed suddenly to flood the paddock in 1986. Jean François Baldé was the lucky recipient of one of them and took it to fifth place in the championship.

but broke his foot at the fourth GP in Austria and couldn't get back in the groove for the rest of the season. As Mang's challenge dissolved, Sito Pons's season picked up from a poor trio of GPs after his home race in Spain. He turned out to be the most consistent rider, winning two GPs and finishing second three times. At the end of the year, it was Lavado who had the title, by a margin of six points from Pons. As Pons recalls,

> I was happy with the 1986 bike, but it was the first year back in the 250. I remember the race in Sweden. I am fighting with Carlos Lavado for the world championship; he's first and I'm second. It's raining just before the race and we are eyeing each other to decide which tyre to put on the bike. Lavado put on rains and I put on slicks. Some sections of the track are wet and he goes in front, then the tracks dries and I go in front, but with five laps to go it starts to rain again, and Lavado wins.

THE 1987 SEASON

A New RS250

Having held off from producing the Spencer replica for the general racing community, Honda relented and produced a completely new RS250 in 1987. The bore and stroke went to the square 54 × 54.5mm that was

1986 was a tough time for Toni Mang (2) but at Assen he beat up-and-coming rider Sito Pons (19) in the battle for second place behind Yamaha rider Carlos Lavado.

Only Moriwaki would ever get permission to build as strange an NSR as this one. Hiwatashi rode it into thirteenth place at the 1986 British GP.

associated with the machines that ran crankcase reeds. The cassette-type transmission was fitted, with an access cover behind the clutch drum. The flat-slide carburettors were replaced by round-slide units of the same 38mm bore. The twin exhaust pipes both exited on the right-hand side of the bike and swept up and back, parallel with the rear seat fairing.

White hollow-spoked magnesium wheels finally replaced the Comstar units, and they were held in place up front by 39mm diameter forks that were poorly damped, had no adjustment and were structurally too weak. Honda stated that this was necessary to keep the cost of the bike low. The front wheel was 17in and the rear 18in in diameter. The standard spares kit that was delivered with the bike had nothing more than a couple of pistons, some spare rings and spark plugs. This was in contrast to the Yamaha spares kit, renowned for its generous proportions, and enough to keep the bike running for a significant part of the season.

Problems with the New RS

Out of the crate, there were many problems with the 1987 RS250R. The suspension was very poor, leading many people to replace the rear shock and some people going as far as swapping out the front forks for sturdier 41mm units. For a 90-degree V-twin, the engine vibrated very badly. Ignition failure was often attributed to the awful vibration that was produced over 12,000 rpm. It took mechanics a little time to realize that they needed different jet sizes on each cylinder to compensate the differing length of inlet tract for the vertical and horizontal cylinders. In the US, riders such as Kork Ballington, Randy Renfrow and Rich Oliver were running the RS, but the championship title went to 19-year-old John Kocinski on a Team Roberts TZ250T. In Europe, the Rotax bikes were still hot favourites to win at top non-GP races, but consistency helped Gary Cowan to win the British 250 title, despite only winning a single race.

Changes to the NSR

The NSRs were having an easier time in the GPs as Yamaha's YZR and TZ challenge faltered badly after the successful year of 1986. The most significant change to the engine was the loss of the ATAC chambers from the exhaust pipes and the arrival of a powervalve-like mechanism to raise or lower the height of the exhaust port. As on the 500, this was operated by a drawbridge mechanism in the cylinder exhaust tract. There were also some frame changes, with the profile of the beams becoming more oval-shaped, as the upper outer edge of the spars were chamfered.

Success for the NSR

Despite a lease price of $300,000, strict rations needed to be imposed for allocation of the bikes. The teams got their money's worth; it was a GP-winning bike, taking twelve of the fifteen GPs that year. However, this was more due to the power and characteristics of the engine than the sublime handling. Toni Mang took the title, in a year of exciting racing between the Hondas, as well as occasional battles with the Yamahas of Wimmer, Cadalora and Lavado, and the new Aprilia of Loris Reggiani.

The NSR had a tendency for the front wheel to fold in on corners, and it had taken extensive frame and geometry changes by Sepp Schlogel, Mang's chief mechanic, to solve the problem. The season was a personal triumph for Toni Mang, the wily old fox taking his fifth world title at 36 years of age, with the other young lions on NSRs snapping at his heels.

Powervalve-equipped, sand-cast cylinders grace the 1987 NSR250.

1987 RS250 owners had a machine low on gadgets and low on performance.

Toni Mang used this NSR to take the 1987 world championship.

THE 1988 SEASON

Changes to the RS

For 1988, Honda carried out some of the changes it had applied the previous season to the RS. The ATAC exhausts were dropped and the powervalve was fitted. Cylinder port timing was changed to match the new variable height exhaust, with some fiddling around with the transfer port timing, as well as the exhaust port. The bridge in the exhaust port was widened from 2.9mm to 3.1mm; there had been occasional problems with piston rings breakage on the 1987 model. An exhaust pipe now exited on each side of the bike.

The frame was not changed, but the TRAC anti-dive system was finally discarded and the front fork grew again to 41mm in diameter, with bump and rebound damping adjustments. The bike weighed in at 226lb (103kg) dry and produced just over 70 bhp.

Although the 1988 bike was significantly better than the 1987 model, it suffered from a resurgence from Yamaha in the US, with John Kocinski walking away with the AMA title, followed by seven other Yamahas and an Aprilia. Aprilia also cleaned up in the European championship and it was only in European National racing that the RS could hold its own.

Dominance of the NSR

The performance of the RS was in sharp contrast to that of the NSR in the GPs, where it was dominant. Honda had continued to develop the NSR and, for 1988, they concentrated on improving the handling of the bike and reducing the width of the engine. The new engine was 3mm narrower and repositioning of the transmission shafts also made it shorter, putting slightly more weight on the front tyre. The radiator was curved, to reduce frontal area and ensure that the front wheel did not foul the engine under braking. The rear swing-arm was 20mm longer, although the overall wheelbase of the bike came down 10mm in response to the feedback of the 1987 GP riders, who had complained of slow steering. The bike produced around 80 bhp at 12,000 rpm and weighed just 200lb (91kg).

Riders for the NSR

There was a queue of riders lining up to pay the enormous lease price for the NSR, and Toni Mang, Sito Pons, Dominique Sarron, Jacques Cornu and Reinhold Roth were allocated the bikes. HRC also ran their own rider, Masahiro Shimizu, to get direct development feedback from the GPs. It turned into an exciting season-long battle between fellow countrymen Sito Pons and Juan Garriga, for Honda and Yamaha respectively. Pons proved to be the slightly stronger of the two, winning four GPs and taking the title by ten points at the last GP.

One advantage that Pons had over both Garriga and the other Honda riders was Antonio Cobas, who modified the chassis of the NSR to match Pons' riding style. Most significant was a revised linkage on the rear suspension that resulted in a bike that turned quickly but was stable into corners. With these changes and his own skills, Pons was easily the best NSR rider of 1988, a year that marked Toni Mang's retirement after breaking his collarbone in a crash at the Yugoslavian GP. It was just one fall too many and Mang withdrew from the GP world, still winning GPs and earning the respect of his adversaries.

HONDA'S RS125

Changes in Class

The year 1988 saw the arrival of a new RS to join the happy Honda family – the RS125. Single-cylinder 125 racing had been run at national level in many countries for many years, but these machines had never been run before at GP level. The FIM had been looking for ways to rationalize the sport for many years, and the first victim of this drive was the 350cc class, which was discarded in 1982. A few years later, the 50cc class became the 80cc class and, with the 125cc class becoming restricted to single-cylinder machines in 1988, it was clear that the days of the 80cc class were numbered.

None of the Japanese manufacturers had concerned themselves with the 125 class of the GPs since the classic races of the 1960s, with the exception of Yamaha's brief interest in the early 1970s. It had become the domain of the European machines, mainly from Italy, with the European generation of engine tuners – Harald Bartol, Jorg Muller and Jan Thiel – cutting their teeth on them and squeezing 48 bhp out of the tiny twins.

Honda's 125s

Honda had produced a number of 125 race bikes during the late 1970s and 1980s, all with a pedigree deeply rooted in the motocross division. This included the 1981 RS125RW-T, a twin-cylinder water-cooled motocross engine in a twin-loop cradle frame, weighing 170lb (77kg) and producing around 40 bhp at 14,000 rpm. This machine could easily have been a GP contender at the time, but Honda were not interested in this class, and the bike was only run in the non-championship Malaysian GP of that year.

From 1976, Honda had produced a single-cylinder 125 using an air-cooled motocross engine and called the MT125. The engine used piston port induction and drove a six-speed gearbox to produce 26 bhp at 10,500 rpm. Its only weak spot was a tendency for the exhaust port bridge to pick up on the piston skirt, leading to a slight seizure. Standard modification was an extra hole drilled through the piston skirt to improve lubrication. The MT125 was produced through to 1981, when it was replaced by the water-cooled RS125RW. The motocross engine used reed-valve induction into the base of the cylinder, conventional contemporary practice with reed-valve engines.

With an initial power output of 30 bhp at 11,300 rpm, the RS125RW was very successful in the single-cylinder classes run in several Asian countries. When it became known that the GP class would also be restricted to single cylinders, Honda decided to extend the market for the RS125 to include GPs, providing a cheap and reliable bike and thus guaranteeing the success of the class.

An RS125 for the GPs

In order to test the waters and do a shakedown of the bike prior to the big season start in 1988, Ezio Gianola was asked to campaign the prototype in 1987 against the Garelli and MBA twins. The 1987 model had marked a major change of cylinder

The revelation of 1987 in the 125 class was Enzo Gianola on the Honda single, fighting a field of twins and beating most of them.

dimension, from the short stroke 56 × 50.6mm dimension to the square 54 × 54.5mm that was becoming standard within the company. It was felt that the increased cylinder wall area offered by the square dimensions outweighed the potential advantage in engine speed offered by the short stroke dimensions. This was a general trend that was to result in a migration to the same dimensions for all GP engines during the 1990s. As was so often the case, Honda got there first.

At the first race in Spain, Gianola managed a sixth place, prompting his team manager to say, 'Either we have the best rider in the world, or the other teams have been wasting their time developing twin-cylinder engines.' At the fast circuits, such as Hockenheim, Salzburgring and Monza, the RS was totally outclassed, but it could hold its own at the tight circuits. Highlight of the season was a second place at a wet French GP at Le Mans, after many riders had slid off. With the information collected by Gianola, Honda built a modified version for 1988, available over the counter to anyone with $9,000.

Configuration of the 1988 RS125

The engine of the 1988 RS125 used reed-valve induction into the crankcase. Bore and stroke was the conventional 54 × 54.5mm found on the RS250, and the engine was fed fuel through a 36mm flat-slide Keihin carburettor. No exhaust valve or ATAC chamber was fitted to the exhaust side of the engine. Power was taken off the right-hand end of the crankshaft, via a wet clutch to the six-speed transmission. The water pump was also driven off the right-hand end of the crankshaft. The CDI ignition was fitted to the left-hand end of the crankshaft.

There were similarities in the frame to that of the RS250, a twin-beam frame, with fabricated struts extending down to the front engine-mounting points just under the exhaust pipe. A cross-member above the engine acted as mounting point for the rear sub-frame and one end of the rear shock absorber. The rear suspension was not a sophisticated rising-rate design, but a straight linear monoshock design as used during the 1970s by Yamaha. The swing-arm was heavily triangulated to ensure adequate stiffness. The standard Showa rear shock could be adjusted for rebound damping only, whereas there was no adjustment at all on the 31mm diameter front forks. A single disc front and back on the spoked wheels completed the package that weighed 152lb (69kg) dry and produced a claimed 36 bhp at 12,000 rpm.

The bike was a good starting point for an international rider, and GP riders could have a quite competitive machine if they spent another $9,000 on magnesium wheels, White Power suspension and a little bit of work on the bench of a good engine tuner. The top GP riders were offered the lease of a factory kit, which included a dry clutch conversion as well as new cylinder, head, piston, 38mm carburettor, exhaust, and so on. At least seven riders took this option in 1988.

Success for the RS in 1988

In 1987, Honda claimed to have sold around one thousand RS125s, most of them in the Far East. With Gianola's success in 1987 and the presence of the RS in GPs for 1988, Honda could expect a rapid growth of this market in Europe. Their expectations were met, and the RS became the mainstay of all 125 racing throughout the world, much as the TZ Yamaha did in the 250 and 350 classes during the 1970s. During its inaugural GP year, the RS was not strong enough to beat the factory Derbi, derived from their successful 80cc racers and ridden by Jorge

The 1987 prototype of the RS125 that was to become the mainstay of the class for the next 10 years.

Martinez. However, the next eleven places in the championship table were taken by the RS, with the exception of a Rotax special that stole fifth. It had been a baptism of fire to be proud of.

THE 1989 SEASON

Changes to the Bikes

The cause of the inactivity is unclear, but the 1989 RS250 remained unchanged from the previous year's model. The crisis surrounding the NSR500 may have absorbed resources that might otherwise have worked on the production 250. Alternatively, it might have been felt that the second consecutive world 250 title would sell all the machines Honda intended to produce. Whatever the reason, time stood still for the RS250.

Some minor modifications were made to the RS125, including refined port timing and some changes to the wet clutch. The special kits that were produced for the top GP riders included cylinders with a powervalve in the exhaust tract, as well as exhaust, piston, cylinder head and ignition.

Success for Pons

If Pons was in good form in 1988, he was devastating in 1989. He took the title by a margin of over seventy points, with seven wins and four second places from fifteen races. He was beaten twice by John Kocinski in the

Most riders started the 1988 season with absolutely standard RS125s. Hans Spaan has White Power rear suspension fitted, but the wire wheels lasted well into the year.

two GPs that he contested; as it turned out, this was a warning of things to come. Luca Cadalora, also riding the YZR Yamaha, managed to take two GPs, but the rest were taken by Pons, with Jacques Cornu winning in Belgium, and Reinhold Roth victorious in Czechoslovakia and Holland.

The NSR was truly dominant, despite some confused development based on the plethora of ideas coming from the teams running the bike. As Pons says,

> Having several different teams can be a problem as HRC then has as many different ways of developing the bike as there are teams. In 1989, they came with some quite strange frames, and so on, which we knew would not work, but maybe they had been talking to other teams. We ran the special new downdraught carbs at just one race – Laguna Seca in 1989. They didn't work so good.

After the consecutive world titles, Sito Pons moved up to the 500 class in pursuit of the ultimate in fame and glory within the motorcycle racing sport. He was never to achieve the same level of success in the half-litre class that he enjoyed in the 250 class, because of injuries sustained in high-speed crashes in 1990 and 1991.

Success for the RS125

The RS125 came of age in the 1989 GPs, winning six races, and bringing Honda the

Close racing at the 1989 French 250 GP. Sito Pons (1) narrowly holds off Yamaha riders Honma (28) and Ruggia (7), with Roth (5) and Cornu (3) poised to pounce.

coveted manufacturer's trophy. The rider's title went to a young Spaniard, who was later to have great success riding Honda NSRs, but who for 1989 was riding a Spanish-framed Rotax-engined special built by Antonio Cobas – the JJ Cobas. Alex Criville was completing his apprenticeship in the small GP classes, and had come second in his first GP on a factory Derbi in Spain in 1987. Coming runner-up to Jorge Martinez in the 1988 80cc world championship had been enough for him to go for the 125 class in 1989, with a spectacularly successful result. This clear demonstration of his enormous talent lead him to move straight on to the 250 class at the end of the season, giving Honda riders Spaan and Gianola, who had chased him all the way to the title, no opportunity for revenge.

More Changes to the RS250

Honda could not afford to let the RS250 mature for another year without some serious improvements, so they had a shot at getting the Honda to turn more sharply, to match the prowess shown by the TZ Yamaha. The steering-head angle was sharpened by half a degree, although the trail remained unaltered, as did the overall wheelbase. The frame was totally redesigned with far more substantial engine-mounting struts and a detachable rear sub-frame. The diameter of the front disks increased to 296mm from the 176mm items on the 1989 RS. After offering riders a choice in 1989, HRC decided to offer just 17in rear wheels on the new model. Both front and rear suspension was altered, the ability to adjust compression damping for the first time being especially welcome to the riders.

It seems that HRC felt that the key to better handling lay in a lighter compact engine; they narrowed it by 5mm and lost 4½lb (2kg) in the process. There was significant change to the transfer port timing, all the ports opening slightly later. Combined with a change in exhaust pipes, this resulted in the power increasing, but the power band moving slightly down the engine speed curve. The RS had always been able to rev through the 12,250 rpm peak power delivery, on above 13,000 rpm. A little of this was sacrificed for pre-peak power. The piston skirt was also lengthened to provide better support in the cylinder. Finally, the little battery that had been provided in 1988 to drive the powervalve mechanism returned after a year of absence, during which electrical power was tapped off the generator.

Updating the RS125

The RS250's little brother, the RS125, underwent some minor engine updates, and considerable work on the cylinder porting. The exhaust port opened fractionally later, but was significantly wider. The transfer ports had previously all opened at the same time, but were now staggered, the two pairs closest to the exhaust port opening simultaneously and earlier than before, while the last pair opened slightly later. The chassis was largely unaltered, except for more bracing on the rear swing-arm and the replacement of the wire wheels by six-spoked magnesium items. Like its big brother, it got the

Close racing at the 1989 Swedish 125 GP. Hans Spaan (3) leads, but it was Alex Criville's (28) race and season on the JJ Cobas.

larger-diameter front brake disc and the cartridge forks with compression damping. Although the wheelbase was unaltered, the RS125 had lost 35mm in length and 1lb (0.5kg) in weight.

THE 1990 SEASON

The 1990 RS machine was a good deal, with clear changes from the previous year, a substantial spares kit and an unchanged price in Japan of 1,650,000 Yen.

Championships and Titles

At last, an RS125 took the world championship, in a season-long battle between Dutchman Hans Spaan and Italian Loris Capirossi. It went down to the last GP in Australia, when Capirossi mobilized the assistance of Team Italia to protect his back from Hans Spaan and so take the title. Spaan commented afterwards, 'It was me against a football team.'

The RS250 had mixed success, claiming the British title with Steve Hislop, but

The manic 250 race at the Salzbürgring in 1990. Zeelenberg (14) hung back on the last lap so as not to lead into the final section, but misjudged his run and ended up fourth.

remaining completely out of the running in the European Championships and the US National series. It was unclear who would be taking over from Sito Pons as the top NSR rider for the 250 GPs. Dutchman Wilco Zeelenberg was the only new NSR rider in 1990; many people were surprised that he had been able to obtain the necessary backing and authorization to lease an NSR. He immediately showed that he was worthy of the investment by claiming two third places in the first two GPs of the year.

Work on the NSR had concentrated on the chassis, and riders remarked on the significant improvement that they felt in handling and braking, the latter becoming a notorious NSR weak spot. During the season, many riders experimented with products from companies other than Nissin, but no one found the perfect set-up. HRC rider Shimizu was running new downdraught carburettors that had also been used once or twice by Sito Pons in 1989, but they did not seem to offer any advantage over the 38mm Keihin flat-slide units used by the other NSR riders.

Kocinski and Yamaha

The biggest problem of all for the NSR riders was the Kocinski/Yamaha combination. It was beatable, but not often. There were incredible races through the season, such as the German GP, won by Zeelenberg, inching past Kocinski as the YZR ran a little wide on the last corner. Austria was won by Luca Cadalora, also on a Yamaha, after a titanic slipstreaming power-train of bikes circulated nose to tail for the last couple of laps. For once, the handling and power of the Yamahas and Hondas were closely matched and close racing was the result.

The most consistent rider, and probably the luckiest in escaping serious injury, was Kocinski, although two mid-season crashes resulted in NSR rider Carlos Cardus taking the championship lead in the closing stages of the season. It was Kocinski, however, who kept a cool head and won the last GP in Australia, while Cardus was left ranting and raving in the pits at the unlucky break that left him with a broken gear-change lever.

DEVELOPMENT AT HRC FOR 1991

Fuel Injection

Although the fact had scarcely been visible from Europe, HRC were very busy during 1989 and 1990 with a project that could significantly change the direction of development of the two-stroke GP racer. During the last three races of 1989 and the first half of the 1990 season of the Japanese National championship, HRC rider Takehiko Kurokawa was running an NSR250 fitted with fuel injection. The carburettors that had been used by Pons and Shimizu may well have been a spin-off from this programme. FIM restrictions took some of the shine off the attraction of fuel injection; it was only possible to use it as a direct replacement for conventional carburettors, rather than as a direct injection into the cylinder. Consequently, the charge had to perform the same scavenging process and was as open to contamination by spent exhaust gases as a carburettor. Nevertheless, the promise of more accurate fuel metering, leading to a significantly lower fuel load and lower bike weight made it interesting enough for detailed investigation.

The NSR250 system used downdraught inlet tracts with twin injectors and a butterfly valve controlling air flow past the injectors. There was some considerable experimentation on the location of the injectors and their angle to the air flow through the inlet tract. The bike was reliable, but not especially fast, the best result being a fourth place at Sugo in May 1990 after qualifying in second place on the grid. In July of that year, the programme was stopped for the 250s, but resurrected a year later for the NSR500.

The RS Production Racers

None of this exotica was found on the 1991 RS production racers. The 125 underwent a moderately comprehensive upgrade, based on the move from a 36mm carburettor to one with 38mm throat diameter. Port timing, crankcases, ignition and exhausts were also upgraded to match the increase of power, which was now claimed to be just under 40 bhp. The suspension front and rear was uprated, with full control of ride height, bump and rebound damping possible with the rear shock and compression damping on the front forks. The modifications had shaved 1lb (0.5kg) off the weight bringing it down to just 150lb (68kg). An official HRC tune-up guide recommended shaving 0.3mm off the top of the cylinder, and using 110 octane Blue Gas, for maximum power from the engine.

The RS250 engine had some changes to the piston and cylinder porting to increase engine component reliability. The ceilings of the transfer ports were raised slightly, but the port height was significantly reduced and the skirt of the piston lengthened after some piston failures during the 1990 season. The reed-valve cages were widened slightly to increase air flow, although the carburettor remained the Keihin PJ38. Efforts were being made to reduce the size of the clutch on the right-hand side of the engine; two teeth were removed from the clutch primary driving gear and a single tooth added to the primary driving gear on the crankshaft, causing the overall primary gear ratio to drop slightly.

The steering head angle of the chassis was pulled in half a degree after the experience that had been gained on the NSR racers. At 22.5 degrees, the steering could only be classified as quick. With a careful weight-saving exercise, including some new magnesium wheels, the 1991 RS250 tipped the scales at a respectable 220lb (100kg), just 2lb (1kg) heavier than the new TZ Yamaha (which had at last changed from being a parallel twin to a V-twin replica of the YZR).

THE 1991 SEASON

The Races

Although the RS125 continued to dominate its class throughout the world, including the GPs, the RS250 seemed to come second everywhere, either to Yamaha or Aprilia. The European championships were by now dominated by Aprilia riders, with Massimiliano Biaggi taking the 250 title. Yamaha claimed the British and American National championships, while Honda took the German championships through the services of Jochen Schmidt, who was on the payroll as RS development rider.

The NSR Hondas were back in winning form, with the combination of Erv Kanemoto, Luca Cadalora and NSR250 taking eight season wins. With Kocinski's move to 500 GP racing, there was no one who could ride the Yamaha competitively, and the only challenge to the NSR came from the occasional inspired ride from Loris Reggiani on the Aprilia. During the winter, HRC again worked on improving mid-range engine response and succeeded at the expense of a few hundred revs over 13,000 rpm. There

The last of the first-generation NSR 250s was ridden by Luca Cadalora in 1991.

were only four NSR riders – Zeelenberg, Bradl, Cardus and Cadalora, plus the HRC rider Shimizu.

The Tuners

With the NSR riders having only the other NSR riders to worry about, 1991 turned into the year of the tuners. Kanemoto worked hard for Cadalora to re-find the 300 rpm at the top end; Sepp Schlogel played with inlet tract lengths and found better bottom-end power for Helmut Bradl; and Kel Carruthers looking at ways of putting his twenty years of preparing Yamahas to Cardus's benefit. Kanemoto worked on the carburettors, boring them out to 39mm and finally 40mm and, with the assistance of asbestos tape on the NSR exhaust, was able to build Cadalora an engine that would rev through to 14,000 rpm, 1,000 rpm higher than standard. Schlogel went the other way, fitting Mikuni instead of Keihin carburettors. The only problem was that the powervalve sensor in the Keihin carburettor still needed to be present, so one of the Keihins was bolted to the fairing for the powervalve drive mechanism to pick up the throttle position.

As the season progressed, the lack of work on Zeelenberg's bike began to show, as he had increasing difficulty matching the

It's that man again, hiding behind yet another world champion. Erv Kanemoto, Luca Cadalora and the 1991 NSR250 were good for eight wins and the championship.

performance of the others. He also suffered more than others from a chattering front wheel that limited his performance during a couple of GPs, and caused him to crash a few times in practice and during the race. As the season drew to a close, it became likely that Cadalora would hold off Bradl, his main challenger through the year, and a fall by Bradl at the San Marino GP made it a virtual certainty. Cadalora became the first rider since German Dieter Braun to add a 250 world championship to a previous 125 title.

OFF-SEASON WORK

As usual, some work was done on the two RS machines during the winter recess. Work on the porting of the RS125 was intended to increase the low- and middle-range power delivery. The floor of the exhaust and transfer ports were matched with the crown of the piston at the bottom of its stroke. This effectively reduced the total cross-sectional area of the transfer ports, but apparently did not affect the engine's ability to flow enough charge into

Loris Capirossi made it two in a row with the 1991 125 championship title.

the combustion chamber. Primary gears and the drum in the gear shift mechanism were strengthened, and nothing much else changed in the engine. Apart from a slightly thicker rear brake disc, there were no chassis changes on the 125.

The engine of the 250 was changed in order to increase the flow through the engine, with the exhaust port opening earlier and the floors of the transfer ports being lowered. On the 1991 RS, there had been a spacer at the exhaust pipe/cylinder joint that could be used to fine-tune the exhaust system, but this was gone in 1992. A new reed-valve assembly was another component in the struggle to get more charge into the engine. On the chassis side, the big news was the use of upside-down front forks for the first time, following Yamaha's lead with the TZ the previous year. Both of the

RS put on 6½lb (3kg) in weight; this was not such a problem for the 250, but a serious increase for the 125.

THE 1992 SEASON

The Production Racers

It was a bad season for the Honda production racers, with the 125 GP class going to Aprilia, and few wins in National racing for the RS250. The kit that was leased to the best RS125 riders no longer included a powervalve-equipped cylinder. It had always been doubtful if the powervalve was much use to a 125 rider, riding continuously in the power band and with just 45 bhp (on the kitted bikes) to play with.

A Completely New NSR

Despite these poor results, there was some hope for the faithful, however – a completely new NSR250 was competing in the GPs and, despite a serious challenge from Aprilia riders Reggiani, Chili and Biaggi, retained the 250 title with Cadalora in the saddle.

The new engine of the NSR was a mirror image of the previous twin, with the right-hand cylinder vertical and the left-hand cylinder horizontal, with the angle of the V closing down from the previous 90 degrees to 75 degrees. This was intended to cure the problem of the different lengths of inlet tract on the old model that had caused so many problems with identification of the correct carburation. The smaller angle between the cylinders meant that the engine itself was shorter, providing a little more room for the correct chassis design. The 75 degrees was a compromise between the shorter length of engine and wider crankshaft and crankcase that would be needed as the angle was closed down and the cylinders fouled each other on the crankcase.

With the narrower angle between the cylinders, it was necessary to employ a balancer shaft to damp out the resonances that would occur in such a naturally unbalanced engine. This was fitted at the front of the engine and was driven off the right-hand end of the crankshaft. By placing the shaft at the front of the engine, it was possible to design the optimum equal inlet tracts for both carburettors. For the front cylinder, this meant a reduction of 20mm compared to the previous model. The clutch was now driven on the left-hand side of the bike and transmission gears were widened slightly to guarantee reliability. Re-design of the gear shift mechanism resulted in the shortening of several of the spindles in the mechanism and the saving of 250g. Experience had shown that the 1991 NSR was liable to overheat at some of the hotter circuits and the cooling system capacity was increased by 25 per cent to ensure that the engine ran at 55 degrees centigrade.

Even more startling changes were made to the chassis, with the adoption of the single-sided swing-arm that had come out of the Elf endurance and GP projects of the 1980s. It had always been a problem for Honda to find a way to get exhaust pipes of the right size fitted to the engine, with the swing-arm usually restricting the dimensions of the pipes. For the horizontal left-hand cylinder, there was now a wide open space, as the Pro-arm swing-arm swept to the right-hand side of the rear wheel to hold the hub on that side of the bike. It was even claimed that the swing-arm was lighter than a conventional swing-arm and should be more stable under the forces experienced when cornering hard. Castor was set at 22 degrees and trail was 90mm. The total bike weighed in at 212lb (96kg) and was claimed to produce just under 90 bhp, up slightly on the previous year.

The 1992 NSR250 was a mirror image of the first-generation NSR, and just as successful.

On paper, and stationary in the pit lane, the new bike looked every bit a winner. On the track, although there were no complaints about the handling, the engine seemed slow. Also, all the work done the year before by Kanemoto, Schlogel and the others could no longer be applied to the new engine. Whereas the 1991 NSR had been able to rev through to 13,800 rpm, the 1992 NSR was topped out at 13,000 rpm. Power was about 85 bhp at 12,800 rpm. Only Kanemoto seemed to get the measure of the new engine and Cadalora managed five wins from the first six GPs, before the strong threat of the Aprilia riders with their faster machines could be coupled to reliability. The second half of the season was tough for Cadalora, with Reggiani and Chili winning four GPs and team-mate Biaggi taking his first GP win at the last race in South Africa. Cadalora's early-season performance had saved him, and he retained his world championship title.

DEVELOPMENTS FOR 1993

The RS250

It was natural for the RS250 to follow the NSR's line of development, and, for 1993, 1,690,000 Yen would buy a version of the 1992 machine that was 15½lb (7kg) heavier. Externally, the 125 did not seem to have changed much, but detail work on the cylinders and exhaust had liberated a further 2 bhp, taking the claimed output to 41 bhp.

Most of the work centred on the shape of the ports and the exhaust shape; the only change to the port dimensions was a small increase in the height of the exhaust and transfer port roofs. A different ignition box resulted in a slight widening of the power band, making the bike a little easier to ride.

The NSR

The NSR didn't seem to have changed much either. Since the early 1990s, it had been realized that the design of the air-box that surrounded the carburettors could offer some significant improvements in power. Initially, it had been assumed that the air-box was functioning as a header of cool stable air from which the carburettors would breathe. It soon became clear that a correct design would result in an increase in pressure within the box and provide the engine with a very light supercharging effect. Throughout the 1990s, various designs of the boxes and of the ducts supplying the air were tried on the NSRs. In 1993, the air was drawn through ducts from the front of the fairing, but the turbulence in the tract led to extremely sensitive carburation. There were complaints that the bike under-steered on the exit from corners, especially when fitted with Michelin tyres (as it was for Biaggi).

THE 1993 RACES

The NSR was still the best machine in 1993, but the riders lacked the consistency that would have brought one of them the world title. Tetsuya Harada had a fantastic start to the season and managed to sustain this performance through to the Dutch TT. It did fall apart during the second half of the year, but only Capirossi was able to close the large gap the Japanese Yamaha rider had managed to create. It came down to the last GP of the year, and Harada triumphed as Capirossi's tyres faded. The Yamaha YZR 250 seemed to work well only in combination with a dedicated Yamaha rider. Kocinski had been that rider in 1990, and Harada had managed it again. But Yamaha were to struggle in the years ahead, as glory in the 250 class came to be fought out between Honda and Aprilia.

THE 1994 SEASON

Changes to the Bikes

There were only detail changes on the RS models for the 1994 season. The main concern was to regain the horsepower that had been lost when the regulation was changed to permit only low-lead 100 octane racing fuel. For Honda it was a struggle, more so than for Aprilia and Yamaha. With painstaking work on the porting, exhaust, ignition and cylinder head, they were able to add a couple of bhp to the peak power of both the RS models. The 125 got a rear wheel with a larger rim and full floating front brakes.

The same problems resulting from the new fuel regulations were found on the NSR. Sensors were fitted to the engine to detect detonation. The engine was on a razor edge between performance and failure and the sensors enabled a potential failure condition to be detected. The NSR was no longer the fastest bike on the track. The Aprilias started off faster and got faster through the year. The under-steer of the year before seemed to have been largely fixed through changes of chassis geometry and stiffness of the frame. The engine was mounted slightly higher in the frame and the steering head moved back 3mm. Initially, there were also some problems with the front forks, exhibiting either too much dive or feeling too hard. Within a couple of races, the problem was fixed.

In total, there were eight NSRs on the GP starting grids, but the season developed into a three-way battle between Okada and Capirossi on NSRs and Biaggi on the Aprilia. Capirossi lost touch as the season drew to a close after falling in the American and Czech GPs. Going into the last GP at Catalunya in Spain, Biaggi had an eight-point advantage over Okada and won the race in style.

THE 1995 SEASON

A Completely New 125

While the RS250 underwent only very minor changes in its transformation to the 1995 model, the RS125 was a completely new machine. In view of the bike's lineage, which dated back to the mid-1980s, and under increasing pressure from Aprilia and Yamaha's re-entry into the class, Honda decided to build a completely new machine. Nakamoto, designer of the new generation RS and NSR250, was also responsible for the 125. The biggest changes were the addition of a balance shaft in the engine, cassette-type gearbox and a totally new chassis. The balance shaft was added to remove the strong vibrations that had always been a characteristic of the bike. The shaft was located above the transmission mainshaft and was driven directly off the right-hand end of the crankshaft. The

Hans Spaan prepared a machine that enabled Haruchika Aoki to take the 1995 125 championship title.

complete transmission assembly could now be removed from the bike with the engine *in situ*. This required the clutch removal from the right-hand side of the engine and removal of the engine crankcase cover on the opposite side of the engine, from which the gears could be pulled out.

The twin-beam spar frame had the same dimensions as the 1994 model, but was clearly a scaled-down version of the frame used by the RS250; it showed an identical use of extruded and cast sections, as well as the rear suspension, sub-frame and engine support struts. The monoshock linear-rate rear suspension was replaced by a rising-rate design, with a triangulated box-section aluminium rear swing-arm, the rear shock mounted vertically behind the engine as on the RS250. Upside-down front forks were fitted to the front end of the bike, where the steering had been sharpened by closing the rake down to 23.5 degrees with 84mm of trail. The overall weight of the bike was unchanged at 156lb (71kg). Riders were very happy with the chassis change, as it gave them greater stability into and out of the corner. The engine seemed to have lost a slight edge in the transformation, especially on the top end.

The NSR's Season

The NSR seems to have been neglected a little during the winter of 1994–95. It was only at the last moment, as practice started for the Australian GP, that some special parts – exhausts and a rear swing-arm – arrived for the NSR riders. The season turned out to be the worst for Honda in ten years as Max Biaggi ran off with a total of eight GP wins for Aprilia. Only Waldmann and Romboni of the NSR riders won a GP in 1995. Waldmann, clearly the best of them, took three, largely due to Sepp Schlogel, who had to make chassis modifications to try and cure the chronic under-steer that had again reared its ugly head. Romboni may have been more of a force to be reckoned with if he had not fallen at the German GP and broken his wrist; the injury kept him off the track for three races. To make things worse, Harada pushed Waldmann down to third place in the rider's championship, the lowest position since Honda had returned to the 250 class in 1984. Honda also lost the manufacturer's championship to Aprilia.

The 1995 season was one to be forgotten as soon as possible, except for the fine championship win of Haruchika Aoki on the kitted RS125 prepared by Hans Spaan. Concentrating on producing a bike with a user-friendly power delivery, even at the expense of a couple of bhp peak power, Spaan produced a bike that enabled Aoki fully to exploit his cornering capabilities.

THE 1996 SEASON

Changes to the Bikes

The RS models remained unchanged for 1996, except for a slightly better aerodynamic tail unit on the RS125. Work on the NSR concentrated again on the steering problem of the bike, but the initial solution was not appreciated by all the teams. The swing-arm was longer and the pivot point had been changed. The engine had been tilted slightly further forward, placing more of the bike's weight on the front wheel. The engine was also 2lb (1kg) lighter, although the weight returned in the chassis.

All the NSR riders struggled to set the bike up at the start of the season. Schlogel experimented with the rear suspension from the 1995 bike but found that this overloaded the rear tyre, causing it to wear rapidly and last only ten laps. In the end, a modified version of the 1996 suspension was used.

Stripped to the bone – the 1996 NSR250 as ridden by Nobuatsu Aoki. The NSR was quick but not on the Michelin tyres Aoki used.

The Races

Waldmann's team could now get on with the business of trying to beat Biaggi and his Aprilia, who had a seventy-point advantage by round seven, the Dutch TT. Six GPs later, the gap had shrunk to just twelve points as Biaggi blew hot and cold, crashing twice while Waldmann finished every race, often as victor. With just one race to go and another crash behind him, Biaggi led the championship by a single point from Waldmann; he made no mistake at the last GP of the year, beating the NSR rider into second place and claiming his third consecutive title.

Although Honda had not won the rider's championship, they did recover the manufacturer's title, as French rider Olivier Jacques became consistently fast and reliable through the season. He beat Waldmann three times in the second half of the GP year, and used a new engine that HRC had produced for the last four races. This had a narrower power band, but offered a significantly greater peak power value. It did not match Waldmann's smooth style and only Jacques and HRC rider Ukawa used it during the GPs. It was to form the basis for the 1997 NSR engine, and was immediately a source of concern for Waldmann, who persuaded Honda to allow him to keep the old engine for the new season.

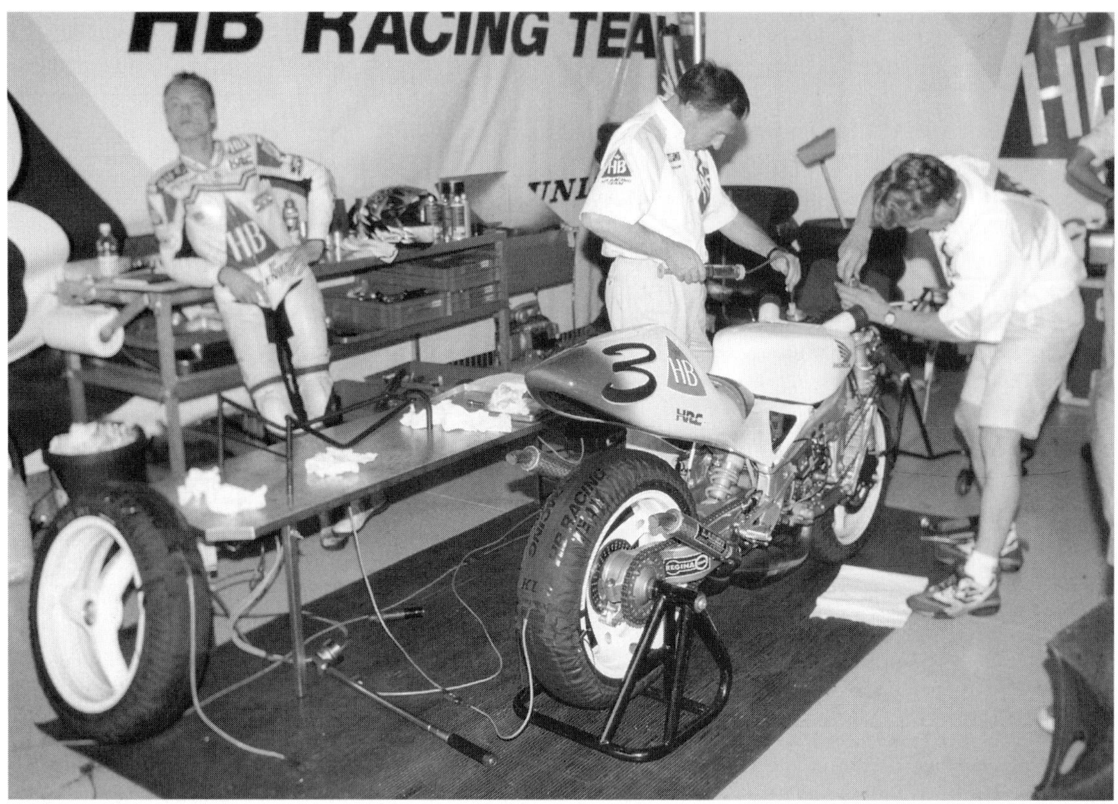

Ralf Waldmann waits for the most experienced NSR engineer in the world, Sepp Schlogel, to ready his 1996 NSR.

THE 1997 SEASON

As the sport continued to move towards using less polluting fuel, the 1997 RS models were designed to run on unleaded fuel and consequently ran new cylinders, heads, exhausts and ignitions. It was claimed that there was no loss of power, but initial impressions were that the engines were slightly flatter than the 1996 models. The NSR had a single year of grace; the regulations were due to come into force in 1998 for the world of GPs. In Japan, unleaded fuel was stipulated for the All-Japan championship, giving the manufacturers a chance to de-bug their engines before competing on the world stage. For the 1997 GP season, Biaggi made a late decision to switch from Aprilia to Honda, and HRC had to scrabble to make another set of bikes as well as those leased to Waldmann, Jacques and Ukawa. Once again, there were handling problems during testing and the early GPs, but Aprilia seemed to have their own share of problems and Biaggi and Waldmann were able to pull a slight lead in the championship.

Mid-season, everything seemed to be going wrong for the NSR teams and Tetsuya Harada started a string of good results that took him and his Aprilia to a nine-point championship lead with just three GPs remaining. Biaggi was plagued all season by acute front wheel clatter that shook his confidence in the front tyre, the most critical component in the support of his riding style. Even the special frame HRC produced for him just before the start of the year did little to solve the problem. At the British GP, he was visibly tip-toeing through the corners, far slower than the other riders, but still unable to prevent the inevitable crash. Then, miraculously, the Aprilia challenge faded in the last GPs and Ralph Waldmann, struggling without a spare bike in his cash-strapped team, had a disastrous Indonesian GP, unable to set up the NSR to work effectively. It was down to the last race, and in a repeat of the 1996 season, Biaggi's cool head and ability to perform under stress saw him take a steady second place and his fourth world title, but this time for Honda and the NSR blood line. It was a sweet victory for both Biaggi and Honda.

Since their arrival in the 125 and 250 class back in the 1980s, the Honda NSR and RS racers have been the yardstick against which the performance of all-comers has been measured. The Hondas have occasionally been bettered, but more often their challengers have been found wanting. And the spirit of excellence that was so clearly present in Freddie Spencer's 1985 RS250R-W lives on today.

At last the number one plate could be seen on the NSR again, but it had been earned on an Aprilia. Biaggi's NSR was plagued by chatter of the carbon-fibre wheels all season

Appendix I

MOTORBIKE SPECIFICATIONS

	RS500				
	1983	**1984**	**1985**	**1986**	**1987**
Series Id.	NC8	ND7A	ND7B	ND7C	ND7F
Bore (mm)	62.6	62.6	62.6	62.6	62.6
Stroke (mm)	54.0	54.0	54.0	54.0	54.0
Carburettor	PE34	PE34	PE36	PE36	PE36
Primary gear	2.368	2.368	2.15	2.15	2.15
1st gear	2.214	2.214	2.214	2.214	2.214
2nd gear	1.706	1.706	1.706	1.706	1.706
3rd gear	1.421	1.421	1.421	1.421	1.421
4th gear	1.238	1.238	1.238	1.238	1.238
5th gear	1.125	1.125	1.125	1.125	1.125
6th gear	1.045	1.045	1.045	1.045	1.045
Final gear	2.063	2.063	2.250	2.250	2.250
Trail (degrees)	25.5	25.5	25.5	25.3	25.3
Rake (mm)	90.0	90.0	90.0	89.7	89.7
Length (mm)	2,002	2,002	2,002	2,012	2,000
Width (mm)	640	640	640	620	620
Wheelbase (mm)	1,384	1,384	1,384	1,397	1,387
Weight (kg)	125.5	125	125	127	132

NSR500							
	1984	1985	1986	1987	1988	1989	1990
Series Id.	NVOA	NVOB	NVOC	NVOD	NVOG	NVOH	NVOJ
Bore (mm)	54.0	54.0	54.0	54.0	54.0	54.0	54.0
Stroke (mm)	54.5	54.5	54.5	54.5	54.5	54.5	54.5
Carburettor	PE34	PE34	PE34	PE35	PE35	PE36/ PJ36	PJ36
Firing interval (degrees)	90	90	90	90	90	90	180
Length (mm)	1,980	1,985	1,985	1,995	1,970	1,980	2,000
Width (mm)	570	600	600	600	600	600	600
Wheelbase (mm)	1,375	1,370	1,370	1,375	1,370	1,370	1,390
Weight (kg)	105						115

NSR500V			
	1996	1997	1997
Series Id.	NVAA	NVAB	NX6A
Bore (mm)	68.0	68.0	68.0
Stroke (mm)	68.8	68.8	68.8
Carburettor	PJ40	PJ40	PJ40
Trail (degrees)	22	22	22
Rake (mm)	89.0	89.0	89.0
Length (mm)	1,960	1,960	1,975
Width (mm)	600	600	595
Wheelbase (mm)	1,360	1,360	1,360
Weight (kg)	103	103	109

	1991	1992	1993	1994	1995	1996	1997
Series Id.	NVOK	NVOP	NVOR	NVOS	NVOT	NVOW	NVOX
Bore (mm)	54.0	54.0	54.0	54.0	54.0	54.0	54.0
Stroke (mm)	54.5	54.5	54.5	54.5	54.5	54.5	54.5
Carburettor	PJ36	PJ36	PJ36/ FI	PJ36	PJ36	PJ36	PJ36
Firing Interval (degrees)	180	<70	<70	<70	<70	<70	<70/180
Length (mm)	2,010	2,010	2,010	2,010	2,010	2,010	2,010
Width (mm)	600	600	600	600	600	600	600
Wheelbase (mm)	1,410	1,410	1,400	1,400	1,400	1,400	1,400
Weight (kg)	130	>130	>130	>130	>130	>130	>130

RS250

	1984	1986	1987	1988	1989	1990	1991
Series Id.	ND5A	ND5B	NF5A	NF5B	NF5C	NF5F	NF5G
Bore (mm)	56.0	56.0	54.0	54.0	54.0	54.0	54.0
Stroke (mm)	50.6	50.6	54.5	54.5	54.5	54.5	54.5
Carburettor		PE36	PJ 38	PJ38	PJ38	PJ38	PJ38
Primary gear			2.636	2.636	2.636	2.636	2.435
1st gear			2.235	2.235	2.111	2.111	2.111
2nd gear			1.619	1.619	1.619	1.619	1.619
3rd gear			1.333	1.333	1.333	1.391	1.391
4th gear			1.154	1.154	1.154	1.200	1.200
5th gear			1.074	1.074	1.074	1.115	1.115
6th gear			1.000	1.000	1.000	1.037	1.037
Final gear			2.400	2.467	2.400	2.188	2.400
Trail (degrees)	26.5	24.5	23.0	23.0	23.0	23.0	22.5
Rake (mm)	100	87	81	80	84	84	84
Length (mm)	1,950	1,960	1,967	1,944	1,940	1,935	1,945
Width (mm)	600	600	600	644	645	640	640
Wheelbase (mm)	1,350	1,340	1,340	1,342	1,330	1,330	1,330
Weight (kg)	97	103	103	104	104	102	100

NSR250

	1985	1986	1987	1988	1989	1990	1991
Series Id.	NF5	NF5	NF5	NF5	NF5	NF5	NF5
Bore (mm)	54.0	54.0	54.0	54.0	54.0	54.0	54.0
Stroke (mm)	54.5	54.5	54.5	54.5	54.5	54.5	54.5
Carburettor							
Length (mm)	1,945	1,910	1,920	1,920	1,920	1,920	1,930
Width (mm)	600	530	530	580	600	600	600
Wheelbase (mm)	1,345	1,330	1,325	1,320	1,320	1,320	1,330
Weight (kg)	97	95	92	<92	<91	<91	<92

	1992	1993	1994	1995	1996	1997
Series Id.	NF5H	NX5A	NX5B	NX5C	NX5G	NX5H
Bore (mm)	54.0	54.0	54.0	54.0	54.0	54.0
Stroke (mm)	54.5	54.5	54.5	54.5	54.5	54.5
Carburettor	PJ38	PJ38	PJ 38	PJ38	PJ38	PJ38
Primary gear	2.435	2.521	2.521	2.521	2.521	
1st gear	2.111	2.333	2.214	2.214	2.214	
2nd gear	1.619	1.812	1.750	1.750	1.750	
3rd gear	1.391	1.588	1.500	1.500	1.500	
4th gear	1.200	1.368	1.292	1.292	1.292	
5th gear	1.115	1.227	1.143	1.143	1.143	
6th gear	1.037	1.173	1.046	1.046	1.046	
Final gear	2.400	2.058	2.250	2.250	2.250	
Trail (degrees)	22.5	22.5	22.5	22.5	22.5	22.5
Rake (mm)	86					
Length (mm)	1,945	1,954	1,954	1,954	1,954	1,954
Width (mm)	640	640	640	640	640	640
Wheelbase (mm)	1,330	1,340	1,340	1,340	1,340	1,340
Weight (kg)	103	103	102	102	102	102

	1992	1993	1994	1995	1996
Series Id.	NX5A	NX5B	NX5C	NX5D	NX5G
Bore (mm)	54.0	54.0	54.0	54.0	54.0
Stroke (mm)	54.5	54.5	54.5	54.5	54.5
Carburettor					
Length (mm)	1,950	1,950	1,940	1,930	1,930
Width (mm)	600	600	600	590	590
Wheelbase (mm)	1,340	1,340	1,330	1,320	1,320
Weight (kg)	>95	>95	>95	>95	>95

RS125							
	1987	**1988**	**1989**	**1990**	**1991**	**1992**	**1993**
Series Id.	NF4	NF4	NF4	NF4	NF4	NF4	NF4
Bore (mm)	54.0	54.0	54.0	54.0	54.0	54.0	54.0
Stroke (mm)	54.5	54.5	54.5	54.5	54.5	54.5	54.5
Carburettor	PJ36	PJ36	PJ36	PJ36	PJ38	PJ38	PJ38
Primary gear	3.150	3.150	3.150	3.150	3.150	3.150	2.952
1st gear	1.823	1.823	1.823	1.823	1.823	1.823	1.824
2nd gear	1.500	1.500	1.500	1.500	1.500	1.500	1.500
3rd gear	1.291	1.291	1.291	1.291	1.291	1.291	1.291
4th gear	1.153	1.153	1.153	1.153	1.153	1.153	1.153
5th gear	1.074	1.074	1.074	1.074	1.074	1.074	1.074
6th gear	1.000	1.000	1.000	1.000	1.000	1.000	1.000
Final gear	2.188	2.188	2.250	2.117	2.117	2.117	2.250
Trail (degrees)	25.3	25.0	25.0	25.0	25.0	25.0	25.0
Rake (mm)	95	95	95	90	90	90	90
Length (mm)	1,862	1,860	1,860	1,825	1,830	1,830	1,830
Width (mm)	510	510	510	560	560	560	560
Wheelbase (mm)	1,260	1,260	1,260	1,260	1,260	1,260	1,255
Weight (kg)	70.0	69.0	69.0	68.5	68.0	71.0	71.0

	1994	1995	1996	1997
Series Id.	NF4	NX4	NX4	NX4
Bore (mm)	54.0	54.0	54.0	54.0
Stroke (mm)	54.5	54.5	54.5	54.5
Carburettor	PJ38	PJ38D	PJ38D	PJ38D
Primary gear	2.952	2.952	2.952	2.952
1st gear	1.823	1.875	1.875	1.875
2nd gear	1.500	1.524	1.524	1.524
3rd gear	1.291	1.301	1.301	1.301
4th gear	1.153	1.167	1.167	1.167
5th gear	1.074	1.077	1.077	1.077
6th gear	1.000	1.000	1.000	1.000
Final gear	2.250	2.250	2.250	2.250
Trail (degrees)	25.0	23.5	23.5	23.5
Rake (mm)	90	84	84	84
Length (mm)	1,830	1,800	1,800	1,800
Width (mm)	560	570	570	570
Wheelbase (mm)	1,255	1,215	1,215	1,215
Weight (kg)	71.0	71.0	71.0	71.0

Appendix II

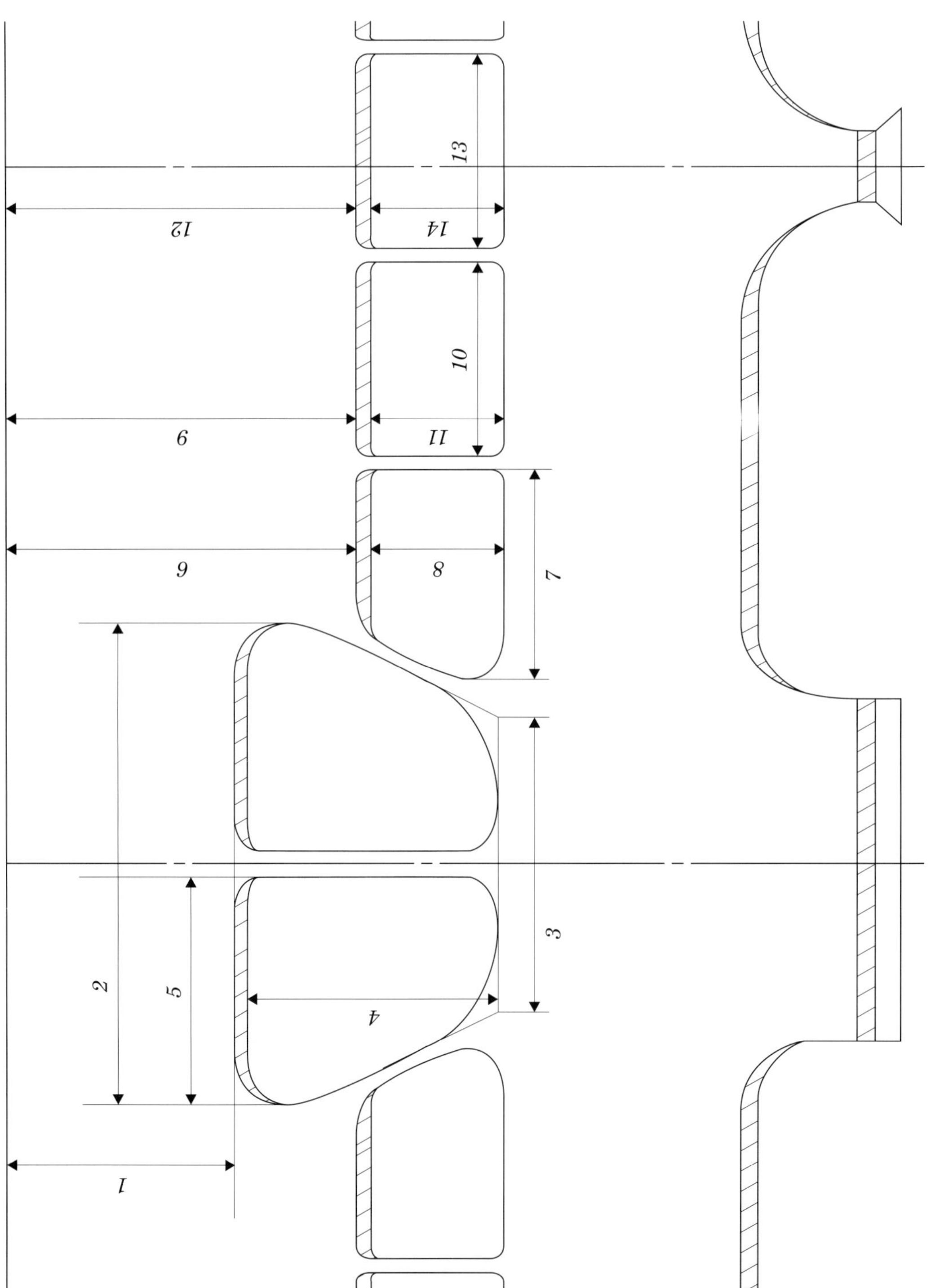

Table of port timing (all dimensions in mm).

MODEL	YEAR	1	2	3	4	5	6	7	8	9	10	11	12	13	14	MODEL CODE
RS250	85	25.5	52.0	44.8	25.3	24.5	39.3	21.0	11.5	39.3	18.5	11.5	39.3	18.5	11.5 Bore 56	ND5
Piston Reed	86	25.5	52.0	44.8	25.3	24.5	39.3	21.0	11.5	39.3	18.5	11.5	39.3	18.5	11.5 Bore 56	ND5
Case Reed	87	27.45	52.5	36.0	28.4	24.8	41.95	22.5	11.65	41.45	20.5	12.15	42.95	19.0	13.9 Bore 54	NF5
	88	27.8	52.5	36.0	27.7	24.7	42.0	22.5	13.5	42.0	20.0	13.5	42.0	19.0	14.4	NF5
	89	27.8	52.5	36.0	27.7	24.7	42.0	22.5	13.5	42.0	20.0	13.5	42.0	19.0	14.4	NF5
	90	27.8	52.5	36.0	27.7	24.7	42.5	22.5	13.0	42.5	20.0	13.0	42.5	19.0	14.0	NF5
	91	27.75	52.5	36.0	27.7	24.8	41.95	22.5	11.25	42.45	20.0	10.75	42.95	19.0	13.5	NF5
	92	27.45	52.5	36.0	28.4	24.8	41.95	22.5	11.65	42.45	20.0	11.15	42.95	19.0	13.9	NF5
New	93	27.8	52.3	36.0	27.9	24.7	41.5	22.5	14.2	42.5	21.0	13.2	43.0	19.0	12.7	NX5
	94	27.1	52.0	36.0	27.9	24.5	41.3	23.0	13.7	42.4	21.0	12.6	43.4	19.0	12.5	NX5
	95	27.1	52.0	36.0	27.9	24.5	41.3	22.0	13.7	42.4	21.0	12.6	43.4	19.0	12.5	NX5
	96	27.1	52.0	36.0	27.9	24.5	41.3	22.0	13.7	42.4	21.0	12.6	43.4	19.0	12.5	NX5
	97	27.1	52.0	36.0	27.9	24.8	41.6	23.5	13.6	42.6	20.5	12.6	43.1	19.0	12.0	NX5
RS125	85	25.5	52.0	44.8	25.3	24.5	39.3	21.0	11.5	39.3	18.5	11.5	39.3	18.5	11.5 Bore 56	ND4
Piston Reed	86	25.5	52.0	44.8	25.3	24.5	39.3	21.0	11.5	39.3	18.5	11.5	39.3	18.5	11.5 Bore 56	ND4
Case Reed	87	28.0	52.3	36.0	27.2	24.6	41.5	22.5	13.7	42.0	20.5	13.2	42.5	26.6	13.3 Bore 54	NF4
	88	28.7	51.5	35.0	26.7	24.2	42.7	22.5	13.3	42.7	20.5	13.3	42.7	19.0	13.8	NF4
	89	28.9	51.5	35.0	26.7	24.2	42.8	22.5	13.3	42.8	20.5	13.3	42.8	19.0	13.8	NF4
	90	29.0	52.0	35.0	26.9	24.5	42.5	22.5	13.5	42.5	20.5	13.5	43.1	19.0	13.7	NF4
	91	28.8	52.3	36.0	28.1	24.2	42.3	22.5	14.6	42.8	20.5	14.1	43.3	19.0	13.3	NF4
	92	28.8	52.3	36.0	26.9	24.2	42.3	22.5	13.4	42.8	20.5	12.9	43.3	19.0	13.3	NF4
	93	28.75	52.3	36.0	26.9	24.2	42.25	22.5	13.4	42.75	20.5	12.9	43.25	19.0	13.3	NF4
	94	28.0	52.3	36.0	27.2	24.2	41.5	22.5	13.7	42.0	20.5	13.2	42.5	19.0	13.3	NF4
New	95	28.4	52.2	36.0	26.9	28.2	41.8	22.0	14.4	43.3	21.0	12.0	42.8	25.8	13.3	NX4
	96	28.4	52.2	36.0	26.9	28.2	41.8	22.0	13.5	43.3	21.0	12.0	42.8	25.8	13.3	NX4
	97	28.1	52.2	36.0	24.6	28.2	41.6	22.0	14.7	43.0	21.0	13.5	42.6	25.8	13.8	NX4
RS500	83	29.3	57.2	46.9	25.1	26.5	42.8	24.5	12.8	42.3	13.5	13.3	42.65	22.7	20.1 Bore 62.6	NC8
Piston Reed	84	29.3	57.2	46.9	25.1	26.5	42.8	24.5	12.8	42.3	13.5	13.3	42.65	22.7	20.1	ND7
	85	29.8	58.5	46.9	25.9	27.3	42.8	24.0	13.4	43.1	14.0	13.3	43.4	22.0	20.0	ND7
	86	30.0	58.5	50.0	26.7	27.3	42.9	24.0	13.5	42.9	15.5	13.2	42.9	22.0	19.5	NF7

Index

Page numbers in *italic* refer to photographs.